Cover: St. Mary's, Isles of Scilly, lifeboat; Arun Class
(Acknowledgements RNLI)

Dedication

To the Lifeboatmen of Cornwall

On stormy nights, while some folk sleep,
Lifeboat bleepers start to bleep.
There's been a 'shout'; twin rockets flare,
And two big bangs disturb the air,
Re-echoing around the quay
To signify distress at sea.

The crewmen quit warm beds in haste,
(Who knows the perils to be faced?)
But comrades, disregarding fear,
Make for the Boathouse, don their gear ...
Adrenalin is flowing free
As men and lifeboat put to sea.

But any time, by night or day
Maroons may summon them away
To tanker, fishing boat or raft,
Or yacht, or some unlikely craft,
Or any other casualty
At risk from the relentless sea.

Though often tough, rewards are rare;
They do not seek the media's glare.
But here's to those, in urgency,
Respond to an emergency,
Where strangers, just like you and me,
May be in peril on the sea.

(Sheila Bird)

M A Y D A Y !

Preserving Life from
Shipwreck off Cornwall

---

by Sheila Bird

EX LIBRIS PRESS

First published 1991 by

EX LIBRIS PRESS
1 The Shambles
Bradford on Avon
Wiltshire

Typeset in 10 point Palatino
Design and typesetting by Ex Libris Press

Printed by BPCC Wheatons Ltd., Exeter

ISBN 0 948578 31 9

CONTENTS

ABOUT THE AUTHOR

An established writer, Sheila Bird was born within the sound of waves breaking on the Channel shore and has a lifelong relationship with the South-West peninsula and the southern coast of Britain. But life's opportunities have taken her far beyond these much loved shores.

Having been educated in Kent and trained as a teacher in Dorset she had three spells of working overseas as well as teaching in various parts of southern England. Her worldwide experiences, which gave her the chance of travelling aboard some of the big liners and cargo ships in the 1960s and 1970s, heightened her perception of our own countryside, history and heritage, particularly our maritime heritage, and led her to to contributing features to a variety of local and national magazines and newspapers. This hobby evolved spontaneously into a full-time career as a writer, and subsequently publisher and broadcaster, specialising in the south-western counties.

Being prepared to go where this new career took her has given rise to an interesting and fulfilling lifestyle, working on location and identifying closely with people and communities in the south-west. In preparing this book she has interviewed scores of people, liaised with the Royal Navy and Coastguards and worked closely with the RNLI and the lifeboatmen of Cornwall, whose dedication, courage, humour and spirit of camaraderie she believes are second to none.

INTRODUCTION

The wide waters of the Atlantic, great mother of storms, crowned
throughout the year with a great diadem of attendant clouds. There is
nothing in this world of ours so old, and yet unchanged as the seas.

A.G. Folliott Stokes, 1909

Throughout the ages, the sighting of the Isles of Scilly and the grand and
rugged coastline of Cornwall must have gladdened the heart of many a
returning seafarer, after many months at sea. In the days of sail it was a wise
skipper who checked his charts and instruments, kept a clear head and sharp
look out, for these capricious waters have sent countless ships to their doom.
Indeed, history has demonstrated that the whole coast of Cornwall, with its
proudly jutting headlands, spectacular rocky bays and fine river estuaries,
looking so benign and beautiful in the sunshine, can suddenly adopt a
menacing profile and become a death trap for shipping. And all too frequently the fate of sailors and their ships was revealed along the coastline, in
the cold, clear light of a cruel Cornish dawn.

In compiling this book, I have outlined some of the navigational and other
hazards encountered by the early seafarers, and followed the theme of the
prevention of shipwreck and the saving of life from the sea. The continuing
story of the preservation of life from shipwreck is a heartening one; it is one
of selflessness, dedication, courage and real life adventure.

Sheila Bird
Falmouth, Cornwall
1991

Some of our noblest services performed by life-boats have been done on the coasts of Cornwall and Devon, where the great Atlantic wave is felt, perhaps more severely than on any other part of the coast of the British Empire.

Richard Lewis, Secretary of the RNLI, 1867

PERILS OF THESE WATERS

Cornwall, almost surrounded by water, is a strong maritime county, with trade and communications mostly by sea until comparatively recent times. Shipping has plied the waters around the peninsula for centuries, but it was the explorers in Elizabethan times, notably from Bristol and Plymouth, who opened up the world trading routes and brought about a vast increase in the number of vessels passing these shores. This was an exciting era of adventure, endeavour and free enterprise, but charts were often inaccurate and navigational techniques crude and elementary. There were no international standards to abide by and men sometimes set off in rotting, overloaded, undermanned vessels bringing about an increasing catalogue of disasters, which highlighted the need for better charts and navigational equipment and the efficient organisation of rescue work around our coasts. Surveys were carried out, and more accurate charts compiled giving details of depths of water, the nature of the coastline and positions of navigational warnings, such as they were at the time. Charts needed continual updating, to take account of changing situations, and there was experimentation in the warning of navigational hazards. But then as now, commonsense, simple ideas costing comparatively little were overlooked on financial grounds as this letter to the *West Briton* in 1874 demonstrates:

Preserving Life From Shipwreck......

Sir,
    In August 1869, *The Times* did me the honour of publishing a letter of mine on the above subject. In that letter I suggested that all navigating charts should have the rocket apparatus and lifeboat stations, laid down as well as places pointed out on the coast to which a captain, in cases of accident, such as finding his ship driving hopelessly ashore in a gale of wind, or fire, or springing a leak etc., might endeavour to run for, as being the points from which assistance could most easily be rendered from the shore for saving life and property. The very flattering manner in which this communication was received, induced me — in order for me to put my idea in something like working shape — to visit the whole of the coast of my

9

native county — Cornwall, which enabled me to lay down all such places on one of the Admiralty charts, and to write a key or guide to it. Copies of them I forwarded to the heads of departments at the Admiralty, the Board of Trade, the Lifeboat Institutions, Lloyds, the Salvage Association, and others. I afterwards sought and obtained interviews with these gentlemen. The courtesy and kindness I received from them will ever be most gratefully remembered: indeed, the cause seemed everywhere to bring its own welcome. So impressed did these gentlemen appear with the feasibility of the plan that in all subsequent interviews the conversation turned principally on the ways and means of getting it carried out; many were the valuable suggestions made for doing so; indeed I may go further and say that between two departments it became simply a matter as to which should bear the cost. Shortly after this I left England, but being anxious to know what was being done in the matter, I made enquiries and received for reply — 'It stands just as you left it, the money arrangements seem to be the only difficulty in the way.' It is this, Sir, coupled with the accounts of the frightful loss of life and property on our coasts, on which every file of English papers brings us, which induces me to ask your influence in forwarding the cause.

The 4-masted barque Pamir, *constructed in Germany in 1905, was just one of many splendid vessles familiar to these waters. Sadly, she was destined to become the victim of shipwreck (Sheila Bird Collection)*

Shipping Traffic

Over the last two or three hundred years, watchers on the shore might have witnessed the magnificent spectacle of the fast and stylish Post Office packet ships, various ships of war, convict ships, emigrant ships, brigantines, sloops, schooners, steamships, liners, cable laying vessels, local smacks and all manner of craft passing up and down the Channel as part of the work-a-day scene, for the seafaring history of Cornwall plays a key role in our nation's maritime heritage. The sheer volume of traffic passing these shores increasingly constitutes a danger in itself.

Smuggling and Piracy

In earlier times, piracy was a hazard to be encountered in these waters, and it was particularly rife around the Isles of Scilly. Smuggling and wrecking took place all around these shores. In 1816, four smugglers from Cadgwith were press ganged, taken to Plymouth and put aboard Lord Exmouth's fleet, which sailed for Algiers, in an attempt to put a stop to the antics of the Barbary pirates, who were in the habit of seizing men from British ships for slavery.

Wide Ranging Hazards Encountered At Sea

Some hazards of the sea are predictable. Unseaworthy vessels continually came to grief over the centuries, and surprisingly, many of the small sloops of war, introduced into the Post Office Packet Service after it was taken over by the Admiralty in 1823 were not fit to go to sea. The frequency of their loss without trace, together with passengers, crew, gold bullion and valuable mails, led to them becoming colloquially known as 'coffin brigs.' And as the *West Briton* pointed out in April 1864, when reporting on the harbour of refuge issue, "No harbours that could be constructed could possibly prevent disaster happening to 'old baskets,' filled up to the 'very eyes', with crews so constantly engaged in pumping that when a gale springs up they are too exhausted to be able to save their craft or keep her off the land."

Fire has always been a hazard much feared at sea. Vessels were sometimes put at risk by their cargoes igniting, as happened aboard the Scilly packet in August 1831, as a result of lime being loaded from the kiln before it had cooled. Today we might describe this as being the result of human error, but no one knew what caused the *Happy Return* of Gweek to drift across Mount's Bay in 1813, blazing in fearful grandeur to the masthead, until she took the ground at Newlyn, and the fire was quenched at water level. Perhaps it was an 'Act of God', that befell the sloop *Friend's Goodwill*, after she became becalmed, then stormbound, after leaving Padstow in 1831. For a bolt of lightning split the mast asunder, knocked the navigator senseless on the deck, then set the ship ablaze. And it would have burnt right out had it not been for a timely torrent of rain, which quelled the flames. Vessels were often caught by groundswell, as with the *Narrow Escape* of Clovelly, another ship

11

with an optimistic name and a sad fate. For after leaving the port of Boscastle fully laden with Delabole slate in 1826, she was dashed to pieces on rocks near Tintagel.

Some perils came unwittingly, from those whose duty it was to protect us, as East Cornish fishermen knew all too well, having been victims of erring aim when Naval personnel from Devonport were out on torpedo practice. It similarly paid to give St. Mawes a wide berth when the coastguards were testing their firing skills.

The Wartime Situation

Situations of war invariably brought greater hazards and a wider range of casualties, for as *The New York Times* pointed out, 'Even in peacetime the long coast of the British Isles is stormy and treacherous. In time of war the work of the lifesavers is a continuous test of skill and courage.' In the First and Second World Wars, Falmouth, Penzance and some other Cornish ports became temporary Naval bases, and boatmen with local knowledge were pressed into service by the Admiralty. In the First World War most of the casualties were caused by enemy submarines; in the Second World War the RNLI's lifeboats, and later the fast and splendid Air Sea Rescue launches also searched for brave young airmen, mostly from the Cornish R.A.F. stations, whose aircraft had crashed into the sea.

Victims Of The Relentless Ocean

A walk through Mylor, St Keverne, Morwenstow or any Cornish churchyard in a maritime setting, will unfold a poignant tale of shipwreck and the cruel sea. Various Christian organisations, Seamen's Missions and The Shipwrecked Mariners' Society raised money and offered practical assistance to seamen and victims of shipwreck, and this excellent, caring work is still carried out by the Fishermen's Mission at Newlyn today. Modern ships and sophisticated technology mean that shipwrecks are fewer, but the sea does not mellow with age; rocks, currents and storms are as dangerous today as they ever were. Sir William Hillary, founder of the RNLI , said in 1824: 'So long as man shall continue to navigate the ocean, and the tempest shall hold course over the surface, in every age, and on every coast, disaster by sea, shipwreck and peril to human life must inevitably occur.'

The Situation Today

Modern reports tell of the stress factor in today's hi-tech, overcrowded shipping scene, and research on safety at sea is important in a changing situation. In 1990 top ship designers from all over the world met for a three day conference organised by the School of Engineering at Exeter University to discuss ways of improving safety on passenger and cargo ships, and the best methods to deal with accidents.

Ships will always be vulnerable, but those who find themselves in distress at sea will have a much stronger chance of survival, thanks to instant communications, bringing a quick response from the rescue services.

NAVIGATION

Navigation is that noble art
That guides a ship when far from land,
And to any distant part
When practised by a skilful hand.

Joshua Coxon: *The British Seas*, 1892

Highlighting Hazards
Navigation of the waters around Cornwall and the Isles of Scilly could be a dicey business at any time, but it was exceptionally dangerous at night. Our forbears set about the daunting task of marking and illuminating hazards, particularly the formidable array of rocks around the south-western tip of Cornwall centuries ago, with the limited technology available at the time. Sir John Killigrew of the influential Falmouth family of Arwenack erected Cornwall's first real lighthouse at the Lizard in 1619 as a commercial venture, inviting revenue from passing shipping. This was rebuilt by Thomas Fonnereau in 1752. But the responsibility of highlighting navigational hazards was taken on by the Brethren of Trinity House, London, who were mostly retired mariners.

Trinity House
Little is known of the origins of Trinity House, an ancient and venerable brotherhood, concerned about sailors and safety at sea, which was chartered during the reign of Henry VIII. They were responsible for creating markers for highlighting navigational hazards, the building and upkeep of lighthouses as well as the licensing of pilots. This institution, like others of its day, was rooted in religious ideals, and much time was spent in praying for the souls of sailors and those who struggled against the raging tempest.

The Emplacement of Lighthouses, Lightships and Other Navigational Aids
Trinity House was responsible for the construction of three types of lighthouse in Cornwall; beacons mounted on tall scaffolding and placed at the mouth of estuaries, towers erected on the shore, adjoined by white-painted

Lighthouses on St. Agnes and the Bishop Rock had provided warning lights to the south and west of the Isles of Scilly, and in 1887 this lighthouse was constructed on the highest point of Round Island to offer protection along the dangerous northern fringes. (Photograph James Gibson; Sheila Bird Collection)

keepers' cottages surrounded by walls and towers constructed on rocks out at sea. There could be some confusion in identifying individual lighthouses until George Manby, the inventor of a mortar propelled ship to shore line hit on the simple and effective notion of giving each its own signal (others also laid claim to this distinction). Lightships were positioned to signify danger and serve as a torch upon the high seas; to float, but not to navigate. Buoys, fog bells, cannons and fog trumpets, which were initially powered by fish oil and later by electricity, have done much in making the sea lanes safer. Traditionally, mariners made use of conveniently placed objects in the landscape, such as hills, church towers and houses, and for many years the tenant of Carn Brea was legally obliged to display a beacon light for the benefit of shipping.

The Elder Brethren had a lighthouse built at St. Agnes, Isles of Scilly in 1680, which, after two and a quarter centuries came out of service, to be superseded by the automatic flashing light on Peninnis Head. In a great feat of engineering, a lighthouse was emplaced on the Eddystone Reef in 1698, and the Longships Light, off Land's End, was built by Lieutenant Henry Smith under lease from Trinity House in 1795, which meant that four lighthouses were highlighting hazards off the Cornish coast at the beginning of the last century. The nineteenth century was to be the great age of

THE ONLY BUOY THAT IS LONELY IN THE
EVENINGS AT FALMOUTH.

The wise mariner will give this one a wide berth — if he can find it! All things nautical were enjoying a popular appeal around the turn of the century (Sheila Bird Collection)

lighthouse achievement, with vastly improved technology, enabling the Bishop and Wolf to be constructed as rock based towers, despite the problems created by the angry, swirling seas. On the north coast, lighthouses were positioned on Godrevy Island, Trevose Head and later at Pendeen. St. Anthony was built at the entrance to Falmouth haven, and the Seven Stones

Lightship was emplaced. Most recently constructed is Tater Du, which looks so distinctive from the deck of the *Scillonian* as she sails in and out of Penzance.

The prevention of shipwreck by drawing attention to dangers, and the evolving role of pilots played a vital part in the story of the preservation of life from shipwreck off Cornwall.

The Evolving Role of Pilots

Negotiating the dreaded waters around the Isles of Scilly struck terror into the heart of many a mariner, and thus the custom of piloting and bartering evolved spontaneously, until it reached the situation that pilotage became the specialised, major occupation of Scillonians. The skills were handed down from father to son, and seafarers were grateful for the service, aware of the practical and safety advantages of employing those with expert knowledge of shifting shoals, rocks and other hazards. As it was customary for the first man aboard the incoming ships to gain the contract, speed was all important, and the design of gigs and pilot cutters became more and more refined. Scillonians were not at all happy to receive a communication from Trinity House in August 1807, concerning an Act of Parliament 'For the better Regulation of Pilots, and of the pilotage of ships and vessels navigating the British seas.' This they felt, was counter productive to them and their system which had evolved to meet the special needs of the Islands. It was to create divisions between licensed and unlicensed pilots, with and without their own craft, and the problems rumbled on for many years, eventually bringing about several categories of pilot. However, resented changes and new situations become established to the extent that they are viewed, in retrospect, with great nostalgia. J.G. Uren of Penzance placed on record in 1907;

> Nothing more forcibly shows the great change which has come over the Mercantile Marine than the decay of the old Channel Pilot. He was as essential to the Master Mariner of the bygone day as was the compass. Knowing the lay of the land, the set of the tide, and the run of every current between the Lizard and the Downs, from Cape Cornwall to Great Ormes Head, he took charge of the ship as soon as she was into the narrow overcrowded waters, and steered her safely into port.

School of Navigation in Penzance

James Sautry, who had thirty years practical experience of the Art of Navigation and Nautical Astronomy, ran a School of Navigation in Penzance, assisted by his son, Edward. Here young sailors were taught to apply Geometry and Lunar Trigonometry in the finding of latitude and longitude,

THE PILOT. *Vaughan T. Paul's series, Penzance.*

Pilots, with their specialized knowledge of the vagaries of local waters, adapted to the needs of passing shipping. They were renowned for their skill and daring, and played a vital role in the preservation of life from shipwreck (Sheila Bird Collection)

to calculate tides and ascertain the variation of the compass in all parts of the world. They were instructed on how to keep a journal at sea, and how to employ Townson's Great Circle Sailing, which was much in vogue at the time.

HARBOURS OF REFUGE

The first object in advance that pleasantly catches the eye of the voyager on nearing the port of his desires, is the lighthouse.

The West Briton: March 1864

Havens of refuge have always been important along Cornwall's wild and inhospitable coastline, but they are few and far between, and by a strange irony, most have hazards such as sandbars or rocks at their entrances, which have to be carefully negotiated before safer waters are reached. Another hazard, particularly in the days of sail, in poor visibility, was the resemblance of one headland to another, which sometimes resulted in ships running headlong into disaster on unexpected shores. Impending storm sent ships off Land's End scurrying for the comparative safety of St. Ives Bay or Mount's Bay, but a sudden shift in wind direction could turn a hoped for safe haven into a death trap.

The Capricious Waters of Mounts Bay

Mount's Bay, which takes the full force of the Westerlies has been called a 'maritime trap', and when two ships with all hands were added to its countless victims who met their doom on Loe Bar in 1810, a contemporary newspaper commented; ' We have reason to believe that had the harbour at Porthleven been completed these two vessels would have been saved.' Piers at St. Michael's Mount and Newlyn were periodically washed away, and in May 1814 a dry dock was opened at Penzance to deal more efficiently with storm battered shipping than had hitherto been possible on blocks on the windswept, open shore. Other ports of refuge, particularly Falmouth, turned their attentions to ship repair.

Falmouth Harbour

The vast natural haven of Falmouth, on the seemingly gentler south coast, has been able to provide shelter for hundreds of vessels on many occasions. But Black Rock constitutes a navigational hazard right at the harbour entrance, and even inside the haven, conditions can become tricky, particularly when winds funnel up the estuary. January 1814 saw the transport *Queen* wrecked on Trefusis point, inside the harbour, in just such conditions, with catastrophic loss of life. This is an area where headlands resembling each other led to confusion and casualties, but the erection of St. Anthony lighthouse and the red and white striped daymark on the Gribbin clarified the situation, particularly in regard to vessels making for the ports of Falmouth or Fowey.

Fowey Harbour

Fowey, described in early times as 'one of the easiest of access and safest harbours of its size in the whole Channel,' was without a harbour light in the middle of the last century, a situation described as 'a singular omission,' and 'a maritime puzzle' by *The West Briton* in March 1864. Warming to the theme, this newspaper with a social conscience continued. 'Fowey harbour is undoubtedly blind; Blind by nature, blind by art, a vexatious defect, involving, doubtless, the loss of much profitable custom by ocean wayfarers, who would look in, and storm driven ships seeking shelter, but find it not, for this barbaric, inhospitable, and impolite neglect.'

Padstow Harbour

In 1845 there was a calculated 40,000 vessels passing annually between Padstow and Lundy Island, with so many shipwrecks that a public meeting was held in Wadebridge to discuss ways of making Padstow a more accessible and efficient port of refuge. This eventually led to a number of improvements, including the cutting back of large sections of rock at Stepper Point. Padstow and Hayle both have dangerous sandbars, which have defied attempts at clearance.

Government Efforts to Improve Harbours

In 1857 a Government select committee recommended the construction or improvement of harbours around the British coast, suggesting various suitable places, including St. Ives or Padstow. In its review seven years later, attention was drawn to the Board of Trade's observation that 'frequent attention has been paid to lighthouses, harbours, anchors and all the other means which have been devised for the prevention of shipwreck, and yet the terrible reality remains that about one thousand ships and their cargoes are annually lost within the narrow limits of the United Kingdom.' This involved the loss of thousands of lives, and millions of pounds in lost revenue. It was decided to set up a Royal Commission, composed of scientific, mercantile and seafaring men, with the recommendation that the Government should contribute to the scheme, but that shipping interests should shoulder most of the costs.

Shipping Industry's Reluctance to Contribute

However, the shipping fraternity did not feel under any obligation to do so, for reasons summarised thus in the *West Briton*:

> The shrewdest and best informed men in that (shipping) trade, contend that wrecks are chiefly due to causes that harbours could not prevent, and that the construction of such works would neither lessen casualties nor reduce the premiums of insurance. Their reasons are

19

founded upon various facts, which are very important in character, but liable to escape general observation. The great proportion of vessels lost are coasters of small value and comparatively ill found: and where this is not the case, the vessel is best off by keeping the sea. The coasting and short foreign trade is being rapidly transferred to steamers which can keep off a lee shore and are seldom lost by stress of weather. Therefore the argument is deduced that harbours of refuge are required for bad vessels rather than good ones, and to tax shipping generally for them would be to tax the better class for the benefit of the worse, and to discourage the development of steamers. Besides, a harbour is only of use when a vessel can get into it, and the chances are against this being generally the case, not to mention the fact that mist, snow, and thick weather may prevent their being seen. This is one side of the question, and on the other are to be set those considerations of national economy and humanity which dictate the use of all possible means for the saving of life and property....

There is also another difficulty — making one harbour serve for any great extent of coast. The number of wrecks at any place depends much more on the amount of shipping than on the nature of the coast — a fact proved by the supposed safe spots producing about as many wrecks as the reputed dangerous ones....Other arguments against any general harbour scheme are founded upon the disproportion existing between the average annual loss at any particular spot, and the average annual cost of constructing and maintaining a harbour there....On the Cornwall coast the cost would be £17,600 a year, and property saved about £7,000. The general result of all these observations is to lead to the the the inference that if harbours of refuge for saving life are to be made, the number of such harbours and the consequent cost must be greater than was at first supposed; and that the Government would have to provide the money.

The Attitude of Those Who Never Went To Sea
It was reported by The *West Briton*:

The shipping interests appear to have good cause for their refusal to bear the cost; and the Board of Trade, coming to that conclusion suggested that it would be advisable to let the House of Commons have an opportunity for reconsidering the subject, as, however desirable it was to save life and property , the benefits which would accrue for constructing the harbours named would in all probability be utterly out of proportion to the millions spent. This is the position in which the question is left, and is likely to remain, except in cases where local wants are so imperative as to call for the expenditure of local capital.

The Voice of Those Who Cared
While these procrastinations were going on, the catalogue of casualties continued to grow, and there were particular requests for the establishment of a port of refuge on Cornwall's formidable and unyielding Atlantic coast, as dangerous a section of coast as could be encountered anywhere. A letter to *The West Briton* in February 1863 drew attention to this:

> Sir,
> I observe your correspondent stating 'Lundy desires a harbour of refuge for coasting vessels etc. in the extreme north of Cornwall. Many there are who join with him, but hitherto, nothing to the purpose has been done to secure such a desirable object. True it is that surveys have been made, plans have been drawn, calculations gone into, but no place possessing the natural qualifications for a great national work has presented itself. At the same time, there are several places where pretty little coves might be secured at the cost of only a few thousands, where ships might run into in rough weather to be safe. Of this class is that of Boscastle, now a small tidal harbour, where about 30 acres of good anchorage might be secured by running a breakwater of 40 or 50 poles from Willa Park to Maychard Gull Rock. The doing of this has been discussed for the last 40 years.....

PRESERVING LIFE FROM SHIPWRECK

The Inventors of Inshore Life-Saving Apparatus
The wrecking of H.M. Frigate *Anson* on Loe Bar in 1807 was to have far reaching effects on our maritime history. Having left Falmouth on Christmas Eve to take up her position off Brest as a lookout ship for the Channel Fleet, she took a buffeting in Mount's Bay for several days. On trying to return to Falmouth, Land's End was mistaken for the Lizard, and the vessel ended up as another victim of Loe Bar. It was the harrowing experience of seeing so many people perish in the surf so close to the shore, while he and others stood helplessly by, that caused Henry Trengrouse to dedicate the rest of his life to the invention of an effective inshore rescue apparatus, sacrificing his money, his business and his health in the process.

The potential of a line which could be propelled from the shore to stricken ships had occurred to others, who independently came up with various designs. Back in 1791 Lieutenant John Bell had earned a medal from The Society for the Encouragement of the Arts for a device which fired a rope by means of a mortar, but the invention had never saved any lives. Captain

George Manby, a military man from Yarmouth, and contemporary of Horatio Nelson had similarly invented a mortar-propelled shore-to-ship line, which was installed at Penzance, St. Ives and Hayle in 1816. Although this invention had won a Government award of £2,000 and achieved a degree of success, it was also cumbersome and dangerous to operate, and was abandoned after causing fatalities during testing.

Henry Trengrouse of Helston

Henry Trengrouse carried out various line throwing experiments across the mouth of Porthleven harbour, conveying people backwards and forwards in flexible chairs and tight-fitting cork garments, watched on one occasion by the Mayor of Helston and other dignitaries, who were impressed. Thus heartened by this success he contacted The Society for the Encouragement of the Arts, inviting them to test his 'Apparatus for preserving Lives and Property in cases of Shipwreck,' and enclosing a short, printed essay on the subject. Trials were carried out at Woolwich in front of high-ranking naval officers, who saw a mackerel line propelled 180 yards by an eight ounce rocket, and 212 yards by a pounder. Furthermore, The Society demonstrated that a rocket one and three quarter inches in diameter was capable of carrying a cord right across the Serpentine in Hyde Park. For this Henry Trengrouse was awarded a large Silver Medal and thirty guineas. He received other medals and awards, but never really got the credit he deserved for an invention which saved many lives, and was the forerunner of inshore lifesaving equipment.

The Life-saving Role of Seafaring Communities

In earlier times spontaneous rescues were carried out by seafaring communities, when local fishermen, boatmen, pilots and coastguards put their specialised skills and local knowledge to good effect. Whole communities would turn out, sometimes linking hands to form human chains to haul victims of shipwreck from the surf. When Commodore George Walker's ship *Boscawen* was wrecked at St. Ives in 1745, he wrote: 'The people of the sea coast of Cornwall have for some years undergone the censure of being savage devourers of all wrecks that strike their coast. How weak a creature is general belief, the dupe of idle fame! Humanity never exercised its virtues more conspicuously than in this instance in the inhabitants and people of St. Ives. They flocked down in numbers to our assistance and, at risk of their own lives, saved ours.'

In 1817 the inhabitants of Gunwalloe Cove, near Helston teamed together bravely to go to the aid of some terrified sailors who had leapt into the boiling surf from their stricken ship, and in the course of the rescue William Triggs and John Curtis risked their own lives to prevent an exhausted sailor from being sucked back out to sea. The men of the Jackson and Rowe families

Sampson Mitchell, of the Perranporth Rocket Brigade, was able to get a line aboard the Dutch steel schooner Voorspoed *after she had become a victim of a March gale in 1901, thus saving the crew.*
The vessel became an object of curiosity on the beach at Perranporth, and was severely looted by local 'savages'. She was refloated a fortnight later — only to be lost with all hands on her next voyage to Newfoundland (Sheila Bird Collection)

similarly put themselves at risk in 1882 at Porthgwarra, near Land's End, when the fisherfolk made a combined effort to help a barque in distress. They were horrified to see the vessel strike Kite Cairn, then get swept out to sea. In a feat of great skill and courage these men were able to get the ten crew members ashore, just as their ship disappeared beneath the waves.

Due Recognition — And Lack Of It

In 1831 two humble fishermen of Mevagissey received the thanks of the Emperor for saving the crew of the Russian brig *St Nicholas* at Port Holland, and were each awarded fifty ducats. However, a fisherman from the Lizard called Hitchens, who risked his life in going aboard the naval vessel *Exmouth*, a ninety gun screw ship which had gone off course in thick fog and become embayed near Kynance Cove in 1857, did not receive the recognition he deserved. Under his expert guidance, the steam was got up, the anchor slipped and the ship piloted out of danger. For thus heroically saving hundreds of lives and property estimated at around £100,000 the Admiralty awarded him £5.

Ever Vigilant
The observation and diligence of local boatmen often averted total disaster as in February 1848, when the boatmen of St. Martins in the Isles of Scilly noticed the dilapidated French brig *Eagle*, returning fully laden from the coast of Africa with an exhausted crew, anchored to the east of the island in a vulnerable situation. As a gale arose and threatened to drive them on to the shore they went out, boarded her, and brought her in to safety. Pilots, particularly those of Scilly, were renowned for their skill and daring in saving lives from shipwreck. Later that year the Scillonian pilot cutter *Active* went to the aid of the Swedish brig *Charlotte*, which had been driven ashore on the rocky island of Melledgan. They picked up ten of the crew who had managed to climb along the mast and onto the rock, by daringly venturing in and out of the surf.

Prompt and spontaneous action by the local seafaring fraternity saved many lives from shipwreck (Sheila Bird Collection)

The Contribution of Coastguards, Pilots and Others
During the last century, pilots, coastguards and others received official recognition in the form of medals or monetary awards for outstanding service in the preservation of life from shipwreck on a number of occasions. The Coastguard Service was actually an amalgamation of various patrol

groups, set up to eliminate smuggling activities along the coast, but having got spontaneously involved with rescue work, a directive of 1822 stated that in the event of shipwreck, 'every officer and man on the spot, or stationed within a reasonable distance is to afford every assistance for the purpose of saving lives of the persons on board,' and coastguards, particularly those in the Mount's Bay area made an outstanding contribution to rescue work in Cornwall. Naval officers, such as Captain Norcock, R.N., held high ranking positions in the Coastguard Service. When the schooner *Endeavour* was wrecked three miles west of Fowey Harbour in May 1856, this inspecting commander organised a rescue which involved carrying a boat over the cliffs from Polkerris and lowering it down a two hundred foot cliff. Then he and two boatmen battled their way through very rough seas to rescue crewman George Dewy, who had found refuge on an isolated rock.

'To Die Unknown is Dying, Twice Over'
Henri-Alphonse Esquiros, a French professor who had great empathy with Cornwall and its people, wrote in 1865: 'Shipwrecks in these seas, bristling with reefs, were not only very numerous some years ago, but they had a peculiarly grave character. A ship was crushed by dashing against rocks or precipices. What was this ship? Ask this of the winds, the sea, the few insignificant fragments tossing on the immensity of the waves. To die unknown is dying twice over. Such, however, has been the lot of many ships on the Cornish coast, and no one ever knew their name, their country or the number of passengers on board...' After citing examples of brave rescues, he talks of 'a thousand traits of bravery which honour the sailors, and especially the fishermen of Cornwall, 'with the institution of life boats which were becoming established along these shores, heightening the standards of humanity, creating 'an emulation for devotion and sacrifice.'

THE ROYAL NATIONAL
LIFE-BOAT INSTITUTION

A Frenchman's View:

The Life-boat stations are managed and supported by local committees; but most of the committees are under the control and patronage
of the National Life-boat Institution, whose seat is in London. Elsewhere we should expect to find such a service of public utility
organised by the State. In England, the State has undertaken the
material defence of the coasts; it raises batteries, builds forts, and
forms a sanitary cordon of custom house officers against the evils of
smuggling. It has to some extent accepted the ungrateful part of the
task, while it yielded the generous part to individual efforts. The
National Life-boat Institution receives nothing from the Government,
and depends solely on public charity.

As the Institution exists on public liberality, it has been obliged
necessary to arouse the national sympathy in favour of the sailor and
the wrecked. It has recourse to everything that can affect the heart and
the imagination: to music, poetry, engraving, and publicity. Thanks to
this fortunate assistance of literature and the fine arts, the life-boat has
become in the mind of the masses a sacred object, a palladium of the
seas.

Alphonse Esquiros: Cornwall And Its Coasts, 1865

**The Formation of the National Institution for the Preservation of Life from
Shipwreck**
Mankind has always been touched by tragedies at sea, and at the beginning
of the last century, concerned, influential people nationwide, spearheaded
by Sir William Hillary of Douglas, Isle of Man, were pressing for a properly
organised rescue service to be established around the coast of Britain. And
thus it was that a meeting was held in March 1824, at the London Tavern,
Bishopsgate, at which the Archbishop of Canterbury moved a resolution
that, 'An institution be now formed for the Preservation of Life in cases of
Shipwreck on the coasts of the United Kingdom, to be supported by donations and subscriptions, and to be called the National Institution for the
Preservation of Life from Shipwreck.' The Sovereign had graciously con-
sented to become its patron, and an impressive list of notable people had
pledged their support. Royalty and the gentry have always maintained close
links with the organisation which, after the Merchant Shipping Act of 1854,

requiring better regulation of maritime affairs became more clearly defined as the Royal National Life-Boat Institution founded in 1824 for the Preservation of Life from Shipwreck, to avoid confusion with the Shipwrecked Fishermen and Mariners' Royal Benevolent Society.

Keeping Lifeboats In The Limelight
Lifeboats caught the imagination of the public, and were the topic of the day, particularly after the noble exploits of Grace Darling, the lighthouse keeper's daughter, had been highlighted by *The Times*, for bravely taking the heavy oars of her father's sturdy coble during their heroic rescue of the survivors of the *Forfarshire*, wrecked off the coast of Northumberland in a raging storm in September 1838. The Institution had become aware of the need for favourable publicity, noticing that donations fell away when lifeboats were out of the limelight. Lifeboats stylishly drawn through the streets of inland towns and cities generated much revenue, and indeed Falmouth's first lifeboat was donated by the citizens of Gloucester. The arrival of new lifeboats created great excitement and aroused feelings of pride, as befitted a maritime nation such as ours. This produced more revenue and was a fine public relations exercise in itself. The money raised was used to build lifeboats and support lifeboatmen. The general public identified closely with the hazards of sea travel, which, in the days before aeroplanes, might have implications for them.

Early Lifeboat Coverage In Cornwall
Cornwall had the Institution's lifeboats stationed at Penzance in 1826, Padstow in 1827, Bude and St. Mary's (Isles of Scilly) in 1837, St. Ives in 1840, Sennen Cove in 1853 and Lizard and Polkerris (Fowey) in 1859 (some of these places had previously had private lifeboats). But in his Report of 1851 the Duke of Northumberland, who had been untiring in his efforts towards the lifeboat cause, had highlighted the inadequate coverage between Falmouth, on the south coast of Cornwall, and Hartland Point in North Devon. Furthermore, *The Times* criticised the Duke of Cornwall, who was then a minor, for not giving lifeboats the backing that dukes, squires and burgesses elsewhere had provided for their coastal areas. This aroused public awareness to the extent that there were nineteen lifeboat stations in Cornwall by 1870. These early Cornish lifeboats, manned mostly by fishermen, boatmen and coastguards along some of Britain's most treacherous coastline, achieved a fine record of outstanding service. And the strong tradition of family service remains in Cornwall today.

EARLY LIFEBOATS AND EQUIPMENT

Let not the waterflood overflow me,
neither let the deep swallow me up.
(This quotation, abbreviated to, 'Let not the deep swallow me up', was chosen as the inscription on the RNLI Gold, then in 1917, Bronze Medals, awarded for outstanding service)   *Psalm 69 verse 15*

For some time before the setting up of a national institution for the preservation of life from shipwreck, it had been recognised that workaday fishing and other craft used for locally organised rescue operations, even when converted, were not really suited to the lifesaving role. Extra speed and buoyancy were required, particularly where there was a need to get in close to a stricken vessel in very rough seas. So this gave rise to a challenge to design a boat specifically for the purpose. Various people responded to this, and a tombstone in Hythe churchyard in Kent, proclaims Lionel Lukin to have been the first man to have built a lifeboat and be the inventor of the principle of insubmersible boats, patented in 1785, by which so many lives had been saved. But the Frenchman Bernieres had invented a self-righting craft in 1765, and others might contest these claims. However, Henry Greathead is generally regarded as having achieved this distinction. For this boatbuilder from Shields won a competition to design a lifeboat, which was launched in January 1790 and saved hundreds of lives before being wrecked on rocks forty years later. Over the next fourteen years, thirty Greatheads with slight modifications were sent to stations in England and Scotland as well as places overseas.

Henry Greathead's lifeboat, which came to be known as the *Original*, incorporated ideas gleaned by the committee of judges and was thus the outcome of pooled design strengths, as was the aim of the competition, set up by a group of gentlemen who were concerned about shipping disasters occurring at the mouth of the Tyne. The *Original* was a thiry-feet, ten-oared, double-ended boat with a curved keel, but she did not incorporate the self-righting principle. Later lifeboats were to be self-righting.

'It Flies, It Skims The Waves'
'Through its shape and the nature of its progress, a floating lifeboat differs greatly from ordinary boats.' wrote Alphonse Esquiros in *Cornwall and Its Coasts* (1865). 'Graceful, elegant, with a prow and stem raised, it flies, it skims the waves. Storms and the most awful seas are unable to terrify such a boat.' And he went on to point out, 'It is not solely on account of its shape, or the number of its oars, that the lifeboat proves lighter and is endowed with greater speed than ordinary boats...it is because it is swollen with atmospheric air.'

28

Injected with Renewed Zest

A horrifying lifeboat disaster in South Shields in 1849 led to a shake up in the administration of the lifeboat service, whereby young and enthusiastic Richard Lewis became Secretary, the 4th Duke of Northumberland President, and Commander J.R.Ward the Inspector of Lifeboats, keeping in close touch with what was happening at the local stations. The Duke of Northumberland set up a competition for the best self-righting lifeboat, offering a prize of a hundred guineas. This was won by James Beeching, a boatbuilder from Great Yarmouth. Then it was the task of Mr. Peake, a Master Shipwright from Devonport Dockyard, to take note of the finer points of all entries, then come up with a design incorporating the best ideas. Thus evolved the prototype for lifeboats used around our coasts for many years, combining buoyancy and self-righting properties with the ability to self-dislodge water.

Perfecting the Finer Points of Lifeboat Design

The early lifeboats were pulling or pulling-and-sailing craft of varying lengths, with hung ropes festooned from gunwhale tops which acted as external ropes for casualties in the water to grasp or use as a stirrup for stepping aboard. In those days of muscle power, the design and performance of oars could be a matter of life or death for the crews themselves. Launching was a crucial manoeuvre, requiring disciplined synchronisation with the strokeman. The oars needed to be strong, but not so tough that they could strike the bottom with rigidity and cause a capsize during those first few, vital strokes, which propelled them through the dangerous rise and fall of oncoming waves, about to explode into flying surf upon a stormy shore. The oars were long, weighted and skilfully fashioned from complete sections of young trees, and painted blue on the port side; white on the starboard. Experimental work was carried out to improve the finer points, for the loss of them rendered the lifeboat vulnerable. However, various swivel and clip devices were not generally liked by the crews, whose second nature, as men of the sea, was their readiness for quick, unhampered manoeuvre, vital when trying to get out of a tight spot, or getting in close to a casualty.

Basic Equipment

Spare oars were an essential part of any lifeboat's equipment, as were grappling irons, anchors, drogues, compasses and lifebuoys, still basic equipment in today's sophisticated lifeboats. The drogue, a long, conical canvas bag, trawled astern by rope, would act as a brake or sea anchor, controlling and stabilising the lifeboat, lessening her chances of being swept broadside on to the waves, or being catapulted end over end in a following wind. Drop keels, incorporated in later lifeboats, were aids to manoeuvrability, helped with trimming, and had the advantage that they could be jettisoned in an emergency. And in the RNLI, there are still times when oil is poured on the proverbial troubled waters during rescue operations in turbulent conditions, to create a calming effect on the surface of the sea.

Practice and Maintenance
It was formerly the responsibility of the salaried coxswain to maintain and repair the lifeboat, backed up if necessary by local boatbuilders. Periodic practices gave the lifeboatmen the opportunity to put the lifeboat through her paces and demonstrate their prowess to the District Inspector and admiring watchers on the shore (particularly the ladies). These practices took place, whatever the weather, and resulted in the loss of lifeboatmen on more than one occasion in Cornwall. There used to be rowing contests between various Cornish lifeboat stations, but the situation got out of hand and it was thought to be prejudicial to the efficiency of the lifeboat coverage if an emergency should arise at that time.

Life Preservers
The importance of suitable clothing for sailors in distress and those who went to their aid was recognised some time ago, as this report of 1813 in *The West Briton* demonstrates:

> An experiment of great importance to seamen in general, was made at Falmouth on Monday last. A mattress so contrived as to answer the double purpose of a seaman's bed and a life preserver, was exhibited before a great number of spectators, who were fully satisfied that the inventor has attained the desirable object which he proposed. The buoyancy of this life preserver and its capability of supporting a human body for any length of time was evident. A hole in the centre, into which a cushion falls, admits the head, and the cushion is so contrived as to answer the purpose of a cap which preserved the head from injury. It is recommended to the Packet service and is likely to come into general use.

Functional Clothing for Lifeboatmen
In the last century the original air belts worn by lifeboatmen were replaced by two sectional cork lifejackets, which kept the head and shoulders of a fully clothed man above the water without restricting his breathing. The insulating properties of cork also helped retain body heat. The traditional weather proof oilskins, sou'westers and thigh boots may have been wind and waterproof, but they were cumbersome and not entirely satisfactory. The design of effective, non-restrictive buoyancy and weatherproof garments has been an ongoing challenge for the RNLI. After much trial and error with fibrous kapok as a promising material, there emerged a satisfactory design in the 1920s, which remained in use for about forty years. Concerned about the

The crew of the Porthoustock lifeboat wearing their cork lifejackets and warm, woolly hats, known to later generations of lifeboatmen as their 'Noddy' hats (Acknowledgements Frank Curnow; Sheila Bird Collection)

comfort and welfare of lifeboatmen Mrs. Edith Manby, a relative of Captain George Manby, whose mortar-propelled life-lines had been sent to most of the Cornish lifeboat stations in the middle of the last century, had organised a team of busy knitters to fashion woolly scarf helmets, which were worn by lifeboatmen all over the country. To show its appreciation, the Institution awarded her a Gold Badge in 1937.

Official Advice to Belt Up Before Departure

The Life-Boat Journal of December 1852 made some pertinent observations on the subject:

> No life-boat station can be considered complete without a set of life-belts for the boat's crew, and the several local committees should insist upon having them, and upon the belts being put on, before the men go afloat. The qualities essential in a good life-belt, for life-boat purposes, are that it should be light, compact, and flexible, so as not to inconvenience the rower, for if it does so we may be sure it will not be worn.

31

Launching the Lifeboat

Getting the lifeboat launched was a strenuous exercise in itself, for horses had to be rounded up and harnessed to the lifeboat carriage before it was hauled across the beach, or on some occasions transported for several miles over the cliffs. In the event of horses being required for a lifeboat emergency, owners were obliged by law to make them available, and failure to do so could result in heavy penalties.

Few places in Cornwall where lifeboat stations were established enjoyed the natural advantage of harbours where lifeboats could remain permanently afloat, and those which did also presented the problem of how to get the crewmen aboard quickly in an emergency. So it tended to be more convenient to keep the lifeboat in a boathouse, to be launched down a slipway by gravity with a crew already aboard, transported on wooden skids across sandy or shingle beaches, or drawn to where they were needed by teams of horses. As horses, lent by farmers, carriers or railway companies became increasingly difficult to obtain, purpose-built tractors were developed, like the ones used at St. Ives.

Launching at Porthoustock was viable by means of skids across the beach when the tide level was as shown here in 1907. But it became increasingly difficult as the build-up of the beach caused it to retreat (Acknowledgements Frank Curnow; Sheila Bird Collection)

TO SIGNIFY DISTRESS AT SEA

Coastguard stations had been experimenting successfully with the firing of cannons as a means of signifying emergencies over a considerable distance, and in 1873, the RNLI sent a cannon to the Mevagissey station for use at night in case of shipwreck. But for subsequent generations, the mortar fired maroons which summoned crews, and which zipped skywards in spectacular style, exploded and shook the little ports of Cornwall, set dogs barking, seagulls protesting and pulses racing, also informed communities of the imminent departure of their lifeboat and gave some encouragement to those in distress at sea.

The maroons were partly usurped by the coming of the telephone, and more recently by the arrival of neat, compact radio pagers (bleepers), carried by crewmen. The mortar fired maroons were phased out and replaced by hand held maroons to supplement the pagers. The word 'maroon', signifying a firework exploding with a loud report, is derived from the French 'marron', meaning chestnut, which expands and explodes when exposed to fire.

Mayday! Mayday! Mayday!

This is the international radio-telephone distress signal used by ships and aircraft today. In 1838, Samuel Morse devised a system of dots and dashes which came to be known as the Morse Code. Morse could also be signalled by arms or hand-flags, as in semaphore. It was reported in 1990: 'Long used in radio communication on land, sea and in the air, this method of transmitting messages will have ceased in the commercial shipping world by the end of the century. The code will be replaced by the Global Maritime Distress & Safety System, which is to be introduced in 1993.'

Pan Pan Medico!

In former times, when ship to shore communication was limited to visual signalling, sailors taken ill at sea were at the mercy of their Captain's interpretation of medical guides, or in a dire emergency contact might be made with big liners carrying doctors, if they were fortunate enough to find one in the vicinity.

Although they would have been oblivious to it at the time, the foundations of an evolving medical tradition were being laid in September, 1907, when the Coastguard reported that the *S.S. Ellesmere* of Manchester, close to the Runnelstone, was displaying signals requesting a pilot and medical assistance, and the *Elizabeth & Blanche II* took a doctor out to the ship.

Western Cornwall has long played an exciting role in developing communications, and after the First World War the Post Office established a medical advice service in association with the Land's End Radio. This led to decisions as to whether doctors should be taken out to ships, or the patient brought ashore for hospitalisation. Today, lifeboats and helicopters from RNAS Culdrose continue those traditions.

In the last century, Admiral Fitzroy, a government minister studied wind direction and made calculations predicting the arrival of these currents at given lifeboat stations, whereupon the news was communicated by telegraph to all the threatened areas, and alarm and caution signals were hoisted at the relevant stations. The signals consisted chiefly of a cone and a drum, both made of coarse canvas painted black, and made rigid with hoops. Barometers attached to the early lifeboat stations, were consulted by fishermen and sailors before they put to sea.

THE LIFEBOATMEN

May we not say that the divine breath of humanity swells the sails of such boats, which carry them through the darkness, and the lightning consolation to the heart of those who are despairing?

Alphonse Esquiros: *Cornwall And Its Coasts*, 1865

An Incredibly Hardy Breed
The toughness and endurance of those early lifeboat crews are, in the light of most people's capabilities today, almost beyond belief. By the nature of things, the emergencies almost invariably coincided with the most difficult of weather conditions, usually in the depths of winter. The men often got soaked to the skin in the process of launching, and could be out in their open boats for hours on end, sometimes all night, buffeted about in the wind and the rain, with little or nothing to eat or drink. But they were a hardy breed, well used to working at sea in harsh conditions, and well aware that their survival depended on their fitness to control the boat and keep going. In those days the shipwreck was usually within sight of land, and rescues were mostly carried out in waters familiar to them.

Lifeboats Traditionally Manned by Fishermen
In the last century, when every Cornish harbour and cove had a thriving fishing industry, and the coastal population had a close relationship with the sea (which is not always the case today), there were plenty of willing candidates to man the lifeboat and therefore great competition to be accepted into the ranks of this elite service. Youngsters held their elders in awe. It was a case of proving their worth, before they, too, were eligible to occupy a much

coveted position on the fishermen's harbourside bench and listen to *men's talk* — of fish and boats and personalities and happenings and how things used to be. This automatically gave rise to the easy relationship and close bonding, vital to the performance of any good lifeboat crew. In selecting a crew, preference was always given to fishermen, accustomed to the daily perils of the sea, and it was a great day when a youngster was promoted from frequent and willing helper, in the right place at the right time, to Lifeboatman. In an emergency everyone, including the womenfolk, turned out to help with getting the lifeboat launched. Coxswains received an annual salary, while crews were paid for each service, according to the severity of the weather. Those who helped with launching were similarly paid a modest fee, which in Cornwall, where life could be particularly harsh, and communities deprived, created a welcome supplement to the frugal family income.

Every Cornish port had one: a bench from which fishermen could keep an eye on things and philosophise. Youngsters, who held them in awe, knew that they had been accepted into a man's world when they were allowed to occupy a space on this élite seat (Acknowledgements John Miles; Sheila Bird Collection)

Ever Ready for the Call
On the occcasion of the inauguration of the Falmouth lifeboat in August 1867, Richard Lewis, Secretary of the Institution said:

When a shipwreck takes place, which is of course mostly in stormy weather, that is the time when the life-boat is called into requisition. As soon as the signal of distress is made, the crew of our life-boats are ever ready to man them, either in the night or in the day, no matter how strong the gale may be. On such occasions the crews who man the lifeboat never falter for a moment, indeed, the great difficulty is to keep the men out of the boat when she is required, and the British tar now displays as much bravery in saving life on our coasts as he used to do in former times in defending the honour and interest of our country. Now, it would be cruel to call on these men to sacrifice their health, to sacrifice their clothing, and to sacrifice perhaps everything that is dear to them, without some acknowledgement for their noble deeds. The Royal Life-boat Society pays each man, when he goes afloat in the daytime, 10s., and each man for night service 20s., so that when a life-boat goes to sea it costs the Institution about £10 or £12 in the day, and £14 or £16 in the night. Again, in order to practice the men in the management of this craft, they are required to go afloat in their life-boat once in every quarter throughout the year, when they are paid 5s. each man in rough weather, and 3s. each if it is calm weather. I should observe, in regard to these payments, that they give the utmost satisfaction to the men. They know very well what they are to expect; we never receive any complaint from them, and they know that when they have to perform services attended with more than ordinary peril, their payments will be doubled. But I should like to impress upon you that the crew are seldom actuated by mercenary or pecuniary consideration, they are generally impelled by a much higher and nobler feeling.

LIFEBOAT STATIONS IN CORNWALL AND THE ISLES OF SCILLY

(In the following pages Lifeboat Stations
are described in order of their establishment)

O Lord, Thy sea is so wide
And my ship so small.
Have mercy!

Breton Fishermen's Prayer

LIFEBOAT STATIONS IN CORNWALL

Inshore Lifeboat
Still Operational
Redundant Stations in Brackets

*** ST

(H

** PENLEE

** SENNEN COVE

* MARAZIO

** ST. MARY'S

(ST. AGNES)

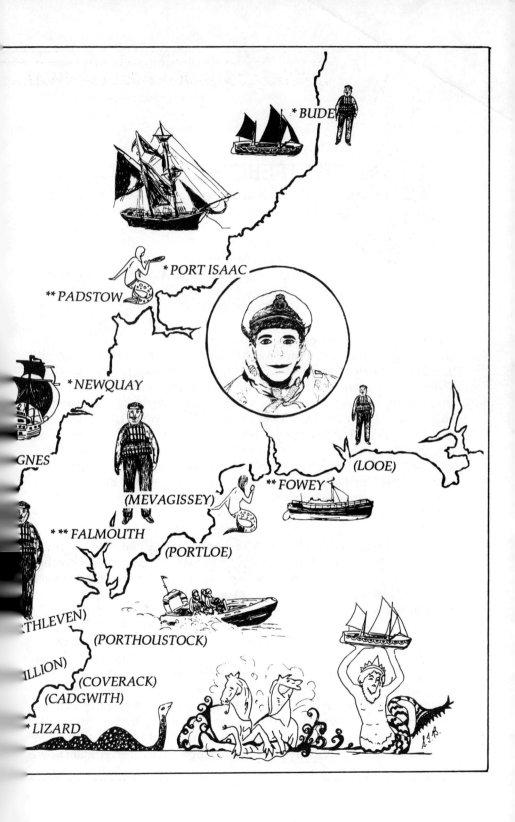

* BUDE

* PORT ISAAC

** PADSTOW

* NEWQUAY

GNES

(LOOE)

** FOWEY

(MEVAGISSEY)

* ** FALMOUTH

(PORTLOE)

THLEVEN)

(PORTHOUSTOCK)

ILLION)

(COVERACK)

(CADGWITH)

* LIZARD

PENLEE LIFEBOAT STATION

(Penzance: 1803-1917 Lapsing 1828-1851): Newlyn 1908-1913: Penlee 1913-)

Break, break, break,
At the foot of thy crags, O Sea!
But the tender grace of a day that is dead
Will never come back to me.
(Alfred Tennyson)

The Capricious Nature of Mount's Bay
'Mount's-Bay lieth N.W. from the *Lizard* 6 Leagues, and 3 Leagues from the Land's-end.' stated Captain Greenvile Collins in his Great Britain's Coasting Pylot of 1693, a survey of the sea coast commissioned by Charles II, in an effort to make these waters safer with accurate charts for the benefit of mariners. This *Coasting Pylot* cited *Gover's -Lake* (Gwavas Lake) as being a good place to anchor, 'because you bring the sunken Rocks of *Carrenbase* and *Lowleigh* South-east from you, which Rocks break off the Sea... Although this, and the curve of the bay offered protection in some conditions, seafarers over the centuries found to their cost that a sudden swing in wind direction could turn an apparently safe haven into a death trap, driving little sailing vessels helplessly on shore before a gale.

Penzance Lays Claim To Having Cornwall's First Lifeboat
An on-going catalogue of disasters in Mount's Bay, with appalling loss of life, led to a special appeal fund being set up to raise £150 for a lifeboat, to which Lloyd's donated £50, and a lifeboat of Henry Greathead's design arrived in Penzance towards the end of 1803. However, after apparently remaining unused, she was somewhat ingloriously seized for debt in 1812 and raised the sum of twenty guineas. *The West Briton* newspaper commented caustically; 'Perhaps the gentlemen of Penzance and its neighbours feel themselves so burthened by providing the poor with provisions at this season that they had nothing to spare for redeeming the lifeboat.' The reason for the lifeboat's neglect probably stemmed from a preference of local seafarers to use their own, trusted craft rather than new fangled designs from upcountry. Be that as it may, Penzance lays claim to being the first place in Cornwall to have a lifeboat. Furthermore, there was the distinction of local men William Rowe

40

and John Freeman being awarded early Silver Medals of the future RNLI in 1824, for saving the crew of eight from the collier brig *Olive* wrecked beneath the Halzephron cliffs in Mount's Bay.

Recognition of Life-saving Endeavour
A local branch of the newly formed National Institution for the Preservation of Life from Shipwreck was promptly established, and a lifeboat of the Plenty class arrived in 1826. But, unfortunately, her career turned out to be short-lived, for she was wrecked on 15th November 1828, when launching to the assistance of the vessel *Phoebe*. Rescues continued to be carried out in local boats, as in May of that year, when Mr. Richard Pearce, the Lloyd's agent put Manby's inshore rescue apparatus and his own six-oared gigs to good use in saving the master and five crewmen of the brig *Albion* of Plymouth, which had been driven on shore to the east of Newlyn in a heavy gale. There was no official lifeboat here when the schooners *Kitty* and *Stephen Knight* became casualties of the storm around Yuletide 1848, which sent shipping scampering for safe havens. Fortunately the crew of the *Stephen Knight* was able to save themselves in their own boat, but the *Kitty*, with most of her canvas blown away, was driven on shore between Penzance and St. Michael's Mount. The surviving crew of seven was rescued by a shore boat at dawn, in a fine service in which William A. Selly was recognised by the Institution's Silver Medal. Further recognition came in 1851 with the heroic life-saving exploits after the wrecking of the *New Commercial* on the Brisons, which led to the establishment of a Lifeboat Station at Sennen Cove (*see* Sennen Cove). 1851 also brought official recognition to Mr. Richard Pearce, who was awarded a Silver Medal for his repeated services in saving life from shipwreck.

The Siting of Boathouses and Safety Measures Taken
Richard Pearce, Lloyd's agent and Honorary Secretary from 1826 to 1862 was instrumental in raising local funds which resulted in a thirty-feet, ten-oared lifeboat of the Peake class, constructed by Messrs. Semmens & Thomas of Penzance coming into service in 1853, the remainder of the money having been provided by the National Shipwreck Institution. A wooden boathouse was constructed near the railway station in 1856, but because of on-going launching problems, the lifeboat was variously sited around the waterfront at Penzance, Wherrytown, Newlyn and Penlee. In the last century there had been ambitious plans to create a harbour of refuge in Mount's Bay, along the lines of that created in Plymouth Sound but, as it transpired, work was carried out on piers and extensions in Penzance and Newlyn at various times in the eighteenth ,nineteenth and present centuries, with pier and light-houses and other illuminations, and beacons and buoys being emplaced. At one time Mount's Bay was served by lifeboat stations at Penzance, Newlyn,

Porthleven, Mullion and the Lizard; now Penlee and the Lizard (currently sited on the eastern side of that peninsula at Kilcobben) remain, with seasonal back-up by the more recently established ILB station at Marazion, to deal with the increasing number of inshore, recreational mishaps in the bay.

An early lifeboat being launched at Penzance (Sheila Bird Collection)

Living up to their Names

In 1860 that first Peake lifeboat was replaced by another, built by Forrestt of Limehouse, under the auspices of the Institution. When the town celebrated the marriage of the Prince and Princess of Wales in March 1863, they incorporated a double lifeboat naming ceremony, with this boat taking the name *Alexandra*. The other, which was based in Trinity Yard, Old Quay for the duration of the Wolf Rock Lighthouse assembly, took the name the *Duke of Cornwall*. It was a rousing and stylish occasion, with processions and music of the type much relished by Cornish folk. The lifeboat fulfilled the promise of her name in a single service, by going to the aid of the endangered brig *Ridley* of Plymouth in fierce conditions, saving eight crewmen. This service earned Captain T.H. Fellowes, R.N., the RNLI's Silver Medal.

If names have any influence on lifeboats, the next one, a ten-oared self-righting boat, augured well, for she took the name of that devoted and energetic RNLI Secretary, *Richard Lewis*. And, indeed, hers was a proud record of service in which eighty-six lives were saved in the period 1865 to 1884. It is difficult for us to comprehend the determination and endurance of those early lifeboatmen. An example of this transpired in January 1866, when the lifeboat was transported overland to Hayle by a team of horses as a prelude to launching into unfamiliar waters, to assist the St. Ives crew in saving nine lives from the stranded *S.S. Bessie* of Hayle. It must indeed have merited the description at the time, 'Beyond all praise' and a Silver Medal. A Silver Medal was awarded the following year, in recognition of the service to the schooner *Salome*. Another very notable service took place during the terrible gale of December 1868, when the barque *North Britain* of Southampton got into difficulties in Mount's Bay, and was eventually driven on shore. A pilot gig and an eight-oared barge from St. Michael's Mount had put to sea but turned back before the lifeboat was launched from the Eastern Green. As the lifeboatmen reached the casualty, after a long, hard pull, their lifeboat capsized, flinging them into the water. The coxswain, Thomas Carbis, jammed under the ship by wreckage, managed to extricate himself after a desperate struggle and was hauled aboard the *Richard Lewis* apparently lifeless. The stroke oarsman, Hodge, was washed away and subsequently recovered, while the tough, resilient coxswain was revived after being got ashore. By a sad irony, the captain had ordered his men to take to the ship's boats, having seen the gig and the barge retreat, giving up any hope of being rescued. But unfortunately one took a battering and the other capsized, and most of the occupants were lost. Disregarding the setbacks, the lifeboat was launched into tremendous seas for a second time with a fresh crew, and the remaining men were saved minutes before their ship disintegrated. Five Silver Medals were awarded in recognition of this outstanding service, as well as Thanks on Vellum. More Silver Medals recognised the services to the Norwegian brig *Otto* and the wrecked *Marie Emilie* in 1873, when they overcame the hazards of storm and rocks and seven broken oars.

Ever enthusiastic about casting care aside and enjoying celebrations, the citizens of Penzance had launched a lifeboat spectacular to coincide with the opening of their new public buildings in September 1867, with the gaily bedecked lifeboats of Penzance, Hayle, St. Ives and Mullion and their cork lifejacketed crews, drawn through the streets on their carriages by fine horses (*see* Mullion). Later the Sennen and Porthleven lifeboats joined in a hotly contested rowing race, which was won by Sennen.

Tact and Tactics
Mr. Downing, the station's Honorary Secretary obviously appreciated the value of good public relations ventures, for when the Wesleyan missionaries were visiting the West in 1874, they were treated to a trip to Land's End and taken out in the lifeboat *Richard Lewis*. *The West Briton* reported: 'Mr. Downing at these great public gatherings evidently displays admirable tact and judgment towards promoting much goodly fellowship amongst brethren, combined with a most kindly display of generous hospitality.' For their part, the missionaries paid the dubious compliment of recalling the 28th Chapter

43

of Acts, Verse 2": 'And the barbarous people shewed us no little kindness.'

Tact is not always at the forefront of human reactions witnessed by those strangers of deliverance of life from shipwreck, who miraculously appear on the scene, when all seems lost. For coolness and a cavalier disregard for everything, it would be hard to beat Captain Kergulant of the brig *Ponthieu* of Vannes, which went ashore five miles east of Penzance in May 1879, attracting would-be rescuers and an excited crowd of onlookers. Despite the ship being in such a dangerous situation amid heavy seas and rocks, the Captain was unwilling to allow his crew to board a local fishing vessel or the lifeboat which came alongside, contemptuously ignoring them and the watchers on the shore. All except himself left the ship as it began to fall apart and, as their continued pleas were to no avail, the lifeboatmen landed the exhausted crew. Well aware of all the dangers, Commissioned Boatman William Gould of the Coastguard risked his own life to take out a letter from the French Vice Consul, requesting the captain to leave his ship. But this was similarly ignored by the captain as he perched nonchalantly on sections of vanishing debris. He was eventually got ashore by breeches buoy, in complicated manoeuvres after he lost his grip, and had to be snatched from the surf by brave and patient coastguards, who formed a human chain. Once ashore, he refused kindly proffered brandy, caustically commenting that he had more than enough liquid inside him already, and contemptuously ignored a doctor's advice to rest in bed. If he lacked appreciation of the efforts made on his behalf, the French Government did not, for they expressed their gratitude and awarded the humane coastguard a Gold Medal.

A Period of Transition
A fine new boathouse with a bell and turret, which became operational in February 1885, offered the advantage of the new pulling and sailing lifeboat, the *Dora* launching directly into the harbour from the quay. This lifeboat carried out many valuable services before being replaced by the twelve-oared *Elizabeth & Blanche* in 1895, which was replaced by a Watson class of the same name four years later. This lifeboat was transferred to Newlyn in 1908, when the *Cape of Good Hope* came to Penzance, followed by the *Janet Hoyle* in 1912. The Penzance lifeboat station ceased to be operational in 1917. The transfer to Newlyn was an interim step, for the Penlee lifeboat station had been envisaged in 1910; when this was completed in 1913, the *Elizabeth & Blanche* occupied that boathouse.

The service record of the *Elizabeth & Blanche* demonstrates the shift in emphasis from sailing vessels in distress to steamships, calling for more speed and power in rescue craft. *The Brothers*, Penlee's first motor lifeboat which arrived in December 1922, soon proved her worth. And while it was clear that such lifeboats would ease the harsh physical demands made by the

Above: The Elizabeth and Blanche *and her crew on the Newlyn shore c. 1911
Below: After experimenting with various sites around Penzance and Newlyn, the
slipway at Penlee offered a fast and efficient launch, with the whole crew aboard
(Sheila Bird Collection)*

45

earlier boats, the increased capabilities gave rise to a greater range of hazards in this area which has justified its notoriety as a 'maritime trap' amongst seafarers.

The Proud Era of The W&S

The *W & S,* short for *Winifred Alice Coode and Sidney Webb,* which came on station in August 1931, was regarded with great affection among the local lifeboat fraternity, recalling sterling rescues which brought prestige to the Penlee Lifeboat Station. In particular there was the bold, slick service to the *S.S. Taycraig* in January 1936, with the saving of nine lives, which brought a Bronze Medal to the station's longest serving coxswain, Frank Bluett, and the dramatic events surrounding the mission to *H.M.S. Warspite* in April 1947. For Edwin Madron, this was his first service as coxswain. This defiant old battleship, which was generally acknowledged as having a mind of her own, was undergoing the indignity of being towed to a scrapyard on the Clyde in a strengthening south-westerly gale, when she broke adrift and went aground on Mount Malpas Ledge near Cudden Point. The lifeboat launched through the heavy seas, and managed to get within hailing range to warn the skeleton crew of their predicament in a worsening situation on a rising tide, and advised them to abandon ship. The master declined to do so, regarding it as impossible to board the lifeboat in such wild conditions. The weather deteriorated, and the *W & S,* which had been diverted to Newlyn, set out a second time, to discover the casualty in a more vulnerable situation, ashore to the east of Prussia Cove, close to rocks, with heavy seas breaking around them.

Coxswain Madron, pumping oil on the angry waters, heroically took the lifeboat into a narrow channel between the ship and the rocks, where there was a rise and fall of thirty feet, and got two lines aboard. Then, daringly, with great skill and clever timing, the lifeboat was manoeuvred backwards and forwards in anticipation of the movement of the waves, allowing each of the eight men to leap aboard, a process which took thirty-five minutes. For this magnificent St. George's Day rescue, coxswain Madron received the RNLI's Silver Medal, the Mechanic, John Drew, the Bronze Medal and the crew the Institution's Thanks on Vellum. The coxswain also received the Maud Smith award for the bravest lifeboat deed of the year. The wreck was to remain an object of curiosity for some time. The theme was re-echoed in 1954, when two salvage officers who set out for the wreck in a DUKW were shipwrecked and rescued with difficulty by a shore boat. The reserve lifeboat *Millie Walton* carried out a notable service in July 1956, when ten lives were saved from the *S.S. Yewcroft,* which stranded near Cudden Point and broke her back. However, the *W & S* lifeboat returned to continue her fine record of service, mostly with fishing vessels, motor vessels and steamships until she was replaced by the splendid Watson type lifeboat, *Solomon Browne* in September

1960. In December the following year one shore helper was killed and another injured on the slipway while the lifeboat was being rehoused.

One member of the Yewcroft's *crew was rescued by breeches buoy, and the remaining ten taken off by the Penlee Lifeboat after she stranded near Cudden Point, Mount's Bay, in foggy conditions and broke her back in July 1956 (Acknowledgements P.A. Reuter Photos Ltd. and the RNLI)*

The Arrival of the *Solomon Browne*

The *Solomon Browne*, which was basically of traditional design, but with an enclosed cockpit, was constructed by William Osborne of Littlehampton and fitted out with the most up to date equipment of the time. She was forty-seven feet long, had a beam of thirteen feet, a draught of five feet and had twin screws driven by two sixty horse-power diesel engines. The engine room had a double bottom and her hull was divided into six watertight compartments, fitted with 216 aircases, and she subsequently underwent several overhauls. This lifeboat was financed by legacies, principally that of Miss Lydia Browne, and named in honour of her Quaker father, a squire and gentleman farmer from the Landrake area. The naming ceremony was carried out by Lady Tedder. This lifeboat had a particularly fine record of service, launching scores of times during her twenty-one years on station. The crew remembered incidents, such as the thirty-six hour standby during the *Torrey Canyon* disaster of 1967, when they returned exhausted, and faced the daunting task of removing all traces of oil from the *Solomon Browne* before returning home. Stephen Madron explained to me that 'standby' was more wearing than getting to grips with the task in hand. He recalled the Fastnet Race of August 1979, mostly for the frustration of being on standby for forty-eight hours: 'We were ordered to wait in case another emergency arose. Care had to be taken that lifeboats were available when help may urgently be needed. Eventually we were called out to tow one of the yachts back.'

During her time on station, the *Solomon Browne* was particularly associated with medical services, bringing sick seamen ashore or taking doctors out to ships. And in common with other lifeboat stations in recent years, she had an increasing number of call-outs to holidaymakers with little or no experience of the sea. During my interview with Second Coxswain Mechanic Stephen Madron in the Penlee Boathouse in July 1981, I asked him whether he considered some people irresponsible in the way they did silly things, putting their own lives and the lives of others in danger. 'We're here to provide assistance, not to make judgments,' he replied firmly, 'Anyone who feels like that should not be in the lifeboat service.' We mused about our nation of seafarers or would-be seafarers, and he commented, ' There is no training for ordinary people to put to sea. If they get into difficulties, it is because they don't know what they are doing. It's ignorance, not deliberate. I've never met anyone who deliberately got into difficulties,' and added: 'Even the experts sometimes make mistakes,' citing the experienced crew of a famous sailing ship which started sinking off Land's End because the pumps had been blocked with shavings after the last refit.

Stephen's most memorable service was that of the *M.V. Lovat* in January 1975, probably because of the emotional aspect. Shortly after returning from Swansea, where he had been working for Trinity House, the maroons sounded, and as everyone went flying about he heard the ship's name being mentioned, but could not quite place it at first. Then it transpired that the ship had just left Swansea, and he found himself hauling lifeless bodies aboard, and looking into the faces of drinking associates of a few days previously. 'Dealing with dead bodies is a gruesome task which has to be done. Recognising some of the faces of people you were chatting to and drinking with just a short time ago, really brings it home to you.' For this service, carried out in appalling weather conditions, Coxswain William Trevelyan Richards received the Institution's Bronze Medal, and his crew the Thanks on Vellum.

The year 1981 had been a very special one at Penlee, where 'Rescue 21' fund-raising celebrations took the form of 'a tribute to the 21st Anniversary of the present Penlee Lifeboat *Solomon Browne* and Associated Rescue Services' and the production of a special commemorative booklet acknowledging the role of all concerned. A newly received letter of thanks from the RNLI relating to the service to the Belgian trawler *Normauwil* was proudly displayed in the Boathouse. It concluded: 'On behalf of my Committee, I send you the Institution's warm and appreciative thanks for the determination and seamanship displayed by you during this service which was carried out in a strong south easterly wind and rough sea. I wish to add an expression of my appreciation of your skill in carrying out this very difficult rescue with seas sweeping the foredeck of the lifeboat.' And it was signed 'Atholl', Chairman.

A Tragic Night

This area is characterised by sudden changes of weather and periodic storms of terrific intensity. The night of December 19th, 1981 was just such a night. As villagers were anticipating the delights of the Feast of Tom Bawcock and Christmas, the lifeboat *Solomon Browne* launched down the slipway for the last time, to the aid of the coaster *Union Star*, in a distressed condition and drifting out of control towards the shore in hurricane force winds and mountainous seas to the south west of the lifeboat station. A Royal Naval Sea King helicopter made heroic efforts to lift the survivors from the deck of the stricken ship despite being perilously close to her mast and the cliffs in darkness and driving rain, with winds gusting up to 100 knots. The lifeboat appeared on the scene and made repeated runs alongside the casualty in these horrifying conditions. The courageous lifeboatmen, intent on the plight of others, got four people aboard the lifeboat. She seemed to be under control and about to make another run to pick up the rest of the survivors as the helicopter returned to RNAS Culdrose. But her lights went out and radio contact ceased shortly afterwards. Meanwhile the coaster *Union Star* was overwhelmed and settled on her side at the foot of the cliffs near Tater Du. The Coastguards who were on the cliff continued the hazardous attempts at saving life from shipwreck, with Sector Officer Don Buckfield subsequently being awarded the Silver Medal of the Royal Humane Society. The entire crew of the Penlee Lifeboat was lost in this tragedy, together with the eight people who had been aboard the *Union Star*. For their gallantry, the RNLI made posthumous awards of a Gold Medal to Coxswain William Trevelyan Richards, and Bronze Medals to Second Coxswain/Mechanic James Stephen Madron, Assistant Mechanic Nigel Brockman, Emergency Mechanic John Robert Blewett, and Crew Members Charles Thomas Greenhaugh, Kevin Smith, Barrie Robertson Torrie and Gary Lee Wallis.

Coping with The Aftermath

News pictures flashed across the world, touched the hearts of people everywhere, and this harrowing event did more than anything else in recent years to bring the selfless devotion of lifeboatmen and the role of the RNLI to the attention of the general public. Locally, people were shocked and

On 19th December 1981 the entire crew of the Penlee Lifeboat was lost while heroically going to the aid of the Coaster Union Star *in distress during an exceptionally violent storm in Mount's Bay. Those aboard the casualty pictured here, also lost their lives (Acknowledgements RNLI)*

pained; the proud little fishing community of Mousehole, which had been deprived of the cream of its manhood in one cruel night, was stunned. But for every reason, thoughts were quickly focussed on the overwhelming prospect of forming an instant replacement crew. In normal circumstances, men would be absorbed into the crew one at a time, with continuity and natural bonding; coxswains would emerge spontaneously with a close knowledge of the station and the crew, after years of experience. An instant coxswain, in the wake of lost heroes would have a difficult and delicate role to play, also requiring an ability to handle the attentions of the less desirable sector of the media.

Initially, the relief seventy foot Clyde lifeboat *Charles H. Barrett* (Civil Service No. 35) was sent here, with a staff coxswain and crew, augmented by local volunteers. She was replaced by the Watson Class *Charles Henry Ashley* and later the *Guy & Clare Hunter,* another Watson, formerly stationed at St. Mary's, Isles of Scilly, which was already known in these waters. Being similar to the *Solomon Browne,* she had the advantage of being familiar to handle for those who had already served at Penlee, while allowing more local pride to be restored by bringing ex-Second Coxswain Frank Wallis and his brother Phil, former Bowman, out of retirement to work with the newly trained crew. Local fisherman Kenneth Thomas was appointed coxswain when the new Arun lifeboat *Mabel Alice*, financed by Mr. David Robinson of Newmarket arrived in 1983. Edwin Madron, of the celebrated lifeboat family of Mousehole, and brother of Stephen, was subsequently appointed Second Coxswain Mechanic.

The Arrival Of The Arun Class *Mabel Alice*

The new Arun, described by Phil Wallis as 'the king of lifeboats', was to be kept permanently afloat in Newlyn harbour, and a smart, new boathouse was erected at Newlyn. However, it meant a great deal to the people of Mousehole to have emergency relief lifeboats in the traditional boathouse at Penlee, with all its associations, rather than it remaining sadly neglected.

The *Mabel Alice* was soon to demonstrate her prowess, when swift responses were all important to yachtsmen and fishermen in distress. 'Warm and appreciative thanks' were expressed by the Institution, in connection with the service to the yacht *Alto* in September 1984, made in rough squally weather, with poor visibility, acknowledging their devotion to duty, while the Chief Inspector gave them credit for 'a good job, well done.' The following year Coxswain Ken Thomas received recognition for the *St. Simeon* service. In September 1989 The *Western Morning News* reported: 'A yacht was saved by Penlee lifeboat last night when the experienced Coxswain Ken Thomas and his crew carried out a second skilled and courageous rescue in twenty-four hours.' On this occasion, 'Coastguards and an RNAS Culdrose helicopter coordinated by Falmouth coastguard centre also went to the scene and a diver was lowered to talk to the crew.' The service ended with the lifeboat bringing the yacht safely into harbour, across the storm-torn waters of Mount's Bay, following the traditions established here so long ago, but with casualties and rescuers of a very different style.

PADSTOW LIFEBOAT STATION

(Padstow No. 1 Station was established prior to 1825; the No.2 Station in 1899. In March 1938, the afloat lifeboats at the No.2 Station were redesignated the No.1 Station, and the old No.1 Station at Hawker's Cove was redesignated the No. 2 Station. The No. 2 Station was closed in 1962. The current Lifeboat Station at Mother Ivey's Bay, Trevose Head became operational in October 1967.)

Padstow Harbour, though much obstructed by sand, with an entrance narrow and dangerous, and a bar called the Dunbar (Dune Bar) within its mouth, is the only place of shelter on the North coast of Cornwall; and during gales from the North West, when a refuge on this iron-bound shore is particularly required, its entrance is attended with considerable risk, as at these times there is an eddy of wind within the point by which vessels are likely to be taken aback and driven upon the sands. A capstan has, however, been placed on Stepper Point (227 ft. above the sea), and when a vessel is expected a pilot boat waits within the headland, so as to carry a hawser on board in time to prevent these fatal effects. But it is intended to construct a harbour of refuge here.

Murray's Handbook: Devon & Cornwall, 1865

Hazards of The Harbour

When freshening winds veered to the north-west, whipping up angry seas and creating a veritable Hell's Bay between Pentire Point and Trebetherick, the prospect of the golden Camel estuary, with its heavenly aura, must have been regarded as the answer to many a sailor's prayer. But beauty can be deceptive and, sadly, the haven of Padstow has been the last resting place for many sailing ships and their crews, caught out by the baffling winds under Stepper Point, or the dreaded Doom Bar, situated a mile or so inside the heads. But apart from getting caught in this lethal embrace, many ships came to grief by confusing one headland with another, as happened to H.M. Brig *Bloodhound* in December 1811, mistaking Trevose Head for Stepper; the third to have done so in the space of a month, with tragic consequences. This again pinpointed the need for a lighthouse on the jutting headland of Trevose, which had long been recognised as a navigational hazard in its own right.

Application for a lighthouse there had been made in 1809, but time dragged on and ships went down. Then in July 1843 the ship's boat from Trinity House's own vessel *Vestal* was added to the roll of casualties here, during the course of carrying out survey work to assess the need for a lighthouse. The disasters continued while the press and the public agitated for action, and a petition was presented to Trinity House. But it was not until December 1st 1847 that Trevose light shone forth for the first time.

Man-made Improvements

The authorities took on mammoth tasks to improve harbour safety from the middle of the last century onwards, including altering the profile of Stepper Point, to counteract the effect of those baffling winds on vulnerable sailing vessels. Then, in an attempt to turn a problem into an asset, they allowed the stone to be marketed, and similarly capitalised on the removal of the offending sand but, in terms of clearing the navigational hazard, it proved abortive.

The Notorious Doom Bar

The whimsical might subscribe to the theory that Doom Bar appeared here as the result of a curse from a petulant mermaid, retaliating to an unchivalrous rascal of Padstow who playfully let fly with his longbow, and struck her with an arrow as she innocently frolicked in these waters. Be that as it may, the sandbar has been here a very long time. Back in the sixteenth century, Richard Carew in his Survey of Cornwall stated: 'The harbour is barred with banks of sand...', while antiquarian John Leland, also of that period, recorded that, 'Shyppes cum not yn but at the Flowyng Water.' Yet despite all this, Padstow at one time was a flourishing commercial harbour.

Early Life-saving Traditions

Padstow folk will tell you that it was the first place in Cornwall to have a lifeboat, and this might well be the case. Some say that a local clergyman was involved in having a pilot gig placed on the north Cornish coast in 1790, for the purpose of saving life, having had it constructed by the Peters boatbuilding family at St. Mawes. But there is no conclusive evidence, for many of the gigs in the area got involved with rescues.

Padstow Harbour Association's Comprehensive Role

Kelly's Directory of 1889 states: 'The Padstow Harbour Association was formed in 1829, for the purpose of saving life and property by rendering assistance to ships entering the port in distress. It is supported voluntarily and no salvage claims made other than expenses out of pocket. Up to the year 1888 this branch had rendered aid to not less than 86 vessels.' It goes on to tell us, 'A branch of the Royal National Lifeboat Institution is also located here, and the lifeboat has been instrumental in saving the lives of many shipwrecked crews.' The Patron of the Padstow Harbour Association was the Reverend Charles Prideaux Brune, whose family is closely associated with the lifeboat today. With the help of a grant from Lloyds, and subscriptions from the gentry, merchants and mercantile organisations from Bristol and Swansea and many others anxious to improve safety at sea, they were able to carry out harbour improvements. These included emplacement of buoys to define the narrow navigation channel close to Stepper Point, providing three capstans on the inner side of the Point and building a white navigational tower and a daymark on that headland. On-going improvements were the construction of cottages at Hawker's Cove, well placed for pilots and boatmen to assist the incoming vessels, as well as safety equipment, storage sheds, landing stages and slipways. So this organisation tried to cover a very broad spectrum, from the prevention of shipwreck, to help in easing the many practical difficulties to be faced. Having been donated the money, they aimed to invest it wisely, and recover it. But this state of affairs became increasingly difficult to maintain.

In earlier times whole communities turned out to assist in getting the lifeboat launched — as this photograph of the launching of the Padstow lifeboat Arab *demonstrates (Sheila Bird Collection)*

Padstow's Early Lifeboats and Fine Services

The first lifeboat, financed by subscription, plus a grant of £10 from the Institution, and built by John Tredwen of Padstow, had come on the scene in 1827. She was later kept on her carriage in the stone boathouse at Hawker's

Cove, and thought to have been given the rather endearing name of *Mariner's Friend*. There was only one recorded service, in November 1833, when she saved four crewmen from the Brig *Albion* of London. In recognition of this service, carried out in a violent gale, Mr. W. Giles, who was in the lifeboat with seven seamen was awarded the Institution's Silver Medal. Other rescues of this period, also meriting awards, were carried out by the Association's working boat and everyday craft.

In 1856, a six oared Peake Lifeboat, bearing the name *Albert Edward* came on station, under the authority of the RNLI, staying eight years and saving thirty-eight lives before being replaced by a ten oared self-righting lifeboat of the same class, also built by Forrestt of Limehouse, taking on the same name, but requiring a larger boathouse. One of her memorable rescues occurred on December 29th 1865, when the barque *Juliet* of Greenock, laden with sugar and rum signalled her distress off Hell's Bay during a heavy south-westerly gale. *Albert Edward II* battled her way through the heaving waters, and by a clever process of anchoring and drifting, expertly positioned herself under the stern of the casualty, giving the seventeen men the opportunity to jump from their ship, which was parting her timbers and casting casks of rum upon the Polzeath shores. This successful rescue earnt the heartfelt thanks of the captain; a Silver Medal for Coxswain William Hills, to which a clasp was added in 1875, when he retired, and a third clasp for former Coxswain Daniel Shea's Silver Medal, thereby creating a record (Note: Daniel Shea and William H. Tregidgo of Bude share the distinction of being the most decorated lifeboat crewmen in Cornwall, while Matt Lethbridge, of St. Mary's, Isles of Scilly, with three Silver Medals, is the most decorated Coxswain). He had been obliged to relinquish his position on being promoted within the Coastguard service, but remained a very dedicated lifeboatman. Strangely, the only casualty resulting from this shipwreck was one William Ham from St. Austell who, working locally, rushed down to the shore with scores of other excited people, and managed to drink himself to death on rum, despite the medical intervention of a stomach pump.

The Ultimate Price For Devotion

A marble memorial in Padstow Parish Church recalls how Daniel Shea, then Chief Officer of the Coastguard, 2nd Class, together with William Intross, Chief Boatman, Thomas Varco, Commissioned Boatmen, Andrew Truscott, Trinity Pilot and Michael Crennel, Mariner, paid the ultimate price for their devotion to the cause of preserving other people's lives from shipwreck, in February 1867, whilst going to the assistance of the schooner *Georgiana* of Boston, Lincolnshire, which had struck Doom Bar in a strong west-north-westerly wind. Launching into confused seas on the outgoing tide, *Albert Edward II* battled her way towards the casualty with the intention of getting in close on her leeward side. But in those difficult conditions, things started to go wrong; oars broke, and the lifeboat took in water. Unable to return against the outgoing tide, they made for the Polzeath shore, letting out the drogue (sea anchor), in an attempt to gain stability and prevent a capsize. However, the stress of water was such that it caused the canvas drogue to split, suddenly releasing pent up pressure, which catapulted the lifeboat end over end, and flung her crew into the surf, as the horrified crowd watched from the shore. Coxswain William Hills, Second Coxswin Samuel French and six crewmembers survived this ordeal. Meanwhile the schooner was driven onto the rocks, with one man drowning and the remaining four crewmen being rescued by shoreline. 'The Lord hath his way in the whirlwind and the storm,' says the inscription chosen in the church, and 'The will of the Lord be done.' A relief fund was set up; the RNLI donated two hundred guineas and paid funeral expenses.

The lifeboat emerged virtually intact from the incident, and people's faith was undiminished. Their confidence proved to be well founded, for in her remaining sixteen years on station, she saved scores of lives. Seven lives were preserved in an award winning service to the barque *Viking* of Sunderland, which had gone aground in Harlyn Bay in a howling April storm of 1872. It turned out to be an innovative rescue, requiring the removal of the lifeboat upstream to Padstow, before being set on her carriage to be drawn overland to Harlyn Bay by a team of ten horses. A line was established with the casualty, and in heroic, fictional style, the mate tenderly bore the captain's baby son across the tenuous lifeline in a soft muffler secured beneath his jacket. Intent on handing the infant to safety, he tragically forfeited his own life, for he lost his grip and was swept away by a huge wave. The idyllic theme was borne out by the baby being christened Harlyn, and growing up to become the captain of a liner — or so they say.

Dame Fortune's Deliverance
Another romantic adventure of *Albert Edward II*, with just the right ingredients, concerned the Brig *Thomas* of Whitehaven, which was discovered dismasted and eerily abandoned in 1874 by the *S.S. Countess of Dublin*, whose Master decided to put his mate and five of his crew aboard, and take her in tow. But during that stormy night she broke adrift, and the Captain eventually gave up the search for her, and steamed on sadly, thinking them all lost and gone for ever. In the meantime, the brave mate and his five sailors had managed to get the disabled vessel close to the shore off Padstow, where they were spotted, and the lifeboat set out in the teeth of a strong north-north-westerly gale to assist them. Reaching the casualty and taking the men off was a severe test of endurance; but the return trip with the wind in their tail was infinitely more hazardous. In these conditions, with the drogue streaming aft, many people were mindful of that fateful day in 1867.......Then the very thing they were all dreading happened; the drogue rope parted and the

lifeboat was flung forward. But on this occasion Dame Fortune was kinder. Luck, in feminine form, brought deliverance for the sailor whose boat had capsized in a squall off Bray Hill in August 1879, for the Misses E.F., G.R., M.K., and B.M. Prideaux Brune and Miss N. O 'Shaughnessy made their intrepid way out through the heavy surf in their rowing boat, risking their lives to save his, according to the citation, when they were awarded Silver Medals by the RNLI.

A Double Hat-Trick
On two occasions *Albert Edward II* had the distinction of performing three services in one day, the first being January 15th 1869, when she saved six people from the Brigantine *Thomas* of Poole, eight from a gig which had gone to her aid, but got into difficulties in the process, and six from the schooner *Alexandrine*. Then the morning of February 20th 1877 saw service with the schooner *Jeune Prosper*, the lugger *St. Clement* of Nantes and the schooner *Plymouth*, saving a total of five lives. The relationship with this lifeboat was such that when they were offered a new one, the crewmen were a trifle diffident at first. The second *Albert Edward's* final service was with the *Mary Josephine* of Padstow, when three lives were saved.

A Lifeboat With Sandy Associations
The new thirty-five feet self righting lifeboat, *Arab*, arrived in style on August 15th 1883, drawn on her gaily decorated carriage by a team of eight grey

The lifeboat Arab *negotiates the treacherous Doom Bar during a storm (Sheila Bird Collection)*

horses, with her crew wearing life jackets and scarlet caps, led by a rousing military band and the Foresters, all looking splendid in their uniforms, and followed by local dignitaries, Sunday school children and others, decked out in their finery, singing, cheering and clapping in the right places between the lengthy speeches and the blessing of the boat. The lifeboat had already been the centre of attention in Hyde Park, where she had undergone tests on the Serpentine. Her somewhat unlikely name was derived from that of a yacht wrecked on the Goodwin Sands, whose owner had donated the money as a token of his gratitude to the RNLI, having been saved by the Ramsgate lifeboat. His donation also defrayed the cost of building the new boathouse.

The Arrival of an Impressive Steam Lifeboat

The *Arab* served well for many years, ministering mostly to schooners, yawls, brigs, luggers and ketches, which repeatedly fell victim to Doom Bar. However, experimental steam lifeboats, which could be kept afloat were now appearing on the scene, and the increasing number of steamship casualties beyond the range of traditional lifeboats led to the decision to place one here. She arrived with two engineers and two firemen, employed as permanent crewmembers, as part of her compliment of eleven. Thus the screw-driven, fifty-six feet lifeboat *James Stevens No.4*, came on station in February 1899 to supplement, not supplant, the existing lifeboat. Her swift response, manoeuvrability and capability of taking casualties in tow were impressive. With two prestigious lifeboats on station, equipped to handle a whole new range of emergencies, all seemed set fair.

A Second Tragedy

A tall, granite monument, the imposing focal point of Padstow cemetery, situated just above the little town, recalls the brave lifeboatmen who lost their lives at the entrance to Padstow harbour on April 11th 1900, when the steam lifeboat *James Stevens* capsized during endeavours to save the crew of the *Peace & Plenty* of Lowestoft. The ketch, which had been fishing outside the estuary, had made for the protection of Stepper Point as gale force winds intensified and seas became rougher. They were out of the wind, but found themselves confronted with the danger of huge waves sweeping around the Point and racing currents. Big seas breaking over their decks had swept two men overboard, who had been recovered after frantic attempts to get a line to them in these horrifying conditions, and thereafter they had thought it prudent to retreat below and wait for the situation to improve. But unfortunately they had misjudged the length of cable used to pay out the anchor in these hostile conditions, and were unaware that the anchor had started to drag. Their plight was seen from the shore, but they were equally oblivious to the warning shouts of the Hawker's Cove pilots, who were unable to get out to them. Lifelines fired by the Trebetherick rocket brigade fell short, and

The splendid twin-screw tug Helen Peele worked in close collaboration with the No. 2 lifeboat Edmund Harvey, which was kept permanently afloat (Photo: George Marvin; Acknowledgements RNLI)

efforts were made to get closer by getting the apparatus down the cliff and over the rocks. The *Arab* launched, but after a lengthy struggle, took a battering from a rogue wave, which flung the men about and swept away most of their oars. While trying to recover the situation, they fired a flare to alert the steam lifeboat that assistance was required. Observing this, Coxswain David Grubb proceeded towards the harbour mouth, keeping to deeper waters before turning and running in towards the casualty. Having cleared the Point, they were engaged in this manoeuvre when disaster struck. A terrific wave caught her on her stern quarter and she capsized. She remained keel uppermost, with her propellers still rotating, rising and falling with the surge of the waves. The sombre monument in the cemetery bears the names of those brave men who did not survive this tragedy. They were David Grubb (Coxswain) and his son James (Deckhand), John Martin (Chief Engineer), James Old (Second Engineer), Joseph Stephens (Fireman), Sydney East (Fireman), Edward Kane (Deckhand) and John Bate (Deckhand). The names of those lost from the *Peace & Plenty* are also listed here. The catastrophe, which left the entire community stunned with shock and grief, had accounted for eight lifeboatmen and two lifeboats, and created four widows and fourteen orphans overnight. The RNLI Committee of Management voted £1,000 to the local fund set up to aid the distressed families, a relief lifeboat was sent, and volunteers willingly presented themselves.

Prestige of Three Lifeboats for Padstow

Padstow had enjoyed the prestige of having two lifeboats on station, which were now to be replaced by three. These were *Arab II*, constructed at Mevagissey, and the *Edmund Harvey*, which were both sailing and rowing boats with drop keels, and the splendid twin-screw steam tug *Helen Peele*. She was under the command of a Master, his Mate, two Engineers, two Firemen and a Cook, who were permanent employees, while four Deckhands were hired as necessary. She was destined to work mostly in collaboration with the No. 2 lifeboat, *Edmund Harvey*, which was bigger than *Arab II* and kept permanently afloat, which could accompany her on missions outside the harbour. The *Helen Peele* was subsequently fitted with electric light and a mounted line-throwing gun. *Arab II's* function, therefore, was to serve within the heads.

The close relationship between the *Helen Peele* and her surfboat began in 1902, when she appeared at the harbour mouth with the *Edmund Harvey* in tow, having collected her at Southend-on-Sea. On the ebbing tide intent, no doubt, on reaching their destination, and mindful of the expectant crowd, the Master made straight for Padstow town. In doing so he made an early acquaintance with the Doom Bar and the little lifeboat, which was to spend so much time in her wake, assisted in getting her larger counterpart out of trouble. The crew of the *Edmund Harvey* was to experience forty-four hours in their open boat without the protection of their time honoured oilskins a few days before Christmas 1901, after boarding their boat under tow in Padstow wearing ordinary clothes. They were soaked to the skin and freezing cold before leaving harbour, in a bitter north-easterly gale. Hypothermia apparently had not been invented as they stood by a tanker all night, and resisted comforting thoughts of home as they were towed northwards past their own harbour entrance en route for Cardiff in the course of duty. Then, literally to cap it all, northwards of Bude, they encountered snow. In shared physical discomfort, in the context of comradeship, they thought of Yuletide, and started singing carols. Three years later this lifeboat found herself in trouble after breaking adrift from the *Helen Peele* during the night in a violent hailstorm, and was driven under the cliffs at Gun Point. The coastguards and the *Arab II* went to her assistance and, emerging somewhat battered, she was towed back to Padstow.

When a strong west-north-westerly gale was playing havoc with shipping on November 12th 1911, the *Arab II*, which had launched to the aid of the French Brigantine *Angele*, disabled and desperately seeking shelter,

The Arab *lifeboat performing a good public relations exercise, whereby eager local folk in their Sunday best were taken for trips around the Camel estuary (Sheila Bird Collection)*

picked up the crew of the schooner *Island Maid,* which had suddenly rounded the Point at speed and careered headlong onto the Bar. While they were preparing to land these men, the *Angele* came flying around the Point, and did the same thing. *Arab II* landed the rescued men and made abortive attempts to reach the *Angele* on the ebb tide. Then the Coxswain decided to land his tired men and return with a fresh crew. By the glare of the *Helen Peele's* searchlight, crowds on the shore discerned a lone figure, desperately clinging to the rigging of the stricken ship. But volunteers were not forthcoming until the Institution's steam tug's Captain Martin and Police Constable Turner arrived on the scene. As *Arab II* drew near the casualty through the angry seas, the *Angele's* courageous Captain leapt from the rigging and swam out towards his rescuers, who were able to haul this sole survivor to safety. For this outstanding service, Coxswain William Henry Baker was awarded the Silver Medal of the RNLI.

First World War casualties increased the demands on Padstow's lifeboats, with the *Helen Peele* being requisitioned by the Admiralty towards the end of the war, to take part in rescue work with the Grand Fleet. While on

61

Admiralty service, she performed well, saving many distressed vessels and eleven lives.

Lifeboat Personalities
In 1922 Coxswain Edward Oldham of the Edmund Harvey and Second Coxswain Henry Brenton, who had both joined the lifeboat on October 8th 1902, also retired on the same day. Coxswain William Henry Baker of the *Arab*, retired the following year. In 1928, when the Centenary Vellum was awarded, Coxswain William J. Baker of the No. 1 lifeboat received a Bronze Medal for his gallant conduct and skilful seamanship when the lifeboat under his command rescued eighteen from the *S.S.Taormina* of Oslo. This noteworthy year also brought the Bronze Medal to Joseph Atkinson, Master of the steam tug *Helen Peele*, for his gallant conduct and skilful seamanship in rescuing five from the motor fishing boat *Our Girlie* of Port Isaac.

Re-organisation
The three lifeboats were taken out of service between 1929 and 1931, to be replaced by the large and far ranging *Princess Mary* at No.2 Station, and the *John & Sarah Eliza Stych* at Hawker's Cove, where a new boathouse and slipway were emplaced. The *Stych* was a self-righting motor lifeboat constructed at Cowes, which performed good service both inside and outside the harbour, but in February 1938 she was sent to St. Ives and ended her days in tragedy (*see* St. Ives). She was replaced by several lifeboats from other stations, until the *Bassett Green* arrived in 1951.

Heroic Services during and after the Second World War
During the Second World War the *Princess Mary* and other lifeboats here at that time were called out on many occasions to search for lost airmen and victims of attacks on convoys. On November 23rd 1944, the *Princess Mary*, under the command of Acting Coxswain William Orchard went to the aid of the Norwegian steamer *Sjofna*, which had gone ashore, broadside on near Hartland Point. The Coxswain braved the hazards of the surf, and the lifeboat got her bottom scraped when she grounded between the troughs, as repeated attempts were made to get a line aboard, and eventually they were able to get some of the crew into the lifeboat by breeches buoy, while the coastguards saved the rest with their inshore rescue apparatus. For this act of courage, Acting Coxswain William Orchard received the RNLI Silver Medal, as well as the Maud Smith Award for the outstanding lifesaving service of the year. Thanks on Vellum went to Coxswain John Murt, and Mechanic John Rokahr and a special letter of thanks was sent by the Norwegian Government. The rescuers on the shore also received recognition. Coxswain John Murt, John Rokahr and the *Princess Mary* also distinguished themselves in the service of August 12th 1946, in going to the aid of the *S.S. Kedah* of Singapore, which

William Henry Baker, who served in Padstow's lifeboats for nearly forty years, started as a crewman with the Albert Edward *in 1883. He was Coxswain of the* Arab *from 1904 - 1923 (Acknowledgements RNLI)*

had broken adrift from her tug, and was dragging her anchors in foul weather near St. Agnes Head. In conditions described as 'almost impossible', *Princess Mary* attempted to get lines aboard by manoeuvring alongside the casualty, but was thrown against her several times in the process. Then the Coxswain pulled off a smart coup by running in at full speed alongside, getting the ten marooned men to jump, then accelerating fast out of the tight situation. For this courageous act of seamanship, Coxswain John Murt was awarded a Silver Medal for Gallantry, while Second Coxswain William Grant and Mechanic John Rokahr received Thanks on Vellum.

After twenty-three years of service, the *Princess Mary* was replaced in 1952 by the fifty-two feet *Joseph Hiram Chadwick*, a Barnett type, built at Cowes and kept afloat. Interestingly, after being sold out of service and renamed the *Aries*, she became the first small powered craft to make the double crossing of the Atlantic without the use of sail, making the outward journey in thirty-three days and the return in twenty-three days in heavy storm conditions.

'Deo Gratias'

In 1965, it was 'Deo Gratias' in more ways than one, when the *Joseph Hiram Chadwick*, under the command of Coxswain Gordon Elliott was successful in 'doing a Blogg', thereby saving two men from a vessel of that devoutly thankful name. This is lifeboat parlance for the dangerous manoeuvre of running the bow of the lifeboat across the deck of the casualty in a last ditch attempt to save lives. The expression found its way into the language after the celebrated Coxswain Henry Blogg of the Cromer lifeboat achieved the (almost) impossible feat twice, in quick succession. In recognition of this service, Coxswain Elliott was awarded the Silver Medal, and his crew Thanks on Vellum.

The Move To Mother Ivey's Bay

Padstow lifeboats, kept inside the estuary, had always been restricted by the vagaries of wind and tide and sand, and after considerable research involving wave recordings, it was decided to re-site the station at the edge of Mother Ivey's Bay at Trevose Head, with a fast and efficient slipway allowing launching in any conditions, which brought about the amalgamation of the two stations. *The Padstow Lifeboat March* was specially composed by Malcolm Arnold to mark the opening of this impressive lifeboat station, which became operational in October 1967, housing the new Oakley Class lifeboat *James & Catherine Macfarlane* which is now on display at Land's End.

More Recognition

Many fascinating photographs and tributes to Padstow's especially fine lifeboatmen grace the walls of today's splendid boathouse, including special framed certificates presented to the station in 1976, in appreciation of the 'courage, determination and skilful handling displayed by Coxswain Anthony Warnock and Second Coxswain / Assistant Mechanic Trevor England' and the rest of the crew, when the lifeboat was damaged and crewmen injured in heavy seas. Silver Medals were awarded to Coxswain Anthony Warnock and Second Coxswain/Assistant Mechanic Trevor England the following year in recognition of their 'courage, determination and seamanship,' in rescuing the crew of two and a dog from the yacht *Calcutta Princess*, while the Thanks of the Institution went to the other members of the lifeboat crew.

Trevor England was appointed Coxswain in August 1978, and the following year a special framed certificate was awarded to him and his crew in recognition of their services in the course of the lengthy and wearing difficulties surrounding the Fastnet Race. There was further recognition, with a Silver (second) award in connection with the service to the Greek freighter *Skopelos Sky,* in distress five miles north of Trevose Head in an onshore westerly hurricane on 15th December 1979. The Coxswain took the *James & Catherine Macfarlane* alongside five times, but as the freighter's crew could not be taken off, stood by, acting as communications link between the casualty, the coastguard and a helicopter. The helicopter was able to lift off the survivors as darkness was falling and the vessel was driven hard onto the rocks. *The Council of the Gorsedd of Cornwall* also acknowledged this, by awarding Coxswain Trevor England the *London Cornish Association's Shield.* The Tyne Class lifeboat *James Burrough* was on station for the service to the cargo vessel *Secil Japan,* which had grounded on rocks at Deadman's Cove on the stormy night of 12/13th March, 1989, when dramatic T.V. coverage demonstrated to one and all that technology may have grown apace, but the sea can be as dangerous as it ever was. A framed letter of appreciation, signed by the Duke of Atholl, Chairman of the Institution, is a reminder of a night to remember.

ST. MARY'S (ISLES OF SCILLY) LIFEBOAT STATION

(established in 1837, and re-established in 1874 after an apparent lapse around 1855)

Farewell and adieu to you, Spanish Ladies,
Farewell and adieu to you ladies of Spain,
For we've received orders to sail for Old England;
We hope in a short time to see you again.

We'll rant and we'll roar, like true British sailors,
We'll rant and we'll roar, all on the salt seas,
Until we strike soundings in the Channel of Old England,
From Ushant to Scilly is thirty five leagues.

(Sea Shanty: *Spanish Ladies*)

The Dread of Mariners
The French Professor Henri-Alphonse Esquiros summed it all up in one sentence in 1865, when he wrote: 'The ocean which surrounds the Scilly Isles is an object of terror for mariners.' And understandably so, for few coasts anywhere in the world can have witnessed such a tremendous catalogue of shipwrecks as have occurred in this area of rocks, reefs and shoals, storms, conflicting tides and currents. Indeed, many of the colourful names to be seen on the charts are derived from vessels which met their doom here. In former times inaccurate charts contributed to these maritime disasters, and in the seventeenth century fresh surveys were made of our coasts. In his *Directions for Sailing in and out at the several Sounds at the Islands of Scilly*, Captain Greenvile Collins states: 'These Islands lie to the westward of the *Land's-end* of *Cornwall* nine or ten Leagues, and are many Islands and Rocks.' He also gives us some insight into contemporary safety measures and their effectiveness, observing: 'On the Southenmost big Island there standeth an high *Light-house*, erected by the *Corporation of the Trinity-house* of *Deptford-Strond*, and is a most excellent good Light, and may be seen six or seven

Leagues off. Before this *Light-house* was erected, there was not a Winter but there were some Ships cast away: but since the erecting of it, there hath not a Ship been lost, but by Ignorance: so that Navigation is much obliged to the great Care of the *Trinity-House* in erecting this Light.'

A Catastrophic Error

It was a navigational error that brought about one of the worst disasters in our maritime history, as the fleet was returning from the siege of Toulon in October 1707. For in the darkness, having mistaken their position as being off Ushant, Admiral Sir Cloudesley Shovel's flagship, H.M.S. Association, went headlong onto the Gilstone Rock and was wrecked. The tragedy escalated as the seventy gun *Eagle* and fifty gun *Romney* struck rocks, with a knock-on effect for following vessels in the catastrophic confusion. Over 1,800 men lost their lives, including Sir Cloudesley. One fortunate survivor reached the Hellweathers Reef, where he was later picked up.

Renowned for their Skill and Bravery

When storm winds howled or the eerie isolation of fog made conditions particularly hazardous, many a homeward bound skipper must have been thankful to hand over the wheel to a local pilot, whose expert understanding of the area, enabled him to weave his way deftly through the daunting tracery of rocks and reefs. The need for such a service gave rise to the fine breed of Scillionian pilots, who were renowned for their skill and bravery. They, boatmen and coastguards all played a vital role in the preservation of life from shipwreck around the Islands, sometimes forfeiting their own lives in going to the assistance of others.

A poster of 1858 in the present boathouse on St. Mary's throws light on the lifesaving situation of the time:

SAVING LIFE FROM WRECKS
To Boatmen and Others

To encourage prompt and energetic exertions in time of Danger, on the part of Boatmen & Others, by quickly putting off to save the Lives of their Fellow Creatures from Wrecks in SHORE BOATS AND OTHER CRAFT, The Royal National Lifeboat Institution grants REWARDS of MONEY & MEDALS. In all cases the Rewards are given without further delay than is necessary to obtain proof of the merits of each case, and to ensure their being paid to the right parties.

By order of the Committee
Richard Lewis, Secretary
Royal National Lifeboat Institution, 14 John Street, Adelphi, London W.C.
October 1858

Captain Charles Steel R.N., Inspecting Commander of Coastguards was instrumental in setting up a branch of the Institution on St. Mary's in 1837, when a lifeboat was sent by the National Shipwreck Institution, having been financed by them and the Coastguards. This lifeboat had previously been on station at Brighton, and was based at Hugh Town, where a competent crew was always available. In his book *The Scillonian and His Boat,* Alf Jenkins stated: 'The boat sent to Scilly was of no greater length than the gigs. She was heavier and slower, and kept on St. Mary's she was just about the furthest away from any shipwreck.' And pilots, fiercely proud of their skills, went on using their own boats, which also allowed them to pursue their traditional salvage rights, which they depended on for their livelihood in this impoverished area. So the first lifeboat, which stayed for only three years was manned mostly by coastguards, and was replaced by another of the Plenty type, previously at Plymouth, and again financed by the National Shipwreck Institution and the Coastguards. She arrived on March 20th 1840, and was kept in the boathouse at Town Beach. Her only recorded service was on January 4th 1841, when she went to the aid of the steam packet *Thames,* which had become disabled as the result of heavy seas penetrating her boiler room, and was driven onto the Western Rocks. In response to her distress flares, the gig *Thomas* from St. Agnes put out, followed by the gigs *Briton* and *Bee* and, as the tide allowed, the pilot cutter *Active.* After some delay in mustering a full crew, the lifeboat headed out through the raging seas and intermittent squalls, under the command of Captain Steel.

The gig *Thomas,* the first on the scene, managed to get a line aboard the stricken ship, and rescued three women, before a sudden squall swamped the boat. Two other women were in transit on the line but wet and battered, they were hauled aboard, transferred to another boat and taken ashore. Then the gig joined other hovering boats in the lee of the rocks, awaiting a suitable opportunity to rescue the remaining shipwrecked victims but they panicked, and all but one perished in attempts to get ashore in improvised rafts. He was cast ashore on Rosevear where he was recovered, together with eight bodies, by the lifeboat the following morning. It is thought that fifty-seven lives were lost in this disaster, which four people survived, thanks to the gallantry of the rescuers, some of whom may not have got the recognition they deserved. The Institution voted a Gold Medal to Mr. Charles Steel, Inspecting Commander of Coastguard, and Silver Medals to four members of his volunteer crew, while monetary awards went to the remaining crewmen of the lifeboat and the three gigs.

The Re-establishment of a Lifeboat Station
After the tragedy of the *Thames,* which was attended by gigs and cutters as well as the lifeboat, the lifeboat seems to have been neglected in favour of these local craft, which were usually in the water, well positioned for quick

responses in times of emergency. The cutter which picked up survivors from the steamer *Gypsy* out in the Atlantic in 1848 is just one example of this, and mention should be made of the brave men of Bryher who carried their gig *Albion* overland to go to the assistance of the *S.S. Delaware*, wrecked near Mincarlo in December 1871. The lifeboat, which had fallen into neglect, had been sold and the station closed around 1855. But it was the disaster of the *Delaware* and of the four-masted barque *Minnehaha*, which struck Jolly Rock at Peninnis in January 1874, which led to the re-establishment of a lifeboat station later that year. The aforementioned Alf Jenkins stated that the local ship owner and chandler John Banfield could foresee the eventual demise of the Scilly pilot gigs and cutters, and therefore an increased need for a lifeboat. So under his guidance as Honorary Secretary, a new boathouse was erected on the site of an old shipyard at Porthcressa Bank, with a door each end designed for easy launching in the direction of the casualty, according to weather conditions.

This time a new lifeboat arrived: the thirty-seven feet, twelve oared pulling and sailing lifeboat *Henry Dundas*, having been transported from London to Penzance by rail and onwards by steamer. Her formal ceremony of inauguration took place on August 1st, when she was hauled through the streets on her carriage, to the sounds of stirring music. John Banfield's daughter performed the naming ceremony.

Her first service occurred on May 7th 1875, after the splendid German transatlantic liner *Schiller*, returning from New York struck the fearsome Retarrier Ledges in darkness and fog, which obscured the warning lights of St. Agnes and the Bishop. Guns were fired to signify an emergency but, tragically, the thoughtless practice of liners saluting the sighting of land with gunfire caused it to be a commonplace sound to which no one responded. The casualty lay broadside on and as the tide rose the ship's boats were carried away, and scores of people who had sought refuge in the rigging were drowned. The desperate situation was not revealed until dawn, when two gigs set out from St. Agnes, but the seas were such that it was not possible to reach the survivors still frantically clinging to the masts. One gig recovered five people from the water, and proceeded ashore to summon the lifeboat, which appeared on the scene under tow of the *S.S. Lady of the Isles*. But sadly, the sea had taken its toll, and it was their gruesome task to recover some bodies and sacks of mail. Out of a total of 355, only forty-three survived the wrecking of the *S.S. Schiller*. This appalling tragedy put a stop to the practice of incoming liners heralding landfall with gunfire. A century later a German lifeboat came here on a public relations exercise of remembrance.

The Back-Up of a Lifeboat At St. Agnes

The lifeboat *Henry Dundas* went on to render assistance to the brig *Messenger* of Salcombe, the barque *Excelsior* of Hamburg and the *S.S. Castleford* of

Liverpool, before being replaced by a bigger, heavier lifeboat, rowed with the same number of oars. But this was a time of change for gigs, which had hitherto been first on the scene of shipwreck were now declining, and there was a case for a lifeboat station being established at St. Agnes, to cope with the casualties of the Western Rocks. This became operational in 1890, with both lifeboats and other craft often working together (*see* St. Agnes, Isles of Scilly). The initiation of *Henry Dundas II* a few months later was swift, when she saved six from the brigantine *Antres* of Nantes, in trouble near the dangerous Retarriers. But her crew was aware of a heavier, less manoeuvrable lifeboat, and she was soon dispatched to Beaumaris and replaced by *Henry Dundas III*, a few months later. This lifeboat went to the assistance of the *Horsa* of Liverpool and the barque *Sophie* of Frederickstadt with no recorded saving of life.

The Henry Dundas *launches to the assistance of a small craft with three men aboard, which had dragged her anchors and was being driven across the Sound in gale force winds in 1913 (Acknowledgements RNLI)*

In 1899 a new Watson type lifeboat arrived at St. Mary's, taking the name *Henry Dundas IV*, and remaining for the next twenty years. Despite the boathouse having doors at opposite ends, it had become increasingly difficult to obtain the horses needed for launching from a carriage. The advantages of a deepwater slipway, with gravity offering a fast and efficient means of getting a lifeboat launched, led to the choice of Caen Thomas for the construction of a boathouse and slipway, which was extended forty feet three years later. The old lifeboat house was sold for £40.

The lifeboats of St. Mary's and St. Agnes frequently worked together, complimenting each other, backed up by the remaining gigs, as happened in 1903, when the steel barque *Queen Mab* sprang a leak after a brush with the Spanish Ledges, requiring the landing of the Captain's wife and child, additional pumping facilities and towage, for which all concerned received payment. The model of the gig *Slippen* in the boathouse, constructed by Peters of St. Mawes in 1830, recalls the service of December 13th 1907, with its knock-on effects, when the large and prestigious seven-masted steel schooner *Thomas W. Lawson* of Boston found herself in a dangerous situation near the Bishop's Rock. Ill fortune dogged both lifeboats which went to her aid for, in trying to get in close, the St. Mary's lifeboat was dismasted, and had to return for repairs after the Master declined to leave his ship. Then a crewman from the St. Agnes boat collapsed. So pilot William J. Hicks was put aboard the ship from the lifeboat which returned to seek medical aid, after the Master had assured both coxswains that he would signal for help if necessary. As luck would have it, a terrific storm erupted during the night, and all the returning lifeboats found next morning was a mass of wreckage and oil. Local boats joined in the search for survivors, and it was the little gig *Slippen* which found a survivor on Annet, who later died, and which located the Captain and his engineer on Hellweathers. Perhaps the most poignant part of this tragic story is that Frederick C. Hicks, who had gallantly swum across deep and hazardous waters between two reefs with a lifeline, was the son of the pilot who had gone aboard and had been lost in the disaster. In recognition of this heroism, the RNLI awarded him a Silver Medal. The United States authorities bestowed on him a gold watch, and awarded the *Slippen's* crew their Gold Medals.

Combined Operations

In April 1910, a second vessel bearing the name *Minnehaha*, this time a steamship, had an encounter with Scillonian rocks in foggy conditions but fortunately she survived the ordeal. The *Czar*, one of the Bryher gigs which were first on the scene, took ashore passengers and some of the crew; two Falmouth tugs took off more of the crew, and St. Mary's lifeboat stood by. This was a particularly novel example of preserving life from shipwreck, in that it included cattle, brought ashore to the Isle of Samson as tides allowed. The efforts of the people of Bryher were duly rewarded by the shipping company on this occasion. Another victim of foggy weather was the *S.S. Ardencraig* of Glasgow which, in January 1911, struck the Gunners, with the crew taking to the boats as she started to sink in Broad Sound. Both lifeboats went to her aid, but a lighthouse relief vessel, which had been on her way to Bishop Rock when she heard the rockets summoning the lifeboat, and the St. Agnes lifeboat *Charles Deere II* got there first and took off and towed the crew to safety.

In June 1914, yet another liner, this time the *S.S. Gothland* of Antwerp became a victim of fog and of the Western Rocks, but the service was historic, in that the Land's End Wireless Station was used to alert them of the emergency, and notable for the large number of people saved. In response to the distress communication, *S.S. Lyonesse* towed both lifeboats out to the scene, while other boats converged on the area. Coxswain James Lethbridge of the St. Mary's lifeboat defused a second hazard, when one of the ship's boats broke away while being lowered, by leaping into the sinking boat and conveying the frightened passengers onto the lifeboat. It must have been a proud day for the lifeboatmen of Scilly, to have recovered a total of 152 people by nightfall.

Wartime Happenings

Scillonians have long been accustomed to a variety of happenings on their maritime doorstep by virtue of their geographical situation, and never more so than in time of war. In the First World War these mostly became the responsibility of the St. Agnes station. In October 1916, the *Charles Deere James* saved thirteen people who had taken to the boats from the torpedoed steamer *Sola* of Stavanger. But the memory of February 22nd 1917, when a German submarine torpedoed a convoy of seven Dutch and Norwegian steamships, sinking all except one, must have remained with the forty-seven fortunate survivors and those who rescued them for ever. In the Second World War, the French lifeboat *Jean Charcot*, which ran away to sea with refugees landed on these shores (*see* Falmouth). During those wartime years, the lifeboat *Cunard* was on station at St. Mary's, the St. Agnes station having been closed in 1920, partly because of the shortage of men to crew a lifeboat, and also because of the improved power and capability of the new Watson motor lifeboat *Elsie*, which duly arrived at St. Mary's in 1919. In its thirty years of service, the St. Agnes lifeboat had experienced thirty-four launches and saved 206 lives.

Honours Abound

The lifeboat *Elsie* took part in a particularly outstanding service in October 1927, going to the aid of the grain carrying Italian steamer *Isabo*, which had gone ashore to the west of Bryher in dense fog. Bryher men in a gig and two motor boats braved the dangers of jagged rocks in the darkness, and the split, swollen grain which clogged their motors, to pick up many distressed people clinging frantically to sections of debris, and landed them. The lifeboat launched, and made her hazardous way out in search of the casualty. They were joined by a doctor, and at dawn went in close, fired lifelines and picked up survivors from the turbulent waters. For this gallant and dangerous service, the RNLI voted a Silver Medal to Coxswain Matthew Lethbridge and Bronze Medals to Second Coxswain James T. Lethbridge, elder brother of the Coxswain, Motor Mechanic J.H. Rokahr and Dr. W.W. Ivers. Silver and Bronze Medals were awarded to men of the Bryher boats *Sunbeam, Czar* and *Ivy*. The Italian Government also awarded four Silver and thirty-four Bronze Medals for this service, in which thirty-two of the *Isabo's* complement of thirty-eight were saved.

Strange Happenings

One of the most romantic and unlikely shipwreck occurancies concerned the *Lady Daphne* and a bird in a gilded cage, around Christmastide, 1927 (*see* The Lizard). The 'lady' in question was a Rochester ketch barge, which was on passage from the Thames to Plymouth with a cargo of tiles and bricks, when caught in freshening north-westerly weather, erupting into blizzards. These were of such ferocity that, in trying to negotiate the entrance to Plymouth Sound, the Master was lost overboard and the *Lady Daphne* careered on down the Channel, beyond the control of the two remaining crewmen, who frantically ignited flares and anything else they could find to attract attention. Just as they were giving up hope, their plight was noticed from the Lizard shore. The lifeboat launched, but had a hectic twelve mile chase before catching up with the capricious *Lady Daphne*. With great gallantry, the lifeboatmen were able to recover the two survivors before leaving the speeding ketch to her own devices. With wheel set, she hammered on, maintaining a steady course, and was sighted next morning tacking through Crow Sound in classical style. Anticipating an equally skilful rounding off to anchor, the onlookers winced as she centred on, eventually running ashore at Tresco. The anxious lifeboatmen of St. Mary's. who hastened to her aid, were astonished to find her 'manned' only by a canary, who was (apocryphally) singing merrily in his cage. Also strange, but in the blackout conditions of war in December 1939, was the fate of the *S.S. Longships*, which struck the Seven Stones Reef and went down just a few miles from the lighthouse, from which she derived her name. Her crew of twenty-seven was saved by the lifeboat *Cunard*, which had replaced the *Elsie* in 1930, and saved a highly creditable 104 lives in her twenty-five years here. She was replaced by the *Guy & Clare Hunter*, which launched 177 times, and saved 110 lives.

Lifeboat Families

A visit to the boathouse, with its photographs and models helps to bring the ongoing story of the Isles of Scilly lifeboats to life for the public, and a plaque on the wall attributes the boathouse improvements to Mrs. Marion Acatos, of the Guy family, commemorating the service of her grandfather, father and brothers, Ernie, Algie and Roy Guy. Other fishing families, including those of the Trenwith, Ellis, Phillips and Jenkins played their part in the story of St. Mary's lifeboats but, as Alf Jenkins wrote in his book *The Scillonian and His Boat*,

> One family outshines them all ... For three generations the Lethbridge family have served this station, all succeeding one another as coxswain. No greater men have ever dedicated their lives to saving others from the sea than have the Lethbridges, and it must have been a terrible occasion when James Lethbridge, with two sons aboard the lifeboat, went off to search for his own remaining sons, Alfred and George, when they drowned out fishing on a comparatively quiet day (in 1920). For someone who had done so much to saving others from the sea to be struck in this manner is just not fair. But the Lethbridges have carried on, and most deservedly, Father Matt, and now son Matt have been presented with the B.E.M. for their dedication to the Lifeboat Service. 'Find us a better man, for we know not where he is.'

At the time of writing, Matt Lethbridge, Junior, with three Silver Medals to his credit, is the most decorated lifeboat coxswain in Cornwall.

Expert Seamanship
St. Mary's Lifeboat Station, situated in the heart of awesome shipwreck territory, has the enviable tradition of heroic lifesaving at sea, with much recognition. Back in 1934, Acting Coxswain Harry Barrett, who was in charge of the lifeboat for the first time, received a Bronze Medal for a fine service to the schooner *Mynonie R. Kirby*, which had broken adrift from a Dutch tug during a south-easterly gale. Despite the difficulty caused by the weather and drifting debris, a line was fired and six men and a dog rescued. Another parted tow rope towards the end of the war in 1945 brought an award: this time Thanks on Vellum to Coxswain Matt Lethbridge and Second Coxswain James T. Lethbridge, for their fine seamanship in rescuing a salvage party of fifteen of the American Liberty Ship *Jonas Lie*, which had been torpedoed three days previously and taken under tow. Ten years later Coxswain Matt Lethbridge was voted a Bronze Medal for the rescue of twenty-five from the Panamanian steamer *Mando*, which had gone on shore between Manavaur Rock and Gold Ball Rock in a dense fog and a moderate west north westerly wind. The lifeboat *Cunard* launched into the darkness at low tide and was expertly navigated through the islands and rocks to the casualty, mostly by compass. And having got there, it was a case of rising and falling with the waves, and cleverly compensating with the engine, to allow the survivors to jump from the ladder into the lifeboat.

The new lifeboat *Guy & Clare Hunter* arrived at St. Mary's in December

1955 and, during her christening ceremony, a Certificate of Service was presented to Coxswain Matt Lethbridge, who had served for thirty-one years. On July lst 1956, his son Matt Lethbridge, Junior was appointed Coxswain of the St. Mary's Lifeboat, Henry Taylor took over from Henry Thomas as Motor Mechanic in 1958 and William Burrow took over from him in 1961.

Some Memorable Events

March 18th 1967 has gone down in the annals as a black day on the environmental calender, being the day that the giant oil tanker *Torrey Canyon* struck the Seven Stones Reef. It is also a day that the Royal Navy and the rescue services around the coasts of Cornwall will never forget, and St. Mary's, together with some of the mainland lifeboat stations, received a framed letter of appreciation signed by the Chairman of the Institution. The Coxswain and crew were also granted additional monetary awards, and the crew of the *Torrey Canyon* gave a donation towards the cost of erecting a plaque in the boathouse expressing their appreciation for the help given. After this service, lifeboatmen, responsible for keeping their lifeboat in tip-top condition, spanking clean, really knew the meaning of the increasingly common word 'pollution.'

September of that year brought a Silver Medal to Coxswain Matt Lethbridge, Junior, and Silver Medals to his Second Coxswain Ernest Roy Guy and to his Mechanic William Richard Burrow. During the course of covering the final section of Francis Chichester's single-handed round the world trip in Gypsy Moth IV, an ITV crew in the yacht *Braemar* found she was letting in water and placing them in a vulnerable situation twenty-eight miles from the Bishop Rock in gale force conditions. The *Guy & Clare Hunter* launched at 6.48 a.m., and set course past St. Agnes Point; at 9.00 a.m., they received the report that her engines had failed and that the yacht was drifting. When they came up with the yacht an hour and a half later, thirteen miles from Wolf Rock, a motor vessel was taking the casualty in tow, and as the condition of the yacht deteriorated, the lifeboatmen accomplished the difficult task of getting fifteen men and a woman into the safety of the lifeboat. Two men remained aboard the leaking yacht, which was towed into Newlyn by a pilot cutter.

Coxswain Matt Lethbridge, Second Coxswain Ernest Guy and Mechanic William Burrow received Silver Second Service and Bronze Second Service Clasps, and the crew Thanks on Vellum in 1970, for the rescue of ten people from the Swedish motor vessel *Nordanhav*, listing heavily in squally weather, in rough seas and poor visibility to the north of the Islands. When they arrived on the scene, the lifeboat *Guy & Clare Hunter* could see by the illumination of *H.M.S. Ulster's* searchlights that the casualty was listing very heavily, and that prompt action needed to be taken. So he skilfully came in

Above: After the M.V. Scillonian *had stranded on Wingletang Ledges in thick fog on 11th September, 1951, seventy passengers were transferred to the motor-launch* Kittern *and the lifeboat* Cunard. *But it turned out to be a double service, for the launch became disabled, and was towed in to St. Mary's Pier by the lifeboat. The lifeboat then returned to the original casualty, which got away on the rising tide (Acknowledgements RNLI; Fox Photos, London)*

Opposite above: Matt Lethbridge Jnr., with three Silver Medals to his credit, is the most decorated lifeboat Coxswain in Cornwall (Photograph Peter E. Hadfield; Acknowledgements RNLI)

Opposite below: March 18th, 1967, when the giant Liberian tanker Torrey Canyon *struck the Seven Stones is a day that the combined rescue services and environmentalists will never forget (Photograph, The Press Association; Acknowledgements RNLI)*

side, allowing all ten crewmen to transfer, then returned to St. Mary's with them, after a thirty-five mile passage and service taking twelve and a half hours.

A service to the yacht *Moronel* in rough seas and a north easterly gale in March 1972 brought Thanks on Vellum from the Institution, and also particular recognition to crewmember Rodney Terry, who was destined to become the lifeboat's next coxswain. At considerable risk to himself, he jumped from the lifeboat into the yacht, to assist the crew of two who were in difficulties. It was the French trawler *Enfant de Bretagne* which brought Coxswain Matt Lethbridge B.E.M. his Silver Third Service Clasp in 1977, recognising his courage, determination and seamanship in making repeated attempts to reach the crew aboard the casualty, and searching for survivors in dangerous heavy swell and unchartered rocks in the darkness when she broke up after being stranded on a rock about two miles east-south-east of the Bishop Rock Lighthouse. The crew received Thanks on Vellum. The ill-fated Fastnet Race of August 1979 created a long drawn out, wearing service for several local stations, which all received a Special Framed Certificate, signed by His Grace the Duke of Atholl, Chairman of the RNLI.

In 1981, the 52 foot Arun Class *Robert Edgar*, which was kept permanently afloat in the harbour replaced the Watson Class *Guy & Clare Hunter*, which had distinguished herself by launching 177 times and saving 110 lives in twenty-five years. This is the lifeboat in which Coxswain Lethbridge and his crew rescued the crew of two from the yacht *Concerto* in distress twenty-five miles north-north-east of Round Island in stormy conditions with rough seas; a service which brought more Thanks on Vellum in 1982.

Faith in Matt

But it was the relief Arun lifeboat *Sir Max Aitken* which responded to the Coastguard's call, telling of a British Airways helicopter with twenty-six people on board, which was overdue at St. Mary's Airport in July 1983, and helicopters were scrambled from Culdrose. In conditions of very thick fog and a flat, calm sea, the Coxswain had initially expected to come across the helicopter on the surface. But in the event, experience and intuition caused him to investigate a very light mark on the radar screen, which he could not quite account for. As they drew near, lifeboatmen in the bows detected the smell of paraffin and then spotted some survivors in the water. These were hauled aboard, and a doctor lowered from a Sea King helicopter advised that they should be got to hospital speedily. The lifeboat crew must have been proud to have gone to the assistance of fellow Scillonians in distress, and it was particularly touching that those survivors were confident that the lifeboat would save them. This Thanks on Vellum was delivered in a novel way, for the arrangement was that the presentation would take place at the Earl's Court Boat Show. However, this was merely a cover for the popular TV

The Fastnet Race of 1979 will long be remembered by the combined Rescue Services in the south-west, when fourteen lifeboats launched to the aid of multiple competitors in distress, with west-north-westerly winds gusting to hurricane force 12. Pictured here is the St. Mary's lifeboat the Guy and Clare Hunter (© Crown copyright 1991/ MOD reproduced with the permission of the Controller of HMSO))

show 'This is Your Life', when friends and associates recalled some magic moments for the benefit of over fourteen million viewers.

Coxswain Matt Lethbridge retired on 20th January, 1985, after serving almost forty years in the St. Mary's lifeboats; twenty-nine of them as Coxswain, and Rodney Terry, the Second Coxswain, who joined the crew in 1965 became the new Coxswain. In 1987 the station was awarded its 150th Anniversary Vellum.

BUDE LIFEBOAT STATION
(1837-1923: ILB Station established 1966)

The rocks belong to the carboniferous formation, and run at right angles to the beach with Titanic contortions. Stern promontories Compass Point and Beacon Hill spread out wide shadows over the stern waves of the Atlantic. In calm weather this bay is delicious; the sea at high tide advances, describing foaming semi-circles, which enlarge and become appeased as they invade the beach; but let a west wind begin to blow, and the spectacle at once changes. Just as wild horses take to flight before a prairie fire, the impetuous coursers of the ocean, so the sailors say, escape from the presence of these terrible winds with a loud snorting, and rush towards the barrier of cliffs.

Cornwall and its Coasts, Alphonse Esquiros: 1865

With Regal Roots
Bude, set in the heart of awesome, Atlantic shipwreck territory on the grand scale, had the distinction of its lifeboat being known colloquially as the Royal Bude Lifeboat. For when King William IV's attention was drawn to the lack of lifesaving facilities on this notorious section of coast which had claimed so many vessels in recent years, including the Bude pilot boat, he decreed that money from the Duchy coffers would be set aside towards a lifeboat for Bude. And in December 1837 *The West Briton* proclaimed proudly: 'We hail with satisfaction the arrival of a valuable and beautifully constructed Life-boat at Bude, which was built by Mr. Wake, an eminent ship builder at Sunderland. It has been constructed on Palmer's plan, with the approbation of the committee of the Royal National Institution for the Preservation of Life from Shipwreck.' History was to demonstrate that this lifeboat station was a credit to its regal roots.

Faith In Their Own Craft
Man's attempts to improve on nature along this inhospitable coast brought engineering re-alignments here, but at the time the haven was synonymous with the mouth of the Bude canal, opening into a shallow, sandy bay. But a sudden ground-sea or change in wind direction could trap shipping on a lee shore. Local seafarers all too aware of the capricious nature of these waters

80

had faith in their local craft which had evolved to meet these conditions, and were wary of the alien, new lifeboat of northern design, which they thought cumbersome. Tragically, two crewmen were drowned when this lifeboat capsized on the northern side of Bude harbour in October 1844, and the lifeboat was left to degenerate thereafter.

Some Notable Awards
In 1845 the Institution awarded Silver Medals to James Perkins and Thomas Paul of the Coastguard for rescuing three men and a boy from the wrecked schooner *Margaret*, with the use of Dennett's Rockets. The Institution was unhappy about the state of the lifeboat, and after the shake up of the Northumberland Report, published in 1851, plans were afoot to provide a new lifeboat for Bude, with Sir T.D. Acland, Bart., M.P. offering to shoulder the major cost of the carriage. In 1853, the new, twenty-seven foot, Peake lifeboat built by Forrestt of Limehouse duly arrived, having been towed down the Channel to Penzance and brought the rest of the way by the revenue cutter *Sylvia*. She soon proved her worth, and her ability to withstand the dangers of ground-seas in saving two men from the Sloop *Margaret* of Bideford, which brought Chief Boatman William Henry Tregidgo the Institution's Silver Medal. William Tregidgo, J. Stone, J.P. Sharrock, W.R. May and H. Ellis of H.M. Coastguard risked their lives in saving sixteen men and a pilot by means of ropes in 1858, after the *Defence* of Liverpool was wrecked in a storm beneath the towering cliffs of Beeny at St. Juliot, in a service recognised by Silver Medals, bringing Mr. Tregidgo his Second Service Clasp. Two years later J. Dyer was awarded a Silver Medal for gallantly wading into the surf at peril of his life, to rescue the Master of the Schooner *Beverley* of Goole, wrecked under Upton Cliff in a heavy gale. 1860 also brought a Silver Medal (Third Service Clasp) to William Henry Tregidgo, and thereby a record which he still shares with Daniel Shea of Padstow (1859-1866). For both were crew-members, awarded three Silver Medals and both were employed as Coastguards at the time. Mr. Tregidgo's award was in recognition of his service to the Schooner *L'Union* of Bannes and the Lugger Anais of St. Vaast, when he put off with the crew of two boats and rescued eleven men shipwrecked off Newquay in a gale (see Newquay).

The Tragedy Of The Bencoolen
October 1862 witnessed the disastrous wrecking of the Indiaman *Bencoolen*, which was seeking a harbour of refuge after sustaining damage in a hurricane. She made for Bude at great speed, ran aground and rapidly disintegrated within a cable's length of the breakwater, losing twenty-nine of her compliment of thirty-five. *The West Briton* portrayed the pitiful scene:

A little creek, some thirty feet across, at the extreme end of the harbour, was full of fragments of timber, and into this the raft at last was washed, with several dead and only two living men lashed upon it. It took but a few minutes to run round the harbour: a line was passed down the cliff, and one by one twelve men, six living and six dead, were drawn and hoisted up, as carefully as could be, rescued with difficulty from a tangled mass of wreck upon the beach, and there laid upon the grass—so fearfully exhausted were those who still breathed, that only one could speak. These were immediately carried to the village. Those who seemed dead were rubbed and rubbed upon the spot, and every man eager and ready to do his best; one we thought, gasped, but all exertions were in vain, and they were sent in dead.

The lifeboat was brought to the water's edge, but there was delay in mustering a crew, who, mostly inexperienced, eventually decided against launching in such dangerous conditions. This attracted criticism, resulting in a shake up and improvements in facilities here. The name *Bencoolen* is reflected around the town today and the ship's figurehead can be seen in the museum. Fortunately the morale of the lifeboat crew, who had faced criticism mostly from those who never went to sea, was restored by the opportunity of performing a lifesaving service to the smack *Mary & Elizabeth* of Padstow, in very demanding conditions soon afterwards.

The Bude crew with their lifeboat, the Elizabeth Moore Garden, *outside their attractive boathouse.*

A Fine Way to be Remembered
In 1865, the French Professor Esquiros, with a keen eye and an ability to relate to new situations, was touched by the inscription on the wall of the boat-house: 'In memory of Elizabeth Moore Garden, the beloved wife of Robert Theophilus Garden, this life-boat was offered to the National Life-boat Institution by their children.' He made the enlightened comment, 'It was the custom in the Middle Ages to build chapels for the repose of the dead....What testimony more worthy of immortal being, than to attach their names to these liberators of the sea? The thirty-three foot lifeboat, also built by Forrestt of Limehouse had arrived by rail and road two years earlier via Bideford, and appropriately enough, her first launch was on June 19th; the birthdate of Mrs. Garden. Launching was never easy at Bude, with the relentless rollers and frequently erupting groundswell, and the new boathouse, built beside the canal with doors at each end offered alternative means of launching, according to tide and weather conditions, either directly into the water or by carriage, which was sometimes transported overland to Widemouth.

Never Plain Sailing
There were on-going problems with launching the lifeboat, whichever methods were tried, and difficulty in finding suitable men to crew her. Bude's trade by water was mostly connected with the supply of beach sand to inland agricultural areas along the purpose-built canal. Traditionally lifeboats had been manned by fishermen on the spot, to whom working with the sea in all its moods was second nature. But as there was no fishing industry at Bude, the crew was drawn from pilots, hovellers, any sailors who happened to be in port and enthusiastic landsmen. No launch could ever be plain sailing at Bude, but nevertheless a catalogue of brave services were carried out in this vulnerable cradle of the Atlantic: that early criticism must have hit very hard.

Another Tragedy
Tragedy struck the Bude lifeboat again in March 1877, when returning to harbour after launching to the assistance of the schooner *Elizabeth Scown* in terrible conditions. The lifeboat was struck by a very heavy sea, which smashed several of her oars and carried away her rudder; then another heavy sea caused her to capsize, throwing the crew into the water. All managed to regain the lifeboat, except Coxswain James Maynard, who was drowned.

A Variety of Services
There were to be two more lifeboats stationed at Bude, both perpetuating the name of *Elizabeth Moore Garden*, while Thomas Bate, Henry Stapleton and Henry Barrett were to serve as Coxswains. In 1881, Coxswain Thomas Bate received a Silver Medal acknowledging gallant service at risk of his life to the

ketch *Stucley*, wrecked on Bude breakwater, when four lives were saved. After a variety of services to ketches, smacks, schooners, brigantines, yachts, steamships and a Dutch galliot, the station was closed in 1923, having launched forty-four times and saved forty-eight lives.

A Lively Social Life around the RNLI

The Bude Inshore Lifeboat Station was established in May 1966, and the Royal Humane Society's resuscitation certificate was awarded to M. Moyle and A.J. Lovejoy in connection with the service on 30th May, when a bather was rescued. In 1984 a Vellum was awarded in commemoration of the station's aggregate service of one hundred and five years. Although the station is open seasonally, the training goes on throughout the year.

Bude, renowned for its Lifeboat Singers and innovative fund-raising activities which create a pleasant social life around the town, forges close links with fellow lifeboat stations, as well as kindred groups such as gig racing and surfing clubs. This was the first station in the country to link up with Chivenor and Culdrose for a demonstration with the Surf Lifesaving Club. The hard work of Mary McMahon, Chairman of the Bude Ladies Lifeboat Guild for over eighteen years, was recognised by the RNLI in December 1990, with the presentation of an Institution statuette.

ST. IVES LIFEBOAT STATION

(Established 1840: Inshore Lifeboat Station established 1964)

By al the North Se yn Cornewale be sundry Crekes, wher as smawle Fissher's Bootes be drawn up to dry Land, and yn fayr Wether the Inhabitans fysche with the same. At Paddestow Haven, Lanant*, and S. Yes*, the Balinggars* and Shyppes are saved and kept fro al Weders with Keyes or Peres....Ther is now at the very Point of Pendinas a Chapel of S. Nicolas, and a Pharos for Lighte for Shippes sailing by Night in those Quarters.

(*The Itinerary of John Leland, the Antiquary*: 1534-43)

*Lanant =Lelant: S. Yes = St. Ives: Balinggars, Balingers or Bainggars were small, light sea going vessels like sloops, extensively used in the 15th and 16th centuries. They had died out by the end of the 17th century.

The above, engaging mid-sixteenth century quotation provides an insight into the fortitude and ingenuity of earlier seafaring communities in harnessing opportunities and avoiding hazards along this inhospitable section of the Cornish coast, where the few points of refuge had problems of sand accumulation, defying clearance. It also demonstrates that attempts have been made to light up the coast and construct protective piers for centuries.

The Need for a Secure Anchorage
In the seventeenth century Captain Greenvile Collins described the situation of St. Ives as being '4 Leagues to the Eastward of Cape Cornwall, in a Sandy Bay,' where, 'Vessels lie aground at Low water.' *Murray's Handbook of Devon & Cornwall* fills in more of the story in the middle of the last century: 'The pier was constructed in 1767 by Smeaton, the architect of the Eddystone lighthouse; and a breakwater was commenced in 1816, but abandoned after an outlay of £5,000. It would have rendered the bay a secure anchorage, which is now exposed to the North and East. The project, however, may yet be carried out, as the completion of the breakwater was recommended by a committee of the House of Commons in 1859, and the fitness of St. Ives for a harbour of refuge is under consideration.' History shows that a proposed

New Pier on the seaward side of Smeaton's Pier, started in 1864 was unable to withstand batterings from the sea, the Victoria Extension to Smeaton's Pier was completed in 1890, with its octagonal iron lighthouse becoming operational that September, and the West Pier was completed in 1894. Vessels still lie aground at low water.

Time was ...
This incredibly beautiful coastline, so beloved by artists and holiday makers has been the setting for many shipwrecks, some of them in recent times. One of the strangest and earliest recorded shipwrecks occurred co-incidentally on the day of Charles I's execution in 1639, when the *Garland* carrying his personal effects, and those of his queen, was wrecked off Godrevy in a terrible storm, with the loss of the sixty or so souls aboard. The only survivors were a man and a boy, who got ashore and sustained themselves on seaweed and rainwater for a couple of days. This was just one of many casualties here before Godrevy Lighthouse was constructed in 1859. Time was, when the celebrated pilots of St. Ives, or 'hobblers' as they were known around these parts, made a profitable living from pilotage and salvage work; time was when the harbour overflowed with fishing vessels and the fishing so abundant that the Vicar described the smell of fish as being 'so terrific as to stop the church clock,' and tourists had not been invented. Those were the days when rescues were carried out by fishermen, coastguards, pilots and sailors, using a variety of boats including small Naval ship's boats and cork-lined craft.

Humane Endeavours — and their Risks
An example of painstaking lifesaving endeavour occurred in March 1802, when a large eight oared boat was carried three miles overland and other boats came out from Hayle, in attempts to save lives from the stricken East Indiaman *Suffolk* driven on shore at Gwithian. In the event the ship's company was able to get ashore, assisted by local people, having attached a line to a barrel taken in by the tide. A similar attempt the following year cost seven St. Ives men their lives. The Manby Apparatus and all sections of the seafaring community were put to their test in a prolonged sequence of events when the schooner *Rival* was driven on shore at St. Ives in December 1838. After several attempts by various craft had proved abortive, a fresh volunteer crew of pilots battled successfully against the raging elements and not only rescued the Master and four crewmen, but got the battered vessel into harbour. This gallant rescue merited the Institution's Silver Medals for Captain James Berriman, Captain Michael Welsh, Captain Richard Paynter, Captain Edward Richards and Captain Thomas Richards.

The Long-Envisaged Lifeboat Arrives

Although money raising attempts to provide a lifeboat were made early in the nineteenth century, nothing much happened until St. Ives shipbuilder Mr. Francis Jennings Adams won a competition set up by the Royal Cornwall Polytechnic Society to design a model lifeboat, which led to the creation of the real thing. This thirty foot lifeboat named The *Hope* was kept in a shed 400 yards from high water mark, and was in the charge of Mr. Hockin. Rescues continued to be performed, often with masterly seamanship by the seafaring fraternity, which in St. Ives was particularly rich and abundant in that it encompassed the traditional local skills of centuries together with the training of pilots and Royal Naval coastguards. It was not until 1861 that a branch of the RNLI was set up here, and a new boathouse was constructed at a cost of £142. Crowds were enthralled to watch the highly professional crew in their lifejackets performing spectacular capers in and out of the new, clinker built, self-righting lifeboat *Moses*.

The St. Ives Lifeboat in 1870

The Enviable Reputation of the St. Ives Men

Mr. Richard Lewis, Secretary of the RNLI paid tribute to the Devon and Cornwall lifeboatmen in general, and the St. Ives crew in particular in his speech of inauguration in Falmouth in August 1867, when he said, 'Perhaps Cornish lifeboatmen never performed a nobler deed than that rendered by the boat of St. Ives the winter before last (going to the aid of the French brig *Providence*, wrecked on Hayle Bar). She capsized twice, but the St. Ives men were determined to perish themselves, rather than the Frenchmen, who were shipwrecked, should be lost (cheers). That deed excited not only the admiration of the residents of the two Counties, but also of all the Country. Indeed, it was so daring and so persevering, that the Emperor of the French conferred an unusual mark of honour on the lifeboat crew, by sending the coxswain a gold medal, and a silver medal to each of the others. It is gratifying to know that foreigners, who are shipwrecked on our coast, know that great and successful efforts will be made to save their lives; and they cease not, when they return to their own country, to express their gratitude for the help rendered to them by England's lifeboats.' The RNLI voted the Silver Medal to Coxswain N. Levett for this gallant service.

The Vulnerability of Early Lifeboatmen

On her last service in January 1866, the old *Moses* and the Penzance lifeboat, transported overland, jointly and heroically saved the crew of nine from *S.S. Bessie* of Hayle, which had driven on shore at Lelant Sands during a violent storm (*see* Penlee). The *Moses* was replaced by a bigger lifeboat later that year, taking over her name and acquiring more spacious premises allowing her to be launched directly over the Fore Strand. Despite the nautical superstition about it being unlucky to change the name of a boat, she was renamed the *Covent Garden* and later the *Exeter*. She went to the aid of numerous schooners, ketches, luggers brigs, and brigantines and saved many lives, but had a few rough rides along the way. One such occurred in the particularly violent storm of December 1867, which damaged the end of the newly constructed wooden pier and caused the French coal carrying brig *Courier du Nord* to end up on the ridge outside St. Ives Pier amid tremendous waves. Despite these terrible conditions, the lifeboat which was already on alert, battled her way out of the harbour and was successful in grappling the rigging on two occasions. The crewmen were too frightened to trust themselves to this rope, but one man who took his chance and jumped overboard was picked up and landed. Oars were lost, but the lifeboat, at the mercy of the elements, made repeated attempts with four different crews, to save life from the wrecked ship now drifting onto Porthminster Beach on the rising tide. Helpers on the shore were eventually able to grab an apparently lifeless sailor, who later recovered.

Oarsmen in those early, lifeboats, open to wind and weather, were particularly vulnerable in heavy seas, as demonstrated in that daunting December service, for the oars had been lost in the course of saving a crewman who had been washed overboard. A similar situation occurred two months later during the rescue of a pilot and five men from the schooner *Gypsy* for, as they were close to the casualty, a great sea struck the boat and washed out the Coxswain and three men. Coxswain Edward F. Toman was caught under the gunwhale of the boat, sustaining severe injuries, but fortunately there was no loss of life. It is recorded that this Coxswain was granted a gratuity of £25 in 1883.

Honours Abound

In 1871, Coxswain Paul Curnow was awarded a Silver Medal in acknowledgement of his gallant services in general, and for his highly meritorious conduct in saving the crew of six from the brig *Queen* on 11th February in particular. More Silver Medals were awarded to Mr. Charles Martin and to Mr. James Murphy, who remained with the lifeboat which was launched five times with replacement crews, to save thirteen people from the schooners *Rambler* and *Mary Ann* and the brig *Frances* wrecked at St. Ives in a severe storm in February 1873. Rescuing the crew of the schooner *Jane Smith* in September 1880 brought a Silver Second Service Clasp to Second Coxswain James Murphy for his skilful and intrepid style.

Sterling Service

The lifeboat whose name had been changed twice was replaced by a thirty-four foot lifeboat, built in 1886 by Woolfe of Shadwell, which took over the name *Exeter*. She was subsequently improved and fitted with a drop keel. Three years later the Institution awarded a Second Service Clasp to the Silver Medal of Coxswain Paul Curnow, who had saved fifty-two lives in his six and a half years as Second Coxswain and twenty years as Coxswain. When he retired James Murphy took his place. While the lifeboat *Exeter* was away, the *Bessie* of Hayle found herself in distress again, when she and the steamers *Vulture* and *Cintra* were driven on shore at Carbis Bay in a terrific storm in November 1893 and the reserve lifeboat made abortive attempts to clear the harbour mouth in the tremendous seas, also restricted by engineering works. However, the Inshore Rocket team was successful in rescuing most of the shipwreck victims of what became known as the Cintra Gale. This was also a second chance lost for the iron screw steamer *Vulture* of London, which had previously survived an encounter with Lee Oar Rock in 1874.

The *James Stevens No.10,* which arrived in 1900 and remained for thirty-three years, performed excellent service as steam and motor vessels appeared increasingly in the catalogue of services. On the evening of January 7th, 1908, she battled against powerful winds to save the crew of the three-masted schooner *Lizzie R. Wilce* of Falmouth which had struck rocks and gone aground on Porthminster Beach. Thankful to be united with their beds, no doubt, the crew were back in the lifeboat, making for the same place well before the light of dawn, to rescue the crew of another schooner the *Mary Barrow*, familiar to Falmouth, which had fetched up alongside. The *Mary Barrow* survived the experience; the *Lizzie* did not.

The schooners Lizzie R. Wilce *and* Mary Barrow *driven on shore at Porthminster Beach, St Ives, in January 1908 (Sheila Bird Collection)*

The Impressive Service Record at St. Ives

The Medal Chart in the boathouse, in the form of a map locating the positions of casualties, shows at a glance the impressive service record at St. Ives. Numbers five and six recall two fine services of the First World War, when nine lives were saved from the *S.S. Taunton* of Liverpool in 1915, with the *Helen Peele* of Padstow arriving on the scene to save the vessel, and the rescue of a sailor washed ashore in Clodgy Bay from a Government motor launch which struck a rock and blew up in 1918. The Institution voted a Silver Medal to Coxswain T. Stevens for the former and another Silver Medal to Company Quarter Master Sgt. Henry Escott for the latter. The lifeboat crew received an additional reward for the part they played in this service, carried out in a whole north-north-easterly gale. St. Ives, situated on the shipping route for the Bristol Channel, was called upon to render service to a number of torpedo casualties at that time.

The events of July 29th 1921 were to be absorbed into the repertoire of tavern tales, as being the day that a storm played havoc with the Breton fishing fleet, and the day the St. Ives lifeboat went out five times to save forty souls from ten vessels in one day. Not only that; it brought a Vellum to Coxswain Robert Wedge. The vessels in question were the ketches *H.F. Bolt* of Bideford and the *Anne* of Gloucester, as well as the French crabbers *St. Eloi, Suzanne Yvonne, St. Mauday, Eclair, Turquoise, En Avant, Anne Marie* and *Providence*.

Heroism and Tragedy

The events of January 1938 and January 1939, which appear on the Medal Chart, will never be forgotten, for they brought tragedy to this tight-knit seafaring community. On a fateful January night, the lifeboat *Caroline Parsons* battled through stormy seas to aid the crew of the *S.S. Alba*, which in running for shelter had misjudged her position and struck rocks. In urgent conditions of storm and changing tide, there had been delay in obeying the Coxswain's order to get aboard, caused by its crew collecting their kit, which they were promptly instructed to abandon. Shortly afterwards, the heavily laden

The first launch of the motor lifeboat Caroline Parsons *in March 1933 (Acknowledgements RNLI)*

lifeboat with her own crew of nine plus twenty-three shipwrecked men, who had been told to distribute their weight low in the boat, was caught broadside on by a heavy sea and overturned, flinging most of them into the water, much to the horror of those watching from the shore by improvised illumination. The lifeboat crew and most of the other men were saved as the result of brave efforts from the shore, but five people perished and the lifeboat was a write-off. This was the first time a motor lifeboat had ever capsized. For this heroic service, Coxswain Thomas Cocking was awarded the Silver Medal, and the eight crewmen received Bronze Medals.

The second disaster involved the replacement lifeboat, the *John & Sarah Eliza Stych*, transferred from Padstow, which had put to sea in a violent storm at night to render assistance to a vessel reported to be in danger to the north-west of Cape Cornwall, but capsized on the way there with loss of Coxswain Thomas Cocking and three of his crew. The lifeboat self-righted, but the surviving crew, unable to get the engine started, sent up distress flares. As help was on its way, the lifeboat capsized again and another man was lost. Three men were left as they drifted towards Godrevy, but after a third capsize only one — William Freeman remained — and after the lifeboat crashed against the rocks he succeeded in getting up the cliff and raising the alarm at Godrevy Farm. Bronze Medals were given to the sole survivor, and posthumously to the other seven men. Tragedies like this strike even harder when more than one member of a family is lost, and the people of St. Ives were devastated by what had befallen them. The lifeboat station was closed down. The sole survivor, a fisherman, never went to sea again. He died on the fortieth anniversary of the tragedy.

Service during the Second World War

The St. Ives station re-opened at the beginning of the Second World War, with the arrival of the *Caroline Oates Aver & William Maine* in January 1940. She saw service with ditched aircraft, naval and other casualties, and set the precedent for launching here by tractor. After the war the RNLI placed on record: 'That the Institution gratefully recognises the service of the St. Ives, Cornwall Lifeboat Station established in 1840, in the great cause of life saving from shipwreck, and on the occasion of the centenary of the station desires to place on record its appreciation of the voluntary work of the officers and committee and of the devotion and courage of the lifeboatmen of St.Ives, Cornwall, who have never failed to maintain the high traditions of the lifeboat service.' In 1946 the Institution awarded a Silver Medal to Coxswain William Peters in recognition of his courage and seamanship in rescuing two people from the auxiliary ketch *Minnie Flossie*, which had sunk near Godrevy Point the previous October.

The Post-War Period

After the war the pattern of emergencies was changing to include an increasing number of holidaymakers and others indulging in leisure pursuits; work for which Inshore Rescue Boats were subsequently designed, later to become known as Inshore Lifeboats (I.L.B.s). An ILB would have been invaluable for the Hell's Mouth rescue of August 1958, when a party of people, including an injured man became trapped in a cave. The lifeboat towed out a skiff, capable of entering the cave, but in the event it took a battering and left more people in jeopardy. All were eventually saved by the deft use of lines and lifesaving equipment, thanks to the bravery of the crewmen who jumped into the water to convey it all across. For this gallant service, a Silver Medal was awarded to Motor Mechanic Michael Peters and Bronze Medals went to Coxswain Dan Roach and Signalman Dan Paynter Jnr. Also in 1958, Motor Mechanic Peters was awarded the Royal Humane Society's Resuscitation Certificate for a bathing incident on August 15th. He also received the Maud Smith award for the bravest act of life saving in 1958 in regard to a service on August 9th.

An ILB Placed Here

An Inshore Lifeboat established here in 1964, and later equipped with V.H.F. radio telephone, operates seasonally, often working in conjunction with the bigger lifeboat. The ILB capsized whilst on service, on 6th September 1968, flinging the three crewmen and a rescued man into the surf. Fortunately all managed to reach the shore in safety. A framed letter of thanks signed by the Chairman was awarded to the helmsman and crew for this service, which had saved the lives of three men from two speedboats.

Much Recognition for Distinguished Services

The Oakley Class lifeboat the *Frank Penfold Marshall,* which arrived in July 1969, distinguished herself while she was here, and departed twenty years later, much battered, but in a blaze of glory. Meanwhile, recognition for fine services continued. In 1972 a framed Letter of Appreciation from the Institution was forwarded to Coxswain Thomas Cocking in recognition of the occasion he dived overboard from the motor launch *Silver Star* and swam 120 yards to the assistance of a boy clinging to a rock off St. Ives Head. Three years later the service to the trawler *Enfant de Bretagne,* whose engine room was flooded, and had been taken in tow by another trawler, brought more Thanks on Vellum to Coxswain Thomas Cocking.

In November 1977 the St. Ives lifeboat joined the Sennen lifeboat, other vessels and various aircraft in a particularly arduous search for survivors of the the coaster *Union Crystal,* in trouble in a strong gale, heavy squalls and very high seas twelve miles to the north of Cape Cornwall. The coaster subsequently sank and one survivor was picked up by helicopter; both St. Ives and Sennen Cove lifeboat coxswains received the recognition of the Institution (*see* Sennen Cove). The following month the lifeboat experienced a near-capsize after launching into phenomenally high seas to go to the aid of another coaster, the *Lady Kamilla*, in distress twenty miles due north of St. Ives in a west-south-westerly storm. Padstow and Clovelly lifeboats, various surface craft and helicopters also took part in the search for the crew, which had abandoned ship. The *Frank Penfold Marshall* launched at 0.44 a.m., and headed north, before being re-directed to the Portrush/Porthtowan area and while they were proceeding at full speed, a massive breaking sea rolled the lifeboat to port. Although she almost filled with water, Coxswain Cocking firmly retained control, and when the lifeboat righted he resumed the search, which eventually lasted for six and a quarter hours. The Institution awarded Coxswain Thomas Cocking a Silver Medal, and his crew their Thanks on Vellum.

St. Ives was one of seven Cornish lifeboats, which, with Nimrod search and rescue aircraft from R.A.F. St. Mawgan, and R.N.A.S. helicopters and *H.M.S. Anglesey*, searched for survivors of the Fastnet Race in August 1979, in a strong north westerly gale and very high seas. During her nine and half hours' service, she searched for the yacht *Grimalkin*, and saved the yacht *Azendra II* with her sole survivor, and like the other lifeboat stations, received a special framed certificate. 1980 brought framed letters of appreciation from the Institution to Tractor Driver J. Tanner and Head Launcher J. Benney, who had successfully launched the lifeboat in difficult conditions, overcoming a malfunction of a track on the tractor. A letter of appreciation was also sent to Coxswain Thomas Cocking for his judgment in dealing with this launch to the French fishing vessel *Floralie*.

A Contrasting Pattern of Services

By this time, the pattern at St. Ives had tended towards an increasing number of services to holidaymakers and pleasure craft interspersed with major catastrophes in ferocious conditions at the other extreme. A framed Letter of Appreciation was awarded to Helmsman P. Allen in 1981 and letters of appreciation sent to crewmembers I. Lowe and I. Tanner and the Commanding Officer of R.N.A.S. Culdrose in recognition of a combined service saving a man badly injured in a cliff fall near the Western Carricks on 26th August 1981. The following year Helmsman Eric Ward was awarded a Bronze Medal in recognition of his courage and skill when the D Class inflatable lifeboat rescued four from a sailing dinghy which had capsized on the Hayle Bar in windy, rough conditions on April 8th. Crewmembers William Thomas and Philip Allen each received Thanks on Vellum. This year also brought a Second Service Clasp to Helmsman Eric Ward's Bronze Medal, in regard to his courage, tenacity and seamanship, when carrying out a search close inshore amongst rocks for the lone sailor of the yacht *Ladybird*, aground to the west of Wicker Point. The Institution's Thanks on Vellum was accorded to crew members Thomas Cocking Jnr. and John Stevens. Coxswain Thomas Cocking gained a Silver Second Clasp for gallantry, courage and skill displayed during the rescue of fourteen people from the German tug *Fairplay* and the Dutch coaster *Orca* in a strong north-north-westerly gale and very rough seas on January 3rd 1984, after the tug's towline had fouled her propeller. Reaching the tug which was being driven ashore in Hayle Basin, Coxswain Cocking went alongside, took off seven men and landed them. After putting out again, it took seven approaches to rescue the remaining seven from the Dutch coaster. This lifesaving service merited the Maud Smith Award for 1984.

Coxswain Cocking's father had been one of the lifeboatmen lost in the 1939 disaster, and in April 1985 that memorial stone in the cemetery was removed and restored, then re-sited on an external wall of the boathouse. The Duke of Atholl, Chairman of the Institution attended the ceremony of rededication.

Departing in a Blaze of Glory
The glorious swansong of the *Frank Penfold Marshall* is best told in the official language of the Institution;

> Gentlemen, A report has been received from the Divisional Inspector of Lifeboats, South West, concerning an incident on the night of 12/13th March, 1989, when the cargo vessel *Secil Japan* grounded on rocks at Deadman's Cove in a storm force west north westerly wind and very rough seas, which involved St. Ives and Padstow lifeboats and two helicopters.'
>
> H.M. Coastguard informed the St. Ives Station Honorary Secretary at 21.25 that a *Mayday* message had been received from the *Secil Japan*. Her cargo had shifted and she was listing at twenty degrees with a crew of sixteen on board. The Padstow Lifeboat *James Burrough* had already launched and a helicopter tasked from R.N.A.S. Culdrose. The St. Ives Lifeboat *Frank Penfold Marshall* launched at 21.48 and had the casualty in sight. Both Lifeboats anchored close to the *Secil Japan*. The helicopter commenced winching operations with both Lifeboats standing by in support. Four persons were winched into the helicopter but the remaining twelve refused to leave the shelter of the wheelhouse. At 23.15 both anchors parted on the *Secil Japan* when all power was lost. The remaining crewmembers were lifted by a second helicopter from R.A.F. Brawdy and both Lifeboats returned to their respective stations at 02.20.
>
> This service was conducted in severe weather conditions and, on behalf of my Committee, I send you the Institution's warm and

appreciative thanks for a first class service carried out in the best traditions of the Lifeboat service.

Sadly, one crewmember was lost as he was being winched up by the helicopter, raising his arms in anticipation of reaching safety, and slipping through the strop. The dramatic events as shown on television gripped the imagination of the public, and provided a salutary reminder that despite modern sophistication and technology, ships can be as vulnerable as they ever were. The survivors were cared for at the Fishermen's Mission in Newlyn, the Coxswain and crew received a framed letter of appreciation from the Chairman of the Institution and the battered lifeboat was taken out of service.

A Time Of Change

To illustrate the contrasts, the St. Ives 'C' Class inflatable distinguished herself by ferrying no fewer than 112 people ashore from local pleasure boats in a single service on 21st August that year, lasting about two and a half hours. This was a time of change at St. Ives, with the reserve lifeboat *Fairlight* standing in until the arrival of *The Princess Royal* in 1990 and a splendid new beach tractor arriving in November 1989. Eric Ward took over as Coxswain in May 1989, with Thomas Cocking Jnr. being appointed Second Coxswain Mechanic in October 1990. Sadly, there was prolonged wrangling about the siting and design of the new boathouse and slipway before a compromise was eventually reached.

On the day of its arrival in November 1989, the new Bigland beach tractor, looking like an outsize Dinky toy, is pertly poised to recover the St. Ives Lifeboat (Photograph by Sheila Bird)

SENNEN COVE LIFEBOAT STATION
(Established 1853)

A crescent moon may be beckoning in the north west, or a full moon regnant in the east. The night may be dark, with great storm clouds rising ominous above the horizon, or the sky may be a purple dome studded with innumerable stars. Across the wrinkled sea those lesser lights that man has won from the vast storehouse of Nature are flashing their warning rays. Immediately in front of us, gleaming from its granite column, is the Longships Light. Nine miles to the south west is the Wolf lighthouse. It stands on a solitary mass of clinkstone which rises in deep water a few feet above the surface, some seven miles from the land. On the western horizon are the Scilly lights, and away to the right of them a pale star shines intermittently. It is the Seven Stones lightship riding at her moorings in mid-ocean. Of all these warning beacons this one lays most hold of the imagination. Think of it, ye who are apt to grumble at fortune on terra firma.

(*From Land's End To The Lizard*: 1909: A.G. Folliott Stokes)

The Influence of Wind and Wave and Complex Tidal Flow
The rhythmic, sonorous music of the ocean plays upon the stoic, grey shores of ancient Bolerium, as it has done for centuries. For this exposed promontory of the Land's End, jutting aggressively into the wide, wild Atlantic takes the full force of wind and wave and variable weather. Warm air merging with cooler temperatures results in sudden mists, which roll eerily across Sennen Cove, giving rise to folklore and legend, including that of the phantom ship of great foreboding. As if these were not hazards enough, there are complicated currents for unwary mariners to contend with, as pinpointed by Captain Greenvile Collins: 'The first place of the beginning of the Flood in the West of *England* , is at the *Long-ships,* which place divides the Stream, one setting to the Northward, and the other to the Southward. At full and Change the Flood begins East-North-East, and sets nine hours to the Northward: And from the *Long-ships* to the *Rundle-stone* and Gulf, the Tide setteth South East three hours, that is, it is High-water by the shore, before the Flood setteth to the Southward.' He goes on to explain the complex system of currents around the Land's End, 'At the *Seven-stones,* and between *Scilly* and the

Land's-end, the first of the Flood setteth North West, and endeth in the North East nine hours; and the Stream beginneth to set to the Southward at High-water, which is East North East a-shore. It is High-water at the Gulf at Full and Change East North East, and the Tide setteth to the Eastward till half Ebb a-shore. And when it is half Ebb ashore at *Mount's-Bay*, then the North Stream begins in the North West, and ends in the North East nine Hours, till it is high water a-shore.'

'The first place of the beginning of the Flood in the West of England, is at the Long-ships, which place divides the Stream, one setting to the Northward, and the other to the Southward.' (Sheila Bird Collection)

Attractively Named Rocks and Reefs
With few places of refuge along this forbidding north coast, Whitesand Bay afforded shelter to small vessels when conditions were unfavourable in the Channel. Sinister and whimsical names such as the Armed Knight, Shark's Fin, Kettle's Bottom, Irish Lady, Dr. Syntax's Head, the Brisons and the Longships denote just a few rocks and reefs which have claimed a catalogue of casualties. A lighthouse built on the Longships became operational in 1795, and was superseded by the present, handsome structure in 1873.

'In the Midst of Life we are in Death'
A glance at the headstones in any of Cornwall's coastal churchyards will give an indication of Cornwall's maritime story. Dionysius Williams, an eighteenth century astronomer, who helped to chart Mount's Bay and became a Fellow of the Royal Society occupies a place in Sennen Churchyard, as do a

number of victims of shipwreck, including thirty-four-year-old Mary Sanderson of Newcastle on Tyne, whose headstone reminds us that 'In the midst of life we are in death.' The wrecking of the brig *New Commercial* of Whitby on the Brisons on January 11th 1851 highlighted local heroism, and the need for a lifeboat station in the area, a state of affairs made more urgent by the publication of the Northumberland Report shortly afterwards, criticising the lack of lifeboat coverage in Cornwall. The ship's voyage from Liverpool to the Spanish Main came to an abrupt halt as she struck the ledge and started to break up. Captain Sanderson, his wife and the eight seamen managed to reach a ledge, but were suddenly swept away by a huge wave, which took the lives of all save for the Captain, his wife and a half-caste seaman. With tremendous initiative and will to survive, he fashioned a life-saving craft from driftwood and canvas, which he successfully navigated clear of danger and into Whitesand Bay, where he was recovered by Sennen fishermen. The couple washed up on Little Brison struggled desperately to gain height above the angry, leaping waves.

Meanwhile, Captain George Davies, R.N., Inspecting Commander of Coastguards at Penzance had ordered H.M. revenue cutter *Sylvia* to round Land's End and attempt a rescue, as he and other officers and coastguards positioned themselves on Cape Cornwall. A boat was lowered, but despite repeated attempts until nightfall, they were unable to get in close in such rough conditions. Dawn next day saw two pathetic figures still perched on the rock. With a slight change in the wind direction, operations were renewed, and six rescue boats manned by fishermen, coastguards and preventive men converged on the scene, watched by thousands on the cliff tops. Captain Davies, at great personal risk, fired powerful rockets without protection from the kick-back, until he succeeded in getting a line to those in peril on the rock. The Captain fastened it around his wife's waist and urged her to jump. There was some delay until she summoned the courage to do so, but when she did, she chose the wrong moment, for it coincided with a succession of heavy breakers, which placed them all in jeopardy.

However, they managed to haul her aboard the rescue craft, but the poor woman, who had experienced the sedate upbringing of a vicar's fourth daughter, who had bravely endured the ordeal of shipwreck thus far, was exhausted, and she died shortly afterwards. Her husband was strong enough to survive his ordeal. This epic service, one of Cornwall's all time classics, brought the RNLI's Gold Medallion to Captain Davies, destined to become one of their Inspectors, another to Mr. Thomas Randall, Commander of the Revenue cutter *Sylvia*, Silver Medals to all under their command and monetary rewards to the crew of two fishing boats. This stout hearted service also brought recognition for this isolated, hardy seafaring community, which needed these qualities to survive in such a harsh environment by land and sea, and who created the small harbour at Sennen Cove by enterprise, to establish a viable fishing industry.

Sennen Cove's Early Lifeboats

In a flush of enthusiasm in 1852, the National Shipwreck Institution promised to deliver an eight-oared lifeboat of the Peake Class to Sennen Cove forthwith, but in the event a lighter, six-oared version arrived the following year, having been brought by steamer to Penzance and towed around Land's End by Revenue cutter. Her first and last service occurred in May 1856, when she and other shore boats brought the barque *Charles Adolphe* into Penzance, which had been abandoned after a collision off Land's End. She was replaced in 1864 by a larger, ten-oared, self-righting lifeboat called the *Cousins William & Mary Ann* of Bideford, and financed by a Mrs. Mary Ann Davis, who had a husband called George. Her most outstanding service took place four years later, when the Government lighter *Devon* became yet another victim of the notorious Brisons. Seventeen of the eighteen souls aboard perished as the ship disintegrated, but the mate, who had the presence of mind to leap overboard on the *seaward* side of the casualty, was washed up on the rocks, and subsequently saved by the lifeboat firing a line, and hauling him aboard inside a buoy. This brave feat brought Silver Medals to Coxswain Matthew Nicholas and Coastguard Officer Sylvester Morrison. And, apocryphally, the sole survivor's name was George Davis, the name of the donor's husband. This lifeboat, known to one and all as *Cousins*, cut a dash in hotly contested lifeboat races in West Cornwall, frequently emerging triumphant.

Attempts to Defy the Vagaries of the Elements

Getting the lifeboat launched was never easy at Sennen Cove, which was initially done from a carriage, drawn by a team of horses across the beach at Whitesand Bay, backed into the water, then turned bow on to the waves for a quick getaway, vital to avoid capsizing in the surf. Over the years the boathouses were re-sited, enlarged and adapted to accommodate different sized lifeboats in an attempt to defy the vagaries of the elements, which always make themselves felt around these parts. A new boathouse was constructed in 1874 at a cost of £250, and the replacement lifeboat *Denzil & Maria Onslow* came on station five years later, having been publicly launched at Penzance en route. At that time Sennen Cove was remote, with a very self-contained, seafaring community, somewhat suspicious of outsiders. However, this station was administered in conjunction with that of Penzance until 1913, when the former Honorary Secretary Colonel T.H. Cornish, also a member of Sennen Cove Harbour Commissioners, took up duties here. As a much needed safety measure in 1890, the Institution donated £5 towards the cost of a lantern to guard the fishermen approaching the cove from the south and west from the dangerous rocky ledges. Twenty years later an Acetylene Beach Light was supplied.

The pulling and sailing lifeboat Denzil and Maria Onslow *approaching the ever-restless Sennen shores (Acknowledgements RNLI)*

The 'Davies' Theme Re-echoed

Before being replaced by the *Ann Newbon* in 1893, the *Denzil & Maria Onslow* went to the aid of the cutter *Spring* of Guernsey, which had been rammed by an unidentified schooner and saved the crew in a long and arduous service, and also rendered assistance and saved seven lives from the *S.S. Malta* of Glasgow. The 'Davies' theme was revived in September 1891, when they were alerted by signals from the Longships Lighthouse to a vessel in distress during a terrific gale, which was so severe that some of the crew refused to put out, which meant that a call was made for volunteers. These men gallantly set forth, under the direction of Coxswain Nicholas to assist the schooner *Annie Davies*, which was found abandoned in the Bristol Channel. The lifeboat's search for survivors proved fruitless, and her crew had a further test of extreme physical endurance, when the winds increased to hurricane force, and they had to put in at St. Ives on their homeward trip. This service brought Thanks on Vellum to a barrister, a stockbroker and an artist, who had been volunteers.

The Establishment of Slipway Launching

The *Ann Newbon*, built by Woolfe of Shadwell, had a particularly distin-

Above: The construction of a slipway at Sennen Cove allowed the alternatives of launching the lifeboat down the slipway, or from her carriage, drawn by horses across the beach. The slipway was to be modified and rebuilt at various times. Here we see the crew aboard the Ann Newbon, which performed a particularly fine record of service (Acknowledgements John Corin and RNLI)

Above opposite: Local miners and coastguards bravely went to the rescue of the shipwrecked, after the S.S. Malta of Glasgow ran ashore to the north of Cape Cornwall in foggy conditions in 1889, and after abortive attempts to get her afloat, the Sennen Cove lifeboat took off the skeleton crew. The RNLI's Thanks on Vellum went to Edward and William Roberts of St. Just, while monetary awards were made to others who took part in rescue operations (Sheila Bird Collection)

Below opposite: Quite how the S.S. Blue Jacket of Cardiff came to yield herself up at the foot of the Longships in reasonable conditions in November 1898 will always be a mystery. The shipwrecked took to their boats, and all 22 were safely landed by the Sennen lifeboat (Sheila Bird Collection)

guished career here, saving 132 lives in twenty-nine years in a variety of services involving ketches, trawlers, steamships, motor vessels, naval ships, torpedo casualties and a seaplane. Slipway launching was established in her time. A new boathouse built in 1896 incorporated sliding doors, which were safer and more efficient, a carriage house alongside and a slipway. This offered alternative styles of launching according to weather conditions and the location of the casualty.

The Tragedy of the *Khyber*

Mountainous seas and strong currents made it impossible to launch to the aid of the barque *Khyber* in March 1905; a state of affairs which was to bring something positive out of a terrible tragedy, in that it led to a new breakwater being constructed, with added protection for the lifeboat slipway and harbour. The Penzance lifeboat, towed by the steamer *Lady of the Isles*, made a gallant attempt to save the crew, but they were too late. In this story of the preservation of life from shipwreck off Cornwall, it is fitting to portray a perilous situation from the point of view of the shipwrecked, praying for salvation. This was done simply and effectively by A.G. Folliott Stokes, shortly afterwards:

> This was one of the most tragic wrecks that even this iron coast has known. For hours her crew looked into the eyes of Death, expecting the rescue that never came. She was a full rigged ship, homeward bound from Australia. She got embayed, lost most of her sails and being unable to weather the land, anchored a few cables' lengths from a lee shore about eleven o'clock on a dark night. A terrific sea was running and a whole gale blowing from the westward. Though she burnt flares and fired rockets they were not seen. Hour after hour she rode at her two anchors in a hellish maelstrom of breakers. Just as the grey dawn was rekindling hope both cables parted, and she was driven ashore and almost immediately went to pieces. Only three of her crew of twenty-six hands were saved.

These survivors were flung onto the rocks and saved by watchers on the shore. A large headstone close to the wall on St. Levan church completes the story, for here lie Captain Rothery and the remainder of his crew. Some say that a ghostly bell can be heard tolling within the grave.

Recognition of Courageous Services

When the fully-rigged ship *Fairport* of Liverpool was in distress in a whole southerly gale and mountainous seas just after Christmas 1908, the Sennen lifeboat launched twice in a determined attempt to render assistance to the vessel, which had been attended by the tug *Blazer* and the salvage ship *Lady of the Isles*. Then after a successful service, in which the *Fairport* and twenty lives were saved, the lifeboat, unable to return to Sennen Cove in the prevailing, ferocious conditions, had to make for Penzance. This courageous service brought the Institution's Silver Medal to Coxswain Henry Nicholas. In 1915 the Institution presented Mr. John Hocking, who sustained serious injury whilst assisting in a lifeboat launch, with a silver cigarette case.

1919 turned out to be a particularly auspicious year, with much recognition around these parts. The sequence began on St. Patrick's Day, after the *S.S. Falmouth Castle* struck the Runnelstone Reef. Seven men who had taken to the ship's boat were recovered by the fishing vessel *Ben ma Chree*, and transferred to the *Ann Newbon*. Others were rescued by the aid of the rocket apparatus and shore boats. The feat of these shore boats, saving eight lives in difficult conditions in heavy seas was recognised by the Institution by awarding Alfred Jackson a Silver Medal, and Bronze Medals to three others. The RNLI acknowledged the service carried out on 30th November as being one of the finest in the Institution's history, when four men were rescued from the sea and four from the rocks after H.M. Motor Launch 378, which had been in company with other naval vessels, became disabled and drifted onto the Longships during a strong gale. For this service the Coxswain, Henry Nicholas and Second Coxswain Thomas Pender were awarded Silver Medals, and twelve crewmen Bronze Medals. Henry Nicholas Jnr., crew member, who was seventeen, and destined to become Coxswain in 1959, received a Bronze Medal. 1919 also saw preparations and adaptions for the station's first motor lifeboat.

Sennen Cove's First Motor Lifeboat
This motor lifeboat, constructed at Cowes, arrived in 1922. She offered no weather protection for the crew, but carried spars, sails and oars for use in an emergency. 1929 saw the completion of a higher, larger boathouse, with launching and recovery slipways, and a turntable inside. This lifeboat, called the *Newbons*, was to save thirty-six lives and experience wartime service with aircraft casualties, torpedoed ships and naval vessels. The changing social pattern brought about by war, widened horizons and increased material expectations, with the option of well-paid jobs in cosy offices. The onset of tourism meant that Sennen Cove could never revert to being the isolated, contained fishing community it once was. And fewer fishermen meant fewer suitable candidates for the lifeboat.

Absent for her Ceremony of Inauguration
The Watson Class *Susan Ashley* arrived in July 1948. Rather in the style of a bride not making it to the church for her wedding day, she was absent for her inaugural ceremony, owing to the fact that she had been called out on service the previous day in severe weather which had made it impossible for her to

re-house. Visitors to the Land's End area, with its awe-inspiring aspect of the sea, might picture her hammering through these turbulent waters on her way to a gallant rescue, as in March 1964, when the trawler *Victoire Roger* of Ostend ran aground near here on a foggy night amid swirling seas. When the lifeboat arrived on the scene, the casualty was wedged in a deep cleft, making rescue attempts tricky, with very little room for manoeuvre. There was a possibility of anchoring and firing a line aboard, but in the event, Coxswain Mechanic Henry Nicholas daringly ran in twice, grabbed the crew and their injured captain from their doomed ship, and landed them at Newlyn. This enterprise was recognised with the award of a Bronze Second Service Clasp to Coxswain Henry Nicholas and service certificates to the crew.

The Drama of the *Jeanne Gougy*
Two years previously the drama of the *Jeanne Gougy* of Dieppe had been enacted in the vicinity, with media coverage giving the public the chance to identify with the combined operations of the rescue services. The *Susan Ashley* was undergoing modifications and improvements, including the installation of 52 h.p. diesel engines at the time, and the reserve lifeboat *Edmund & Mary Robinson* responded to the nocturnal call. A lifesaving team on the cliffs had been trying to get a line across but, when the lifeboat arrived, the vessel was on her side, crewmen had been washed away, and there were apparently no survivors. The lifeboat and a helicopter from Chivenor carried out a search and recovered three bodies; two were landed at Newlyn, with the lifeboat returning with the Penlee lifeboat *Solomon Browne*, while the helicopter landed the others and refuelled at Culdrose. It was considerably later that someone on the cliff noticed a hand move in the wheelhouse of the submerged *Jeanne Gougy* which led to six men, fortunate enough to have been trapped in air pockets, being rescued in spectacular style by helicopter and breeches buoy. R.A.F. Sergeant E.C. Smith, who was lowered by helicopter to save two injured men, was awarded the George Medal. The French awarded Bronze Medals to Coxswain Henry Nicholas, Second Coxswain James Howard Nicholas, Bowman Edmund George and Richard George, the Mechanic.

Rearing Hulls, Helicopters and Flung Spray
Whatever the time of year, few launches here can qualify for the 'pleasure cruise' wisecracks that are made about practice launches on lovely days. Anyone who has stood on the noisy shore as the rollers roar in and explode on the Cowloes knows the degree of courage required to be a lifeboatman at Sennen Cove. The Rother class *Diana White*, which arrived here in 1974, offered more weather protection than the *Susan Ashley*, and was equipped with radar, MF and VHF/FM radio, echo-sounding and other modern devices. Among the fascinating array of photographs on the wall, displaying

rearing hulls, flying spray and an array of hardy, seafaring faces, is a more sedate one, recalling her naming ceremony, performed by the Duke of Kent.

Despite all the improvements, launching from Sennen Cove is still restricted at certain states of the low tide, and also in severe north westerly gales. However, achieving the almost impossible in the knowledge that survivors of the coaster *Union Crystal* could be fighting for their lives in these menacing waters, Coxswain Eric Pengilly put out in November 1977, into a north westerly gale force nine to ten, with a heaving swell and blinding squalls, joining the St. Ives lifeboat, bigger vessels, a Nimrod aircraft and two helicopters in their search. The sole survivor, the ship's captain, was winched up by helicopter, and the Sennen Cove lifeboat made passage for Newlyn in the maelstrom conditions. RNLI recognition, in the form of a Silver Medal went to Coxswain/Mechanic Eric Pengilly and Thanks on Vellum to his crew. Coxswain Pengilly died on 29th January, 1978, and these awards were voted by the Committee of Management on 22nd February 1978.

Sennen Cove's Illustrious Coxswains

Second Coxswain Maurice Hutchens took over from Eric Pengilly, following other illustrious predecessors from the Nicholas, Pender, George and Roberts families. In 1979 the station was awarded a special framed certificate in recognition of their services with numerous yachts in difficulties during the Fastnet Race. A particularly outstanding service two years later is commemorated by a plaque on the boathouse wall, awarded by the Iceland Steamship Company, 'with sincere gratitude and admiration to the crew of the RNLI Sennen Cove Lifeboat *Diana White.'* This was 'in recognition of an act of outstanding courage and bravery, in saving the lives of the crew of the *M/V Tungufoss* during the hours of darkness in a severe storm in extremely adverse conditions off Land's End on September 19, 1981.' The RNLI awarded the Silver Medal of the Institution to Coxswain/Mechanic Maurice Hutchens 'in recognition of his courage, leadership and excellent seamanship when the lifeboat rescued seven of the crew of the Icelandic coaster *Tungufoss* on 19 September. The coaster was listing forty degrees to port after her cargo of maize had shifted in a south westerly gale and a very rough sea and the Coxswain made approximately twenty runs close into the *Tungufoss* to rescue the seven men, the last three being taken off when the vessel had a list of 60 degrees. The casualty eventually foundered.'

When Maurice Hutchens retired in April 1990, Terry George became Coxswain at the age of thirty-four, thereby becoming one of England's youngest coxswains. Terry is also a cousin of Ken Thomas, Coxswain of the Penlee lifeboat.

Coxswain Thomas Henry Nicholas, of Sennen Cove, pictured in 1921 wearing a kapok lifejacket (Acknowledgements RNLI)

An Area Demanding Exceptional Skills
The contemporary pattern of service includes seasonal cliff and yachting casualties, with fishing vessels and commercial shipping continuing to fall victim to these treacherous waters when conditions are at their most daunting, a situation demanding exceptional skill and courage from lifeboatmen. At times like these, when most of us are glad to be safe and warm at home, how frequently we hear on the local news that the Land's End and Lizard lifeboats are out to the aid of shipping in distress. An example of this occurred in July 1990, after the rescue services had been summoned to assist the cargo ship *Rocquaine*, whose engine room was on fire, two miles west of the

Longships. Engulfing smoke caused a temporary break in the vessel's communications, but in the event she was able to extinguish the fire, with the lifeboat, a helicopter from Culdrose and others in attendance, and was towed into Penzance harbour. As the Sennen lifeboat prepared to head for home, she was diverted to the assistance of a motor boat thirty or forty miles south of Land's End. The *Western Morning News* reported next day: 'A South West lifeboat crew completed a marathon 12 hours on duty yesterday, dashing to the aid of a blazing vessel and then towing a stricken motorboat into port.' This marathon help run to a variety of casualties also demonstrates the capabilities of today's lifeboats, as distinct from those early sailing and rowing lifeboats, which dealt mostly with emergencies sighted from the land.

'They Also Serve........'
Stories of real life adventure on the restless wave depend not only on God and lifeboatmen being 'strong to save', but on us, and the fund raisers who co-ordinate it all. Captain Jim Summerlee, the station's Honorary Secretary spoke of his appreciation of people's generous support, which sometimes comes in unusual ways, as when £400 in £5 notes arrived in an old brown envelope from an anonymous donor. £649 was raised after Mrs. Vashti Watters, great aunt of the Sennen Cove and Penlee Coxswains had directed that money should be donated to those two stations, in lieu of flowers at her funeral. The parents, relatives and friends of four lads who were drowned at Land's End while on an educational trip with their school from Stoke Poges have contributed much to fund raising, and they were delighted when it was agreed that the new, Mersey Class boat for Sennen Cove was to be called the *Four Boys*.

THE LIZARD LIFEBOAT STATION

(Established 1859; incorporating Polpeor (1859-1961):
Church Cove (1885-1899); Lizard/Cadgwith (1961-)
The Lifeboat Station at Kilcobben was renamed The Lizard in 1987)

And now, across the southern heavens there flashes a pale beam of white light, sweeping from left to right, like the luminous arm of some gigantic windmill. There it goes again, a swift but unhesitating beat. We are not superstitious, or we might fancy it the flash of some great angel's wing. Well, and so it is. Not that of the old Reaper, but of the guardian angel of light. In other words, it is the reflection of the Lizard Light, one of the most powerful in the world, visible sixty miles away. That luminous ray, stealing so swiftly across the sky, has brought joy to many an anxious eye on bridge and deck. That silent welcome from the motherland has sent a thrill through the hearts of countless wanderers, who, after many years, perhaps half a lifetime, are speeding homewards out of the great waste of waters.

(*From Land's End to The Lizard*: A.G. Folliott Stokes, 1909)

A Profusion of Navigational Hazards

The Lizard headland, anciently known as Ocrinum, enjoys the distinction of being the site of Cornwall's first real lighthouse, which is testimony in itself to the problems caused by the profusion of navigational hazards in these waters. Captain Greenvile Collins cautioned, 'Right off from the Point of the Lizard lieth a parcel of steep Rocks above Water, called the *Staggs;* they lie off South from the Shore into the Sea, about a short Mile off; they are steep too; you will have twelve Fathom close to them.' This peninsula was usually the first landfall for shipping entering the Channel, and the lights from the twin beacons of the Lizard lighthouse were easily distinguishable from Scilly, which exhibited one, and Guernsey, which showed three. Argand lamps were introduced in 1812, producing lights with considerably more brilliance than the previous oil-fired lanterns. But *Murray's Hand-Book* of 1865 tells us: 'Notwithstanding, however, the brilliant illumination which is hence thrown for miles over the sea, ships, embayed in thick weather between the Lizard and Tol Pedn Penwith, are frequently lost in the vicinity of this headland, and the cliffs are of such a character that it is almost impossible to render from them the slightest assistance.'

To stand on Lizard Point and watch the sea in rampant mood lashing against the rocks and exploding into white foam, and to hear its mighty, majestic chords is awe inspiring; for those aboard one of the old sailing ships, this was frequently an anthem of death. It was just so for all but three aboard the military transport *Royal Anne*, bound for Barbados, which was wrecked on Stag's Reef in November 1720. About 200 victims of that shipwreck lie buried in Pistol Meadow near Lizard Point, which derived its name from the firearms washed ashore on that mournful occasion. But that was one of countless shipwrecks in this area.

In view of the notoriety of these waters and the importance of its geographical situation, it is rather surprising that a lifeboat station was not established here sooner than 1859. None of the gentry took the initiative in this isolated, impoverished fishing community, until landowner and benefactor T.J. Agar Robartes of Lanhydrock got things underway, after the heartrending wrecking of the *S.S. Czar* of Hull on the Vrogue Rock in January of that year, with the loss of thirteen lives, including those of the captain, his wife and child. The coastguards distinguished themselves by bravely rescuing eighteen men on a dark and stormy night in their own boats, and might have saved even more had a lifeboat been available at the time. The Chief Officer of the Cadgwith Coastguard was awarded the Institution's Silver Medal, and his men received monetary rewards.

The Area's Role in Worldwide Communications
The Lizard, with its variously sited lifeboat stations, coastguard stations, Lloyd's Signal Station, Marconi's Wireless Station, Goonhilly Satellite Earth Station and Royal Naval Air Station (R.N.A.S.) Culdrose, was destined to play a key role in worldwide communications, including the co-ordination of Search and Rescue. After the establishment of Lloyd's Signal Station in 1872, every kind of vessel from the humblest little coaster to the most sophisticated ocean liner would come in close to register its name, which was done initially by flags and lamps and later by radio, with the information being relayed to London. Modern technology continues apace, and the old 'whitewashed, castellated pepper box' is now obsolete.

The Establishment of a Lifeboat Station at Polpeor
Having established that there should be a lifeboat station here, opinion was divided on whether it should be at Mullion or at Polpeor Cove, situated on the most southerly toe of the Lizard. Eventually it was built at Polpeor Cove, on land donated by the mother of Mr. T.J. Agar Robartes, with the first lifeboat taking her Christian names, *Anna Maria*. In the first of her two recorded services in 1861 and 1863, she stood by the schooner *Hurrel* of Penzance all night in thick fog and heaving swell, and by preventing the

crew's foolhardy attempt to reach the shore in their boat, saved the men and their vessel, which was able to proceed the following day.

The lifeboat station for the Lizard, initially above Polpeor Cove, on land donated by Agar Robartes and his mother, was reckoned to be well positioned for services on each side of the peninsula, with launching possible in most conditions (Acknowledgements RNLI)

A Tragic Practice Launch, and a Near Repeat
Sadly, this lifeboat, her Coxswain Peter Mitchell and crewmen Richard Harris and Nicholas Stevens were lost on January 2nd 1866, after capsizing on a practice launch during a hurricane. The Coxswain was buried in the churchyard of St. Winwallow, above Church Cove. The Honorary Secretary, the Reverend Vyvyan Robinson, who also served as a crewman, survived this ordeal.

A replacement lifeboat arrived the following month, and also took on the name *Anna Maria*, but the continuation of disasters occurring on the eastern and western sides of the peninsula highlighted the poor access roads to Lizard Town, and the difficult trek across fields to launch for such casualties. Road improvements were made, but it was also logical at the time to establish a station at Mullion, which had been under consideration since the critical Northumberland Report of 1851 (*see* Mullion), and another at Cadgwith, where there was a thriving fishing community, and where there were no problems in raising a crew for a large lifeboat (*see* Cadgwith), which had sometimes been the case at the Lizard. *Anna Maria II* performed services with the schooner *Selina* of Swansea, the *Calcutta* of London, the snow (a small sailing vessel, similar to a brig, with a supplementary trysail mast) *Phillis & Mary* of Blyth, the paddle tug *Slasher* of Liverpool and the Prussian barque *Fomalhaut*, sometimes working in conjunction with the Cadgwith lifeboat. She sustained damage in the last mentioned service, and the third *Anna Maria*, thirty feet in length and rowed by ten oars arrived here in 1873. Her predecessors had been of the same length, but rowed by six oars. Possibly subscribing too literally to the theory that practice makes perfect, the Lizard crew were certainly put through their paces during exercises, whatever the weather, and the lifeboat with the District Inspector and her crew were lucky to emerge relatively unscathed in March 1881, when there was another capsize.

The Hazards of Sudden Blanketing By Fog
This is an area of perverse winds and currents (*see* Sennen Cove), but fog has been responsible for a very high percentage of the casualties. In October 1874. the *West Briton* reported: 'The recent collision off the Lizard seems to have induced the Trinity Board to erect a fog signal. We learn that a spot has been selected near the edge of the cliff, in front of the lighthouse where a steam whistle will be placed as soon as possible. In addition to this it is stated that the electric light will replace the Argand lamps, which have been in use from the beginning of the century.' A second generator, installed in 1881, further increased the efficiency, but the foghorn, powerful as it was could not be heard by vessels close in to the high cliffs. This was thought to have been the case when the large German liner *Mosel* of Brennen, outward bound from Southampton to New York, drove ashore at Bass Point in a sudden enveloping mist in August 1882. With the co-ordination of the lifeboat, ship's boats, Falmouth tugs and coastguards, all the 700 or so people on board were safely landed, as well as some of her valuable cargo. The Coxswain and crew also assisted aboard the liner and ship's boats, with the lifeboat being credited with saving twenty-seven lives. The casualty took a subsequent further battering until she was beyond salvage.

A Lifeboat Station at Church Cove
The third *Anna Maria* was transferred to the newly completed station at Church Cove in 1885, performing one service before being replaced by the *John & Sarah* two years later, which did not perform any. There were launching impediments at Church Cove, which closed down in 1899.

Combined Service with the Cadgwith Lifeboat
The *Edmund & Fanny*, a larger boat which had arrived at Polpeor in 1885, performed a fine service the following year, when she and the Cadgwith lifeboat saved the crew of forty-three and two passengers from the homeward bound *S.S. Suffolk*, which had taken to the ship's boats after she had

struck rocks under Lizard Head in dense fog, having not apparently heard the fog signal. A number of cattle being carried on board also got ashore.

The Colourful Exploits of the *Lady Dufferin*

Dastardly deeds, a raging storm and gallantry all played their part in the downfall of the 894 ton, three-masted wooden barque *Lady Dufferin* in March 1888, also achieving the Institution's recognition of a sterling service. It all began when this Plymouth ship set sail for Montevideo with a cargo of railway track, and ended in a mass of wreckage in Polpeor Cove after mutiny had broken out in the Atlantic and the captain had decided to return to the home port. But the fates were against them, and they were engulfed in a storm. Having thus presented herself on the lifeboat's hazardous, rock-strewn doorstep amid the swirling waves, attempts were made to fire a line to the *Lady Dufferin*. In the event, and at great risk to themselves, the lifeboat was grappled alongside, enabling the seventeen victims of shipwreck to summon up courage and make a jump for freedom. The following month Coxswain Edwin Matthews received a Silver Medal for his long and gallant services.

Fearsome March Gales

After 1892, when the lifeboat station had been re-positioned, and the reno-vated lifeboat was able to launch more quickly down greased skids, she saw service with barques and an increasing number of steamships, mostly caught out by sudden blanketing fog. In March 1893, another Silver Medal was awarded to Captain Davis G. Bell, Master of the *S.S. Gustav Bitter* of London, for gallantly saving one of his own crewmen when his ship was stranded off the Lizard, a somewhat novel situation. The Lizard and Cadgwith lifeboats which took part in this fine service saved the remainder of the crew (*see* Cadgwith). March and October are notorious months for shipwrecks in this area.

The Record-Breaking *Suevic* Service

It was the *Edmund & Fanny's* successor, the *Admiral Sir George Back*, arriving here in 1903, which collaborated with the Cadgwith lifeboats and others in the area in the epic service of the *S.S. Suevic* of Liverpool, destined to become legendary around these parts. She had run onto the Maenheere Reef in rainy and foggy conditions on the night of March 17th, 1907, while homeward bound from Melbourne with 524 people on board. The Lizard and Cadgwith lifeboats were able to intercept some of the ship's boats which had been hastily launched into heavy seas, and embarked on a series of runs between the ship and shore as tugs from Falmouth, and lifeboats from Porthleven and Coverack converged on the scene. All were safely landed, with the Cadgwith lifeboat rescuing 227, the Lizard lifeboat 167, the Coverack lifeboat 44 and the

Porthleven lifeboat 18. Others were saved by the ship's boats and tugs. Saving so many people from one ship created a proud, all time record for the area, and for the RNLI, and it brought Silver Medals to Coxswain William Edward Mitchell and Second Coxswain Edwin Mitchell for their lifesaving achievement, made in six trips. Silver Medals also went to the Cadgwith Coxswain Edward Rutter and the Reverend Henry Vyvyan (see Cadgwith). As a satisfying sequel to the story, the *Suevic's* cargo was removed and her after section, still in working order was cut away, towed to Southampton and fitted to a newly created forward section. And then she steamed on.....

Stately Square Riggers in Distress
By contrast, the lifeboat had a spate of services with spectacular square riggers, beginning with the *Hansy* of Fredrikstad which was driven by a fierce south-south-westerly gale into Housel Bay and wrecked at Carn Table on November 3rd 1911. Most of the people aboard, including the Captain's wife and baby, as well as a cat and dog, were hauled ashore by breeches buoy, in a tricky operation smartly set up from the high cliffs, despite the difficulty of intervening rocks. The lifeboat launched into very difficult seas and, having stood by during this operation, then removed the Captain, Mate and a crewman as the vessel broke up. History relates somewhat engagingly that when the weather moderated, the salvors discovered a pig in the crew's quarters munching his way through a sack of potatoes and two happy goats in a bunk, while the timber which split out from the hold kept the home fires burning for quite some time. Three months later, the lifeboat went to the aid of the French barque *Chile*, in difficulties in thick fog in Pentreath Bay, summoned tugs from Falmouth and assisted in saving the vessel and twenty lives. On May 5th 1913, the elegant, white, four-masted steel barque *Queen Margaret* of Glasgow, which had been tacking off the Lizard in light winds while awaiting a reply from Lloyd's Signal Station, struck the Stags Reef and shuddered to a halt less than half a mile from the shore. The lifeboat was summoned and tugs came out from Falmouth in the hope of getting her afloat again. Twenty-seven people were safely taken off, but the beautiful ship fell onto her port side, then disintegrated. In his book *The Cornish Coasts and Moors* published early this century, A.G. Folliott Stokes quotes an old pilot who told him, 'If only they would sink Lloyd's Signalling Station, there would be no more wrecks on the Manacles or around the Lizard Head, because captains would give that corner a wide berth.' But it was the sudden onset of dense fog off the Lizard which resulted in the Aberdeen full rigger *Cromdale* becoming a spectacular wreck with all sails set, at Bass Point just eighteen days after the loss of the much loved, legendary, *Queen Margaret*. Distress rockets brought the Lizard and Cadgwith lifeboats to the scene, resulting in the former saving five people and the latter twenty (see Cadgwith).

115

The Increased Capabilities of Motor Lifeboats

Having been established somewhat later than its importance justified, this station's recognition was highlighted in 1913 by the decision to have one of the new motor lifeboats based here, with a new boathouse, slipway and turntable constructed in 1914, at a cost of £5,000. But war intervened. In 1918, the arrival of Newhaven's *Sir Fitzroy Clayton* provided the opportunity for the station to become accustomed to motor lifeboats, before the arrival of their own. The *Frederick H. Pilley* arrived two years later, having been commenced at Summer & Payne's of Southampton, who had had to turn their attentions to Admiralty contracts, and completed by Saunders of Cowes. She and her crew were to demonstrate their prowess, being summoned to the spectacular grounding of the five-masted schooner *Adolf Vinnen* of Hamburg on her maiden voyage, and various steamships, including the *St. Patrice* of Havre, providing a distaste of things to come by polluting the waters with fuel oil, and White Star liner *S.S. Bardic* of Liverpool, from which ninety-three people were safely landed. Her last service was a stylish one, rendered to the ketch barge *Lady Daphne* of Rochester, which was careering down the Channel out of control on Boxing Day 1927, after her Master had been washed overboard, while trying to enter Plymouth Sound. The two remaining crewmen's distress signals were spotted at last from the Lizard shore, and after a hair-raising chase, they closed in on her, allowing one man to jump, veering off and coming in close again, grabbing the other man in a feat of clever timing. The abandoned barge was left to her fate (*see* St. Mary's, Isles of Scilly).

The forty-one foot Watson Class lifeboat *Duke of York,* financed by King George's Fund for Sailors, and built by Groves & Gutteridge of Cowes arrived in 1934, and performed many fine services, with casualties of war adding to the hazards of fog. Post-war services were with motor vessels, steam ships, and increasing numbers of pleasure craft, including the trans-atlantic raft *L'Egare II,* which was given a tow, and casualties of aviation. For the strategically sited airfields of the south-west have continuously played a key role in our country's defence, as well as their Search and Rescue functions.

One of the most memorable occurrences of recent times involved the *S.S. Flying Enterprise* of New York when, in January 1952, the drama on the high seas was played out in the grand, heroic style, with more than a touch of mystery. The Lizard lifeboat put out in terrible conditions, and after standing by for seventeen and a half hours, and running low on fuel, she was relieved by the Cadgwith and Falmouth lifeboats, before making for Falmouth rather than her own station, on account of exceptionally bad weather (*see* Falmouth).

Above: The Frederick H. Pilley, *launched down greased skids, prepares to thread her way through a daunting array of rocks off Polpeor (Graham Farr Archives; acknowledgements RNLI)*

Overleaf above: When the 5-masted German schooner Adolf Vinnen *was wrecked near Bass Point on her maiden voyage during a gale in February 1923, the Lizard lifeboat was summoned by rocket. But having battled with the elements to reach them and made contact by grapnel, the crew refused to leave. The lifeboat made for Falmouth, but stood by next day as the shipwrecked were rescued by breeches buoy (Sheila Bird Collection)*

Overleaf below: The Lizard lifeboat closing in for a daring rescue from the runaway ketch barge Lady Daphne *in December 1927 (sketch by Tony Warren)*

Sed to Cut the First Sod'

Photographs, ships' nameplates and a fascinating array of nautical trophies concerned with Lizard lifeboat services are on display at the Top House at Lizard Town, beside the Green. Also on display is a spade with the inscription: 'Sed to CUT the FIRST SOD At the commencement of Construction of the Royal National Lifeboat Station at Kilcobben Cove, The Lizard. Presented by the Contractors Grey Conoley & Co Ltd., to A.J. Greenslade Esq., Chairman of the Lizard Lifeboat Committee, 27th May 1957.' Kilcobben is situated midway between Church Cove and Polpeor Cove.

The Amalgamation of Two Stations, and the Move to Kilcobben

The lifeboat station at Polpeor closed down in October 1961, with 562 saved lives to its credit, and was sold to a consortium of fishermen. The highly successful station at Cadgwith closed two years later, and the two stations amalgamated to become known as the Lizard Cadgwith Lifeboat Station. Traditionally Cadgwith men had helped to crew the Lizard lifeboat, but there was a keen sense of loss when their own lifeboat was withdrawn, which is still felt in the fishing community today. An Inshore Rescue Boat was operational at Cadgwith for a while. After the new Tyne Class lifeboat *David Robinson* arrived in 1988 the name was shortened to The Lizard, for clarity of reporting, and easy identification of the area served. The Cadgwith heritage is recorded in the old boathouse in the centre of the village. The Todden at Cadgwith had been favoured as a suitable site for the new lifeboat station until local fishermen drew attention to the advantages of Kilcobben Cove which, sheltered from the prevailing westerlies, offers deep water at all states of the tide, allowing launching and re-housing in all but exceptional conditions from the east. Thus the Lizard Cadgwith lifeboat station at Kilcobben, with a steep slipway capable of launching the largest of lifeboats, was opened on July 7th 1961 by H.R.H. the Duke of Edinburgh. He named the new lifeboat the *Duke of Cornwall* after his son, and threw in a merry quip about having been responsible for getting both of them launched.

Building on the traditional theme of communications in this area, the Lizard lifeboat featured in the very first television programme to be transmitted live via Telstar to the Continents of Europe and North America on 23rd July 1962. This station, well known for its friendliness and good public relations, launched its lifeboat to welcome home Sir Francis Chichester on May 28th 1967. In 1979, a special framed certificate recognised their part in aiding the victims of the ill-fated Fastnet Race in August 1979. The Lizard lifeboat crew also performed heroically during the service that cost their colleagues at Penlee their lives in December 1981, taking part in the search for them in the most horrifying of conditions, and placing their own lives in jeopardy.

The service to the yacht *Bass*, which was taken in tow by another yacht after losing her rudder in rough seas and a near gale two and a half miles off Loe Bar on 3rd September 1984, brought a Bronze Medal to Coxswain Peter Mitchell. The Oakley Class lifeboat *James & Catherine Macfarlane* found the vessels close inshore to the west of Porthleven, with the casualty sheering badly and shipping water. Coxswain Mitchell passed a heaving line and then a towrope to the yacht, and took her in safely to Newlyn.

Philip Burgess, who joined the crew in 1974 and became Second Coxswain in 1987, took over as Coxswain of The Lizard lifeboat on 3rd April 1989.

119

FOWEY LIFEBOAT STATION

(Established 1859; Polkerris 1859-1922, when it was known as
Fowey (1859), Polkerris (1892), Polkerris and Fowey (1896),
Polkerris (1905). It moved to Fowey in 1922, when it returned
to its original name; Fowey)

The first land we sighted, it was called the Dodman,
Next Rame Head, off Plymouth, off Portsmouth, the Wight,
We sailed on by Beachy, by Fairlight and Dover,
And then we bore up by the South Foreland Light.

(Sea Shanty: *Spanish Ladies*)

An Early Port of Great Importance

Ocean-going vessels have plied these southern Cornish waters for centuries, with Fowey well established as a premier port of national significance in early times. A windmill, situated in an elevated setting above the harbour, referred to as a well known sea mark in 1296, was thought to have reflected the Palestinian influence when ships were constructed here for the Crusades. In the 1530s the antiquarian John Leland placed on record: 'In the Midle of the Toun apon the shore self is a House buildid quadrantly in the Haven, which shadowith the Shippes in the Haven above it from 3. Partes of the Haven mouth and defendith them from Stormes.'

Volume of Shipping; Confusion of Headlands – and Tragedy

The sheer volume of shipping in itself constituted a hazard to navigation, and continues to get worse. In conditions of storm and poor visibility, ships, particularly those returning from long voyages with inaccurate chronometers, often fell victim to the welcoming headlands of home, with the Dodman, or Deadman as it was formerly known, being particularly notorious. The similarity of headlands caused confusion, sometimes resulting in ships becoming embayed, when they thought they were making for a harbour of refuge. This was tragically illustrated in December 1830, when three foreign ships became trapped in Veryan Bay. The distinguishing beacon tower erected on Gribbin Head in 1832, also served as a leading mark for the port of Fowey, and gave a bearing to the china clay ports of Par, Pentewan, Charlestown and to the fishing port of Mevagissey.

Recognition of Early Rescues

Fishing was traditionally the main industry of St. Austell Bay, but as fishing declined, the local seafaring community turned its attentions to opportunities opening up in the china clay ports. And the increase in shipping gave rise to a need for lifeboat coverage for the area. However, local fishermen, coastguards and pilots had all played their part in preserving life from shipwreck, and an early Gold Medal of the Institution was awarded to Lt. Else RN, in August 1826, after he and his men took to their Coastguard galley and rescued the crew of the *Providence* of Par, shipwrecked near Polkerris. Three years later, the Silver Medal was awarded to the Chief Officer of the Coastguard, Mr. G. Crosswell, for the rescue of the crew of five from the seine boat *Diligence*. More recognition came this way in May 1856, after the schooner *Endeavour* of Ipswich was driven ashore under high cliffs near Polridmouth and wrecked, with the loss of three crewmen. Again, the Coastguards of Polkerris were swift to take to their galley in the cause of saving life from shipwreck, but had to return after exhaustive attempts to round Gribbin Head.

On this occasion Silver Medals were voted to Captain Norcock RN, Coastguard, Thomas Henwood, another Coastguard and Boatman Richard Johns, after a small boat had been brought from the farm at Tregaminion on a wagon, and lowered over the high cliff. Clifftop spectators held their breath and marvelled as they watched the three intrepid men venturing through the angry, rock-strewn waters to rescue the sole survivor.

Based at Polkerris

Then, as now, people had to pay the price of tragedy to press home the need for possible safety measures, and this wrecking provided the momentum for a lifeboat to be established in St. Austell Bay. In view of Fowey's facilities for dealing with the aftermath of shipwreck, not to mention the wealth of seafaring talent, eminently suited to manning a lifeboat, it may seem surprising that the little fishing harbour of Polkerris had the distinction of being chosen to accommodate a lifeboat for the area. The possible difficulties of getting a pulling and sailing lifeboat in and out of the harbour in bad weather, and the situation whereby the instigator and benefactor William Rashleigh of nearby Menabilly made land and building materials available at Polkerris clinched the matter, and the six-oared lifeboat *Catherine Rashleigh* arrived in November 1859, having been sent by rail to Lostwithiel and transferred through the port of Fowey to her destination. Polkerris men may not have had the sophistication and qualifications of the professional seamen of Fowey, but they were tough, daring and had inherited the instinctive skill and understanding of local conditions that only comes with generations of sons following their fishermen fathers. As it transpired, this station was to achieve a particularly proud record of service. For a reason which may have had something to do with rivalries and prestige, the station was initially known as 'Fowey', which was misleading, and was changed to 'Polkerris' in the 1890s. Communities which have taken a pride in being associated with the lifeboat service hate a diminished status, so it then became a diplomatic 'Polkerris and Fowey'. But in 1904 it reverted to the original 'Polkerris'. So what is in a name? Quite a lot, as the Institution has discovered over the years, for brevity and clarity of location are all-important in handling emergencies. Initially the lifeboat was launched down skids from her boathouse, but experience was to highlight the advantages of transporting her overland to be launched as close as possible to the scene of the casualty. The *Catherine Rashleigh's* first service demonstrated the fine seamanship of all concerned in June 1862, and brought the Coastguard Chief Officer Stabb, the Institution's Thanks on Vellum, for saving the Danish schooner *Sylphiden* and her crew of seven.

The Polkerris lifeboat Arthur Hill and her crew in classical pose, flanked by helpers and officials (Acknowledgement: Fowey Lifeboat Station)

Fine Feats of Seamanship
The Polkerris lifeboat achieved the remarkable feat of two services in one day during a hurricane on November 25th 1865, after the brig *Wearmouth* and the barque *Drydens* had both stranded broadside on to Par Sands, with enormous

seas running over the top of their mastheads. In going to their aid, the lifeboat lost six oars, but the Coxswain, Joshua Heath, overcame the predicament by letting the lifeboat drift, then judging the right moment to hoist canvas, skilfully made for Par harbour, where replacement oars were obtained. The crew then made two hazardous journeys through the rough seas, rescuing a total of twenty-two plus a cat which was desperately clinging to an Italian sailor plucked from the boiling surf. For this classical performance, Coxswain Joshua Heath was awarded a Silver Medal.

At this time, the Institution was well aware of the importance of keeping lifeboats in the public eye to maintain interest and attract revenue. Inland places liked to demonstrate their support, and when this lifeboat was deemed unfit for service on account of rot, the generous inhabitants of Rochdale provided the wherewithal for her replacement, which was diplomatically named the *Rochdale & Catherine Rashleigh* at a ceremony in Rochdale in 1866, when spectators watched her being demonstrated on Hollingsworth Lake. This lifeboat, which came to be known as the *Rochdale* and subsequently renamed the *Arthur Hill*, saved thirteen lives in services to the Schooner *Devonia* of Padstow, the Galliot *Dora* of Amsterdam and the Schooner *Hawk* of Chepstow, which she also saved. Her replacement, also taking the name *Arthur Hill*, launched several times, but performed just one service, rescuing four people from the Schooner *Emily* of Padstow. It was during her time on station, in February 1893, that four local seamen, William Robins, Edwin Robins, George Bishop and Frederick Perring were awarded the Silver Medal in recognition of their smart action in saving two Frenchmen frantically clinging to a buoy, after their Smack *Dieu Protégé* had capsized during a reckless attempt to enter Par harbour in very inhospitable conditions. The following year saw a Flagstaff erected at East Cliff, for signalling to Par, where the volume of traffic was increasing with the expansion of the china clay industry. An Acetylene Beach Light was supplied in 1910.

It was sunshine all the way, while the band played on for enthusiastic crowds, including well behaved schoolchildren who came to witness the inauguration of the new Watson Class *James, William & Caroline Courtney*, in May 1904. She was accommodated in a new, purpose-built boathouse, and her carriage, drawn by a team of horses, was equipped with Tipping plates on the rear wheels, which operated on the principle of tank tracks, but with seven wheelplates rotating to grip without sinking into soft terrain. According to the records of 1905, arrangements were made to provide horses for lifeboat exercises at the rate of ten shillings per horse for day services and fifteen shillings for night services, which included the payment for drivers. On the last day of that year the Brig *Mary*, with a cargo of old cannon and scrap was wrecked as she attempted to enter Fowey harbour at the height of a fierce south-easterly gale, and a Silver Medal was awarded to Mr. William Penrose for a very gallant attempt to rescue her crew.

Lifeboat and Steam-tugs Working in Conjunction

Fowey's first steam-tug the *Treffry* came into service in 1870, covering a wide range from Start Point to the Lizard, rendering services to vessels, and sometimes carrying out lifesaving activities. The crew of the *James, William & Caroline Courtney* carried out a service in conjunction with one of Fowey's steam-tugs in February 1907, saving the Brigantine *Adelaide* of Fowey, which had got into difficulties while waiting to enter Par harbour to discharge her cargo of coal after being driven into shallow waters by an unexpectedly erupting gale. It was a case of lifeboatmen to the pumps as she was towed around the Gribbin to Fowey for repairs.

Problems Caused by the Shortage of Horses

She performed services in 1913 and 1914, but the shortage of horses needed for launching during the First World War when so many had been commandeered for the War Effort, the delay to the lifeboat's launch in getting them rounded up and the recognised need for a motor lifeboat in the area, led to the decision to transfer operations to the port of Fowey. In lieu of horse power for launching, pushing poles had been sent here by the Institution on an experimental basis, but they were not an overwhelming success. From its establishment in 1859 to its closure in 1922, fifty-two lives has been saved in twenty-four launches.

Transferred To Fowey

The knock-on disruptive effects of war resulted in a twelve oared, forty foot self-righting lifeboat being sent to the new station at Fowey, instead of the envisaged motor lifeboat. The last Polkerris lifeboat, the *James, William & Caroline Courtney* was sold out of service, and this lifeboat, constructed at Cowes in 1896 for the new Walmer station and subsequently placed in the reserve fleet, was given the same name. She had an arduous and abortive night time call to the Schooner *I.M. Nielsen* of Svendborg, which had struck rocks near Polperro in November 1926, with five of the six crewmen being rescued by coastguards and fishermen as the lifeboat crew was battling against a strong south easterly gale. The remaining crewman, who had jumped from his ship and landed on inaccessible rocks was recovered by a brave fisherman bringing a rope down the cliff face, which allowed them to be hauled up; a nocturnal accomplishment which brought him the Institution's Thanks on Vellum. A motor lifeboat would undoubtedly have been an asset on this occasion, and the *Courtney* was promptly replaced by a Watson type from the reserve fleet, constructed at Blackwall in 1903, and called the *William Roberts*. She performed no services at Fowey, but was replaced in August 1928 by a splendid new Watson Cabin type lifeboat, with twin engines and named the *C.D.E.C.* at the Fowey regatta the following year.

An Up-Market Yachting Haven

Fowey was well established as an up-market yachting haven in the 1920s, and was one of the first stations to experience the rescuing of life from shipwreck, where casualties, often with scant knowledge of the sea, were there for the sole purpose of enjoying themselves. Local craftsmen had been quick to adapt to the promising potential of the leisure industry, which was confined to the wealthy at that time, with the construction of pleasure craft, while boatmen and fishermen sometimes skippered yachts for the gentry.

The first call out for the *C.D.E.C.*, in May 1929, was a sad one, involving a family with a motor launch towing two dinghies, which became separated after the engine had failed off the Dodman. The son reached Mevagissey safely, and the daughter in the other dinghy was picked up safely, but the lifeboat and other vessels joining in the search found no trace of their father, a retired naval engineer. It has been frequently demonstrated that the handling of small boats, including lifeboats, requires a different range of skills from those acquired in the Navy. In August 1930, this lifeboat launched to the aid of the Cutter Yacht *Islander* of the Royal Yacht Squadron, which got into difficulties during a heavy gale in Lanivet Bay during a cruise from Dartmouth to Falmouth, and she was being driven ashore as the lifeboat came on the scene. The *C.D.E.C.* went in daringly close and attempted to get a line to her, but the splendid yacht struck rocks and started to sink. Meanwhile, efforts were being made to rescue the crew of six from the shore, with two men climbing down the cliff, but disaster struck before a strong enough line was established. Waves engulfed the yacht, and her crew disappeared for ever.

Swiftly on the Scene to Avert Disaster

Prevention is the best form of lifesaving, and the early 1930s tended to be a period of towing, escorting and standing by potential victims of shipwreck, and averting disaster, as in May 1931, when she escorted the motor fishing boats *Kenneth* and *Mac* of Mevagissey to their home port in a moderate east-south-easterly gale, with rough seas. The following month she located and helped to refloat the passenger tug *Queen of the Fal*, which had gone aground on Vault Beach, to the north of the Dodman headland in foggy conditions. August of that year saw her standing by the trawler *G.V.E. Leonge* of Camaret, and in 1932 she rendered assistance to eight yachts, escorting six to safety in one day. Thus Fowey was getting a foretaste of leisure-loving sailors taking to the seas with the confidence which sometimes accompanies inexperience. Meanwhile, the professionals, who were moving away from sail, were appearing less frequently in the casualty lists. But a notable exception was the *S.S. Ardangorm*.

Fowey's first motor lifeboat, a 45' 6" Watson Cabin type called the C.D.E.C., arrived in 1928 and is pictured at her ceremony of inauguration the following year (Photograph Fred Kitto & Son; acknowledgements RNLI)

An Impressive Casualty of the Gwineas Rocks

The workaday steamer *Ardangorm* became an impressive casualty on January 4th 1940, not of the Germans, but of the sharp, unyielding Gwineas Rocks off Gorran Haven, unseen in the blackout conditions of war, designed to confuse the enemy. A message had been received at 03.10 that distress signals had been sighted off Chapel Point near Mevagissey, and the motor lifeboat *C.D.E.C.* launched into conditions of poor visibility with a fresh east-southeasterly wind, to discover the 5,000 ton vessel aground on the Gwineas Rocks, with heavy seas breaking over her. The Coxswain advised the Captain that he would be safe until daybreak, but that he and the crew could be taken off by breeches buoy if they desired. The Captain opted to remain aboard until daybreak, with the lifeboat standing by, and in the early dawn the lifeboat went alongside to recover eleven of the crew. They were landed at Fowey, and tugs were requested, but by the time an Admiralty tug arrived on the scene the situation had deteriorated, and there was no hope of saving the *Ardangorm*. So the remaining twenty-five men were taken off, and the lifeboat returned to her station at 16.15. A letter of appreciation went to the Coxswain and crew, and an increase in the usual monetary awards on the standard scale was made to each of them.

A Sensitive Sea Area in the Second World War

This was a sensitive area during the Second World War, with mines, enemy submarines and convoys. In the build up to the D-Day landings, some of the landing craft got into difficulties and there were late torpedo casualties of war to be dealt with. In his book *Storm On The Waters*, published just after the war, Charles Vince stated: 'At the beginning of 1945 U-boats returned to a final attack on ships in British waters, and in the last four months of war, lifeboats were called out over twenty times to the help of ships torpedoed close to the shores of England and Wales. Most of the attacks were made off Devon and Cornwall.'

Almost in the Style of the Movies

Two years after the end of the hostilities, when the reserve lifeboat *The Brothers* was on station, a night time call sparked off a search in heavy seas, following the sighting of distress signals in Par Bay. Sharp eyes detected the faint glow of a hand torch near Killyvarder Rock. Moving in closer they perceived a scene resembling some larger-than-life illustration of a novel, with shipwrecked men up to their waists in rising waters which had started to break over them on the almost submerged poop deck of the *M.V. Empire Contamar*, formerly of Germany, which had been a prize of war. After a number of abortive attempts to get a line aboard, the lifeboat was flung onto the casualty and washed off, having sustained damage to her bows. However, a line was eventually established. This enabled the seven wet and frozen survivors to be taken off, and removed with haste to Fowey where they recovered from their ordeal. This difficult and perilous operation, carried out in heavy seas in the darkness, brought a Bronze Medal to Coxswain Joseph Watters, and monetary awards to the crew.

Some Novel Services

The *C.D.E.C.* returned from her overhaul later in 1947, when a pattern of services to holiday makers was beginning to re-establish after those austere years of the Second World War. Passengers out for a carefree trip around St. Austell Bay in the converted sixty-six foot Naval vessel *Thelado* on August 28th 1949 had something to write home about after she struck a submerged object near the Gwineas Rock and they had to be taken ashore by a flotilla of small boats which came out from Mevagissey. The lifeboat assisted in saving the vessel. This lifeboat's last service was carried out on 2nd September, 1954, when she stood by the well known Mevagissey fishing boat *Ibis*, which had gone ashore at Great Perhaver Beach running north-eastwards from Gorran Haven, having been weighed down by a very successful catch of fish. She was able to get away on the rising tide, none the worse for the experience. Her replacement, which arrived in November of that year, was the Watson Class *Deneys Reitz*, built by Groves & Guttridge of Cowes, and financed by the

Jack Watters, who was born in Redruth, spent most of his life at sea on the old sailing barges, plying around the Cornish and Irish coasts, and had the instinctive knack of navigating without instruments. While working on the Fowey dredger for the Harbour Commissioners, he was invited to become Coxswain of the Fowey lifeboat, and was awarded a Bronze Medal in 1947. He is pictured here in May 1954 (Acknowledgements RNLI)

Southern Africa Lifeboat Fund to the tune of £31,922. However, the *C.D.E.C.* was to return here briefly in a reserve capacity in 1957, when she performed a novel service to a stray R.A.F. target, drifting near Looe Island, salving it as it constituted a hazard to navigation.

As it happened, the *Deneys Reitz* performed her first service – standing by the *M.V. Festivity* of London, and escorting her to safety, before her ceremony of inauguration on July 6th 1955. She was named after a South African High Commissioner in London; a former Boer officer who had fought for the Allies in the First World War.

The Watson Class Deneys Reitz, *constructed by Groves and Guttridge of Cowes, served at Fowey from 1954-1980 (Acknowledgements RNLI)*

Recognition of a Daring Deed
Many subsequent services with this and other lifeboats involved towing, escorting and standing by and therefore preventing shipwreck. The Fowey lifeboat carried out an unusual service on September 12th 1958, after a girl had been cut off by the tide near Charlestown, and the coastguard rescue attempts had proved abortive. The lifeboat was summoned, and Assistant Mechanic James Turpin swam ashore with a lifeline through broken water to make it secure so that the girl and a coastguard who had gone to her aid could be hauled to safety. The Institution awarded James Turpin their Thanks on Vellum. The following year they awarded the Centenary Vellum to the Fowey station. Between its establishment in 1859 and 1990, this station had been awarded twelve medals — one Gold , ten Silver and one Bronze.

Frequently in Demand
Since 1958, the increase in tourism has been reflected in the number of similar casualties; indeed, five people cut off by the flood tide were saved in 1987. Wind-surfing fanatics have joined bathers and occasional skin divers in their need for inshore services of the lifeboat, while sailing dinghies, cabin

cruisers, yachts and catamarans experience leaks, engine failure, steering failure, sail failure, fouled propellers, catch fire, strand, lose a man overboard, fail to cope with adverse conditions or are reported overdue; a situation which keeps the Fowey lifeboat's services frequently in demand. Mrs. Margaret Thatcher, Prime Minister, who visited the station in June 1990 was able to experience a lifeboat alert at first hand when an emergency arose towards the end of her demonstration trip aboard the lifeboat. For as The *Western Morning News* reported, 'She found herself having to hold on tight in the wheelhouse of the *Faithful Forester* as Coxswain Keith Stuart and his crew were suddenly sent into action.' She also gained some insight into the dedication, humour and great spirit of camaraderie existing in the Fowey crew. Keith Stuart followed Brian Willis as Coxswain in July 1989.

NEWQUAY LIFEBOAT STATION

(1860 -1934: 1940-1945: ILB Station established 1965,
operational all the year)

New Kaye, a place so called, because in former times the neighbours attempted to supplie the defect of nature by Art, in making there a Kaye, for the Rode of shipping.

(Richard Carew: *Survey of Cornwall*)

A Dramatic and Dangerous Coastline

The little old fishing port of Newquay has been many things to many people, and the process of realigning nature has grown apace since the end of the last war. Nature has created a grand, exposed coastline to the north and south of Towan Head, subject to the constant pounding of the waves and vulnerable to the whims of wind and weather. Although aesthetically pleasing, this coastline has long taxed the skills of those employed in the art of navigation and survival, with the section to the south west presenting a dangerous lee shore, and northwards, even more hazards, as testified by the vast number of shipwrecks. The Gannel, wedged between Pentire Point East and Pentire Point West afforded some shelter, but also became the graveyard for some ships, including the brigantine *Unity* of Dartmouth in December 1793, the brig *Betsy* in March 1794 and another brig, the *Ann* in March 1807.

The Construction of Quays

Attempts to improve on nature began long ago, when Newquay was a tiny fishing settlement. In 1439 Bishop Lacey of Exeter granted an indulgence for the construction of a 'new Kaye for the rode of shipping,' and in 1615 Thomas Stuer applied for permission to build a pier, later described as 'a little pier, the north point of which is fixed on a rock.' Mr. Lomax, who was Lord of the Manor in 1830, set about the construction of a south pier, which was completed after his death by that engineering visionary T.J. Treffry of Place, Fowey, who also constructed a north pier. Thus Mr. Treffry did much to promote Newquay's seaborne trade, which he linked to the railway system. There was support for Newquay's development as a harbour of refuge after the masters of the brigs *Juliana* and *Erato*, who, when in difficulties in a gale of February 1843, had both found salvation in the timely sighting of the harbour lights. Much money was ploughed into this project, which was never completed.

Some Fine Local Rescues
The harbour improvements increased the volume of shipping, and after the Northumberland Report of 1851 had criticised the lack of adequate lifeboat coverage in Cornwall, Newquay was seen to be an emerging place of some importance, well positioned between St. Ives and Padstow, for the establishment of a lifeboat station. However, ten years were to pass before this was to happen. During the interim period spontaneous rescues were carried out. In 1853 a Silver Medal of the Institution was awarded to Thomas Tegg, Master of the sloop *Caroline,* for rescuing the crew of the schooner *Comet,* which was embayed between the headland of Towan and Pentire during a north-north-westerly gale that February. The Coastguards also performed several award winning services, notably to the schooner *New Jane* of Exeter in December 1854, the *Defence* of Liverpool in March 1858 and to the vessels *L'Union* and *St. Anais* during the Great Gale of March 1859, when *The West Briton* reported: 'At Newquay, two vessels are ashore, a schooner and a lugger. The crews are in the rigging.' Services to the *Defence, L'Union* and *Anais* brought Second and Third Service Clasps to William H. Tregidgo's Silver Medal, to create a record (*see* Bude).

The Establishment of the Long-Envisaged Lifeboat Station
Perhaps these heroic rescues re-activated the plans which had been held in limbo so long, for the six-oared lifeboat *Joshua* arrived in September 1861, and was housed in Fore Street. Although apparently well housed, she was soon to be condemned on account of rot. However, she performed a lifesaving service in November 1864, going to the aid of the schooner *Heroine* of Milford, bound for Devoran, which had been observed by the Coastguard with split sails and topsail yard carried away, being driven rapidly on shore. Reportedly, ' A rocket was fired over her, but the crew did not appear to understand it, or, for heavy seas rolling over the vessel, could not make use of it and it was feared she would break up. The lifeboat was launched, and succeeded in saving the master and crew, consisting of five men.' Her replacement in 1865 was larger and took over her name. Despite a disconcerting capsize during a practice launch in December 1868, when this supposedly self-righting craft did not seem to justify that claim, she saved eleven lives before having her name changed to the *James & Elizabeth* in 1871, thereafter saving another eleven lives from the Greek brig *Calamidas* in two stages. Initially she recovered ten of them from their ship's boat in trouble from the cross seas close to the shore, then returned to the stricken vessel, which was subsequently driven on shore at Mawgan Porth, to take off another man.

The Highly Acclaimed Service to the *Gottenburg*
The *James & Elizabeth* was replaced in 1873 by a larger, self-righting lifeboat which initially took over her name, but was subsequently renamed the *Pendock Neale*. But it was as the *James & Elizabeth (II)* that she saved twenty lives from the barque *Gottenburg* of Hamburg in an heroic and highly acclaimed service, which brought in its wake some bizarre events, followed by inaccurate and sensational published reports, based on hearsay. The painful episode provides rare, human insight into the sharp end of the Cornish lifeboat scene at that time. This is the way the newspapers began to unfold the story in April 1874, with the *West Briton* and others printing this contributed item:

NOBLE SERVICE OF THE NEWQUAY LIFEBOAT

Mr. W.E. Michell, chairman of the Newquay (Cornwall) branch of the National Lifeboat Institution, writes as follows concerning the noble and important services performed on Tuesday, by the lifeboat on that station:' Newquay, April 15, The Vessel was a barque, iron, of 1,500 tons, the *Gottenburg* of Antwerp, from Java to Greenock with about 900 tons of sugar & etc. She had been to Falmouth for orders, and was proceeding to Greenock, when she was caught in some heavy squalls on Monday and thrown on her beam ends. The crew cut away the mizzen mast, fore topmast, and main topmast, but she would not right herself, and began to drift ashore, and yesterday morning was observed from the 'Look out' hill at Newquay, in an apparently helpless condition, drifting before the sea. The Newquay Lifeboat of the National Lifeboat Institution was launched, but so tremendous was the sea, that she was frequently hidden from view when only two or three lengths from the pier. The crew has a hard pull of many miles, and at length we received the welcome intelligence of her safe arrival at St. Agnes, with the vessel's crew of twenty men. I hear that the lifeboat was filled twice by tremendous seas before entering St. Agnes Pier, but her conduct gave the greatest satisfaction to her crew, and the hundreds of spectators who lined the St. Agnes cliffs where no lifeboat had ever before been seen; in fact altogether, the service was one of the most gallant ever performed on these shores.

(signed W.E. MICHELL)

Then the story widened:

SHIP IN PERIL OFF PORTREATH (The *West Briton* 20.4.1874)

Steamer *Queen of the Bay* has returned to Penzance from Falmouth, where she towed the German ship that narrowly escaped being wrecked at Portreath. In connection with this matter a very awkward circumstance occurred, which is not unlikely to end unpleasantly. The *Queen of the Bay* had been engaged by the captain of the *Godenborg*, [*Gottenburg*] acting in conjunction with Mr. Vice Consul Matthews, of Penzance, and Mr. Langford of Padstow, and Mr. Denbigh, the secretary of the company owning the *Queen of the Bay*, who was on the spot, arranged for their steamer to be in attendance early the following morning to tow the vessel to Falmouth. Before, however, the *Queen of the Bay* could reach the scene of action, and under cover of a fog, which partially obscured the *Godenborg*, a little steamer called the *Victoria* of Hayle, came out over the bar, and boarded the *Godenborg*, slipped both her cables, and took her in tow. As soon as the captain discovered that his ship had thus been spirited away from under his very nose, he manned the Newquay lifeboat, in which he and his crew had been landed the previous evening, and gave chase to the delinquent tug. Coming up with her after about two hours' stiff pulling, he at once went on board the ship and cut the tow rope, and, of course, left the *Godenborg* adrift, without any anchors or chains, in close proximity to a highly dangerous coast. At this juncture, the *Queen of the Bay* was fortunately at hand, and being a most powerful and efficient tug, took charge of the ship, in virtue of the previous agreement, and, as has been said, towed her safely to Falmouth. The worst feature of this case is that the Victoria, though within twenty miles of the *Godenborg* throughout the whole of Tuesday, when the ship was in extreme danger, made no attempt to go to her assistance; but, no sooner had the danger passed and the ship riding securely at her anchors, then she came up during a fog and took her away whilst the commander and his crew were on shore, making the necessary arrangement. It is also asserted that the *Victoria* was altogether of inadequate power to tow a ship like the *Godenborg*, with the wind on shore, and in a strong tideway, and had not the *Queen of the Bay* come up, it is doubtful if after all the ship would not have been lost. The weather was such that the Newquay lifeboat was unable to get back to her station, and had to be taken around to Falmouth by the *Queen of the Bay*. On Thursday the lifeboat was brought to Truro and sent overland to Newquay.

On a rather more orthodox note, the newspaper was also reporting, 'At a meeting of the Newquay branch of the National Lifeboat Institution, held at the *Red Lion Hotel*, Newquay, on Saturday, Mr. W.R. Michell, the chairman, presiding, it was resolved to cordially thank the harbour authorities and others of St. Agnes and Truro for the hospitality and assistance afforded by them to the crew of the Newquay lifeboat on her return from her recent service and cruise from St. Agnes to Falmouth with the barque *Gottenburg.'* The report was repeated, together with the fact that it had been 'one of the most gallant ever performed on these shores, and the boat afterwards went round the Land's End and to Falmouth in company with the vessel.'

The reports about the Newquay lifeboat were contributed items; this paragraph appeared in a chatty column about general happenings, without being prominent:

> There are rather strange things said about the lifeboat crew at Newquay in connexion with the recent services off St. Agnes. While all the crew except two were afraid to go out in the late gale to the rescue of eighteen poor sailors, there were, I am happy to say, brave volunteers ready to go in their place. One man I am informed, actually paid another man five shillings to do his day's work while he went on his errand of mercy.

This report apparently prompted 'Trismegistus', a colleague on the *Royal Cornwall Gazette*, who had a *penchant* for strutting where angels fear to tread, to make certain investigations around the town and come up with a version of events published in his own newspaper and the *West Briton*:

THE NEWQUAY LIFEBOAT (The *West Briton*, 27.4.1874)

A correspondent of our contemporary, *The Cornwall Gazette*, makes some astounding revelations respecting the conduct of the Newquay lifeboat crew, which it is hoped will lead to an inquiry by the proper authorities, for it is necessary to the successful maintenance of this important branch of the Lifeboat Institution that the public confidence in its efficiency should be maintained. We insert his remarks as follows:

On reading your account last week of the services of the Newquay lifeboat crew, I was astonished to find, at the conclusion of the notice an insinuation that the ordinary crew of the boat had shirked their duty, more especially as there is no allusion in any other newspaper to a circumstance, which, of course, would be well known and ought to excite indignation. I have, therefore, taken some trouble to elucidate the matter, and my enquiries have brought to light facts which are really astounding, and far exceed anything suggested by your brief note. But those facts have been carefully concealed by the local committee of the Lifeboat Institution who met together *in camera*, and adopted a resolution which was forwarded to the newspapers in the district; and the zealous chairman, moreover, wrote a letter which has been distributed far and wide by the secretary of the parent institution, detailing the gallant deeds of the crew, but carefully concealing the shortcomings, not to say cowardice, of certain persons, who ought to have been in the van when a service of danger was to be performed. I do not complain of the chairman; he is a most zealous friend of the Institution, and so I may add, is Mr. Tregidgo, the hon. secretary; neither of these gentlemen are sparing of their own labour; and the gallant services described by the chairman were really performed, but by whom? I think it is only right that this should be fully known by the public, and I proceed therefore, to relate the information which I have gathered by reliable sources. First then, it is a positive fact that *only two* of the regular crew, who are paid for practising in the boat, actually went out in her. All the others refused to go, and the boat was nearly two hours afloat before she went away! And all this time the distressed vessel was in a critical position, and the delay may have been fatal. Happily, for the credit of Newquay, there were plenty of brave men and true, who, on discovering the state of affairs, volunteered for the service. I have ascertained the names of the crew, and, as it is only fair to the men themselves that they should be published, I give them here. John Boxer and Thomas Matthews, the only members of the crew generally paid for practising with the lifeboat, who went out. Captain Thomas Hawkins, Edwin Hicks, Charles Edwin Trethewy, Henry Pappin, John Carter, Charles Thomas, and Francis Frost, all volunteers of Newquay; Charles Shellers, mate of the *Aurora,* Bideford, then in Newquay; and Henry Clark of Cork, Ireland. I am told that one of the regularly paid crew of the boat, who refused to go out in her, afterwards went overland to St. Agnes and was one of those received with honour at Falmouth and Truro! But *palmam qui mercuit ferai,* say I. And after the crew themselves credit is due in an especial manner to Mr. Tredidgo, for his great exertions, both at Newquay and St. Agnes. I very much regret to hear that this is not the first time the ordinary crew of the Newquay boat have been backward in coming forward! Last year, I am told, they refused to go out to a vessel which was in danger off Padstow, and the excuse made to the Lifeboat Institution was that their boat was unseaworthy. Since that time, however, they have been provided with a splendid new boat, but on the first test their courage oozed out at the ends of their fingers! I am glad to hear that the boat behaved splendidly with the volunteer crew; but this is the greater reason why a searching enquiry should be made into the circumstances which I have related. With a magnificent boat and a brave population there can surely be no difficulty in organising a crew which can be relied upon in any emergency.

The next edition of The *West Briton* stated: 'Last week's *Cornwall Gazette* contained a serious charge of cowardice against the crew of the Newquay lifeboat. We copied the statement in last Monday's paper, and said that if true it called for an inquiry. A Newquay correspondent now informs us that the statement was utterly untrue...' and goes on to report a shortened version of the facts. Meanwhile, the *Royal Cornwall Gazette* published two letters which helped to restore the *status quo*:

Sir, — Seeing in your last impression of the 25th. inst., relative to the Newquay lifeboat, that there were only two of the crew paid for exercising that went in her, I beg to say the number is quite correct; but, in lieu of Thomas Matthews, you will please make known it was your humble servant.

EDWIN JOHNSON HICKS
Woodbine Cottage, Newquay, April 27th, 1874.

The second is all the more effective for its underlying good humour:

Sir, — In your publication of the 25th inst., by 'Trismegistus', I observe some comment is made on the services of the Newquay Lifeboat in connection with saving the crew of twenty men from the German ship *'Gottenburg'*, at this place.

I should not have taken any notice of the remarks, knowing well the quarter they emanated from, had your informant confined his remarks to myself. But as the hon. secretary of this branch of the Royal National Lifeboat Institution, I feel myself called upon to rebut the many charges brought against the crew and committee, and crave the favour of inserting this in your next publication.

Your informant says he has taken some trouble to elucidate the matter, and that his enquiries have brought to light facts which are really astounding. I am sorry he should have put himself to such trouble and come sadly short of the truth after all his efforts only to find a mare's nest [illusory discovery] I am thankful for the word of praise your informant has given to the chairman as well as to myself. Surely he must have been in high spirits at the time. Well, we must be thankful for *leetle* mercies from some parties.

The attacks made on the committee by your informant, stating that they met together *in camera*, carefully concealing all the facts, I emphatically deny, and throw back the accusation from whence it came. We had nothing to do in darkness, nor to conceal facts; the committee had a much more pleasing duty, namely, to recommend the extra pay to the boat's crew and honorary distinctions, and should only have been too happy to have admitted your informant *in camera*, had he only expressed a wish to do so.

First, your informant says 'it is a positive fact that only two of the regular crew went in the boat.' Here he comes short again with all his enquiries, or he would have known that we have no regular paid crew save the coxswains; the boat is mostly dependent on volunteers even for exercise. I am pleased to say that there were five men in the boat who have gone out on several occasions to save life, namely, John Boxer, Edwin Hicks, Henry Pappin, Charles Trethewey, and Francis Prout; these men are as much a part of the crew as any others. As of late, since the railway works have commenced, high wages have been given, so that nearly half of the seafaring men have been employed. So much so, that the masters and owners of vessels have been left to shift for themselves and get sailors from other towns. Thomas Matthews named was a volunteer, and not one of the boat's crew.

Unfortunately, our coxswain, David Hoare, is confined to his bed at the point of death; John Carn, also, prevented by family affliction [his wife was seriously ill]. These men never refused; could not be there. Of the other men who have formed the boat's crew on several occasions, and I am confident had they known it, would have been here to go, namely, William Pascoe, Thomas Tinny, and D. Hockin; these men were working several miles up the line. The only man who has been in the lifeboat that refused, was William Matthews; he had been in the boat when she was launched in the quay on this occasion; but when he saw his son come in as one of the crew, and knowing well what they were soon to encounter, he thought one was enough to go on this perilous rescue. Talking with him on the quay, and urging him to go, I saw tears shed. The same may be said for John Carter, who volunteered and went in the lifeboat; his younger brother, Richard, rushed into the boat, and I heard the same remark from him — one is enough of one family to go, and he went on shore again. Lifeboat service here, on most occasions, is more than usually perilous from the heavy ground sea.

I may mention that your informant did not report all the hindrances the committee had to contend with, and forgot in his zeal to rush into print, to name that one of the lifeboat's crew, Henry Pappin, was threatened by one of the foremen of the works on the quay, that unless he came out of the boat and went to his work, he should lose six months' work. On hearing this, I replied that I would name the same to Mr. Muller, the chief of Sir M. Peto's staff, and all should be made right, and by my urgent persuasion the man went into the lifeboat again. It is only right here to say that to that gentleman, had he been here, nothing would have been more painful to his feelings. It has come to my notice that he even paid for substitutes for the two volunteers who went in the lifeboat from the vessel in the quay.

Respecting the honours paid the crew at Falmouth, Truro, and Newquay, your informant is sadly out, with all his painstaking. In the first place, the lifeboat did not go to Falmouth, being towed into Carrick Roads at midnight with the ship, and at 3 a.m. on the 16th, left that roads and rowed their boat up Truro river to Newham Quay, arriving there at 5 a.m. The lifeboat left Newham at 7 a.m. the next day, passed through Truro very quietly, Newquay being the only place where any demonstration took place.

Mention is made that the lifeboat was kept on the quay two hours, while the ship was in a most critical position. Happily I had been down that morning to see the ship, and I concluded she was three and a half miles from the shore riding at her both anchors; wind, strong gale, at N.N.E., with a heavy sea on the coast, and low water. The committee had the lifeboat launched as soon as she could be got out, and took the responsibility of not sending her then, as, from the fearful groundsea on the coast, it would be a matter of impossibility for the boat to have got out to sea at that state of the tide. The lifeboat went at the proper time, and most gallantly succeeded in saving the crew of 20 men: and here I beg to note, for the information of your informant, that those who are entrusted with the management of lifeboats have an important duty to perform, namely, the safety and protection of those men who go in lifeboats to the rescue as well as those rescued.

One other remark your informant makes about the Padstow case last year, proves that he is a novice, and must have been ignorant of the coast and of nautical affairs. He should keep to his own profession, and not meddle with affairs he knows nothing about. Padstow has a good lifeboat, and the ship in distress was twelve miles nearer to that place than Newquay, and that boat had a crew who, I am certain, would most gladly have gone to their assistance had it been possible.

I am quite willing to resign my office of hon. secretaryship to more abler hands.

> I have the honour to be, Sir,
> Your most obedient servant,
> WILLIAM H. TREGIDGO
> Hon. Secretary
> Newquay, 28th April, 1874.

It was a sad time for Newquay, and the next edition of both papers reporting the funeral of Mr. David Hoare, the much respected coxswain of the lifeboat lent added poignancy to the situation. Most of the local population turned out to follow the cortege and pay their last respects, and the service at Lower St. Columb was attended by all sections of the lifeboat fraternity, members of the Fort Lodge of Oddfellows and many others. Sobering also, is the enduring fact that nobody received formal recognition for the very brave service to the *Gottenburg,* regarded one of the most gallant ever carried out off the coast of Cornwall, and acknowledged in *The Life-Boat* of 15th May, 1875 as being of 'a very meritorious nature', with expenses of the first service (£16.4.0.) being awarded.

Illumination by Fire
Coastguards frequently figured in lifesaving missions around these coasts, as in November 1874, when the smack *Friends* of Bridgwater was wrecked at Mawgan Porth. Chief Officer Barry set the furze ablaze on the cliffs at Trenance to indicate her position to the lifeboat, having first obtained the consent of the tenant, who refused payment for his public spiritedness. When this was intimated to the RNLI, cordial votes of thanks were expressed. In August 1880 the lifeboat crew was to face criticism in leaving the ship-wrecked crew of the smack *Harriet* of Barnstaple weathering the storm in their small ship's boat through most of the night, before picking them up.

More Efficient Launching
Consideration for more efficient launching without getting bogged down in the sand led to the construction of a steep slipway on Towan Head, after the new lifeboat, the *Willie Rogers,* arrived in 1892, and the impressive boathouse with its committee room above was completed in 1899, at a cost of over £700. Adaptations to the slipway cost another £200. The services off this coast, always of a vigorous Atlantic nature, involved an increasing number of steamships, apart from the workaday run of vessels plying these waters, with lifeboatmen often stretched to their limits and lengthy spells at sea, which tend not to receive due recognition. After a sequence of tragic wrecks, there was a strong local feeling that Newquay required a steam lifeboat to cope with the emergencies which turned up on their patch. However, Newquay's little harbour was unsuitable for such a boat which needed to be kept permanently afloat.

The *Willie Rogers* carried out a particularly fine service in January 1899, in conjunction with the steam tug *Dragon,* and later the *S.S. Olivia* of Penzance, in a lengthy sequence of events which led to the rescue of nine crewmen of the *S.S. Voorwarts,* who had not got away in the ship's boats. Those who had, including the captain, were never seen again. Having been taken off, the men were returned to their ship the following day for an attempt to be made to tow the casualty to Swansea. But the tow rope parted, and the ship was now in such poor shape that the mission was aborted. The lifeboat, with the nine rescued crewmen aboard, was towed to Ilfracombe and returned overland to Newquay.

Above: Launching across the soft sands at Newquay presented problems and so a slipway was constructed on Towan Head in 1895; the steepest in the British Isles, with a gradient of 1 in 2¼ (Sheila Bird Collection)

Below: Recovery was by carriage, drawn across the sands, through the streets and up to the headland by a team of horses; both pictures were taken on Demonstration Day. (Sheila Bird Collection)

141

A Period of Chequered Fortunes

The arrival of the *James Stephens No. 5*, built by Henry Roberts of Mevagissey, was a prelude to another period of chequered fortunes, with challenging services, sometimes in conjunction with the Padstow lifeboat. Tragedy struck on March 6th 1908, when the lifeboat capsized twice while returning from exercise, throwing the crew and the District Inspector into the sea. The second time all were able to rejoin the boat, except Harry Storey, who died from shock. By a further mischance, the coal-carrying schooner *Hodbarrow Miner* was in need of assistance at Mawgan Porth that same afternoon, after her captain had been knocked overboard by the main boom while rounding the Longships in a raging northerly gale. Joseph Warricker of Falmouth, already a survivor of shipwreck, took command and emerged the sole survivor of this one, having been dragged from the surf by two coastguards. Those who died were buried in the churchyard at St. Mawgan.

All too often the dividing line between triumph and tragedy can be very tenuous, as illustrated by this report in *The Life-Boat* of 1918:

On the 17th December last a strong North-Easterly gale was blowing, with a heavy sea, and a steamer named the *Osten*, of Denmark was observed drifting in a helpless condition. The weather had been wild throughout the previous night and the regular Coxswain of the lifeboat, who had recently been appointed, was of the opinion that it would be impossible to launch the lifeboat as the gale was dead on the slipway; the steepest on the coast. The ex-Coxswain of the boat, James Gill, however, appeared on the scene when the question of launching the boat was under discussion, and stated that he had been out in worse weather and offered to take charge of the boat on this occasion. Everything was at once prepared and the boat was lowered down the slipway. As she entered the water, and before she could gather way, she was struck by a sea and thrown on her beam ends. The boat at once righted herself, but a succession of heavy seas overpowered her, and she drifted into a position under the cliff. Before the crew could do anything to help themselves the boat was dashed on to the rocks and smashed to pieces, Fortunately, the men were able to get a rope to the shore and the onlookers rushed to their assistance, and all the men were landed in a very exhausted condition. They had had a very narrow escape of losing their lives, and some of them being severely injured: but happily they all recovered from the very trying experience, although some of them were laid up for weeks. In this case the regular Coxswain hesitated to put to sea, but the ex-Coxswain felt that the men on board the vessel required help, and regardless of the danger run, he set an example of self sacrifice which nearly cost him his life. In appreciation of his gallantry, the Committee have awarded him the Silver Medal of the Institution, and have also given to R.J. Trebilcock, the Second Coxswain who nobly seconded Gill's efforts, the Bronze Medal of the Institution. Trebilcock has also been promoted Coxswain in recognition of his actions on this occasion.

As an anti-climax to the story, the casualty was swept down the Channel until she was taken in tow by a patrol boat, and the lifeboat was replaced by the *John William Dudley* of the reserve fleet.

Situations of War
The *James Stephens No.5* had been called out on several occasions to war damaged shipping. The reserve lifeboat *John William Dudley* and the motor fishing vessel *Sweet Promise*, employed under the wartime emergency scheme were both operational here in 1918. *The Admiral Sir George Back*, previously stationed at the Lizard arrived here in 1920.

Although launching down Newquay's steep slipway was swift and efficient, recovering the lifeboat was more of a problem. It depended on a team of horses conveying the recovery carriage considerable distances to the water's edge and hauling the lifeboat, mounted on her carriage across the soft sands and up the long incline to Towan Head to be re-housed. The shortage of available horses after the First World War brought about a decline in services here, and increasingly being handled by neighbouring Padstow and St. Ives, and the station closed in 1934. However, the situation of war, with important airfields nearby, brought a new range of casualties, including ditched aircraft, demanding a quick response. So the station was reopened as a temporary measure in March 1940, when the motor lifeboat Richard Silver Oliver arrived. She was kept in the open air in the harbour slipway in the town, not in the old boathouse on Towan Head, and remained in Newquay until the end of the century. This lifeboat launched to a number of aircraft emergencies, where many young lives had already been lost, but a total of eleven lives were saved. A visit to the church at St. Eval, whose prominent tower was such an important landmark that the merchants of Bristol financed its rebuilding in 1724, gives us a moving insight into those dark and heroic days of war with coastal defence and short range attack. Badges of the Squadrons are displayed on the walls.

Newquay's Third Phase
An Inshore Lifeboat Station was established at Newquay in 1965, and the lifeboat was provided with a V.H.F. radio telephone set three years later. This third phase of lifeboat coverage at Newquay was again in marked contrast, for the emphasis now was on helping those who got into difficulties in the course of pleasurable pursuits. In 1973 Thanks on Vellum were accorded to crew member Norman Bailey in recognition of his courage on May 1st, when

he swam sixty yards from the lifeboat through confused and dangerous seas to Horse Rocks to encourage and reassure the eleven people who were stranded there.

In 1984, when the station received its Vellum commemorating its aggregate century of service, there was also a framed letter of appreciation, signed by the Duke of Atholl Chairman of the Institution, addressed to Helmsman D. Snell and crew members W. Martin, C. Pearce and P. Rockall in recognition of their skill in rescuing an angler washed from rocks off Fistral Beach and administering First Aid in very difficult conditions.

PORTHLEVEN LIFEBOAT STATION
(1863-1929)

SEAGULLS

Spirits of old mariners
Drifting down the restless years
Drake's and Hawkin's buccaneers,
So do Cornish seamen say.

Shocking Shipwreck Territory

If, as the old rhyme suggests, the souls of shipwrecked mariners return to haunt the scene of the disaster in the guise of seabirds, Porthleven will never be in danger of losing its wide-winged, vociferous seagulls, for this is notorious shipwreck territory. In December 1807, the forty-gun frigate *H.M.S. Anson* became another victim of the Loe Bar, to the south-east of Porthleven, with catastrophic loss of life. The horror of this was to have far reaching beneficial effects, in that feelings were aroused concerning the indignity of ordinary seamen being buried unceremoniously in any old patch of unconsecrated ground, which led to an Act of Parliament. Not only that, but the shock of impotently witnessing this pitiful event, led to Henry Trengrouse designing his inshore rescue apparatus, which subsequently saved hundreds of lives (see page 11). So this area has earned a proud place in our nation's maritime history.

Pressure to Create a Harbour — and Criticism after its Construction

In view of the vast number of shipping casualties, it was felt that the little fishing port of Porthleven should be upgraded to provide refuge from the storm, and after two vessels had been tossed ashore on the Bar in November 1810, *The West Briton* commented: 'We have reason to believe that had the harbour at Porthleaven (*sic*) been completed these two vessels would have been saved,' and pointed out one of them had been beating about in the bay for twenty-four hours, having been unable to clear the Lizard. Repairs and improvements, including the construction of a new jetty, breakwater and floodgates were carried out by the proprietors of the harbour, Messrs. Harvey, to ease the situation causing damage to ships, for which they had been obliged to pay compensation, and to allow for deeper draught vessels. There was great rejoicing in October 1858, when the sluice was opened for the first time. Then, as now, the public expected Man's engineering skills to re-align the powers of nature. Interestingly, *Murray's Hand-book* of 1865 informs us: 'The harbour has been constructed at a great expense, and, from its position on a wild, dangerous coast, would be of extreme value if more easy of access. In tempestuous weather, however, when such a refuge is required, it is scarcely possible to enter it, since the mouth is narrow, and the sea sets into it with extreme violence.' The *Hand-Book* of thirty years on is more dismissive, stating: 'Considerable expenditure has been made on the harbour, which its difficulty of access in rough weather hardly seems to justify.'

Putting Their Lives on the Line

Local people, who had put their energies towards the prevention of ship-wreck, also made outstanding efforts in saving life from shipwreck. As early as 1824, Gold, Silver and monetary awards were made by the Institution in recognition of their heroism in saving eight lives from the brig *Olive* of Tenby, wrecked in Halzephron Bay the previous year. Further recognition for coastguards, seamen, pilots and fishermen came the following year, in bravely bringing the crew of the whaler *Phoenix* safely ashore. But sometimes those who sought to help paid the ultimate price, as in March 1841, after the brig *Anne* of Dartmouth had taken the distressed schooner *Mary Stewart* in tow, and had to release her in Mount's Bay on account of the weather. When the schooner's plight was known, the revenue cutter *Sylvia*, a fishing vessel and the Coastguards hastened to her aid. But, sadly, the Coastguards' boat capsized almost immediately, and five of her crew were battered to death on the rocks near Prussia Cove within sight of their horrified families. In the event eleven lives were saved from the original casualty by the revenue cutter and the fishing boat.

When local fishermen and others noticed the brig *Mersey* of Brixham being driven towards the shore in strong winds and heavy seas in February 1861, they indicated to those on board the safest place to run for. A cask tossed overboard and brought ashore by the pounding rollers enabled contact to be made, by which the crew of nine was promptly hauled to safety. And not a moment too soon, for the vessel was pounded to pieces within the hour. The entrance to Porthleven harbour was particularly difficult for sailing ships to negotiate when the weather came from the south-west. At the height of a particularly longwinded gale in November 1865, which had already claimed a number of ships in the area, the barque *William* of Sunderland made a hair-raising attempt to make for the harbour, during which a sailor lost his nerve and attempted to jump for the jetty. He missed, and a local man who instinctively rushed to his aid was also swept into the sea. The outcome was that the sailor lost his life, the vessel collided with the inner jetty allowing the shaken crew to stumble ashore, and Peter Pascoe was awarded a Silver Medal and £2 for heroically rescuing his impetuous brother, Anthony.

Lifeboat coverage had come to Porthleven in 1863, with the arrival of the *Agar Robartes*, whose name had been derived from that exceptional benefactor of Cornish lifeboats. She was sent by rail and used as part of an elaborate ceremonial through the streets of Helston in celebration of the marriage of the Prince and Princess of Wales. In December 1866, she launched into heavy seas in stormy conditions, and assisted the Russian Finnish barque *Salmi* into Falmouth, thereby saving the vessel and all who sailed in her.

'So Deserving a Class of Men'
It is particularly touching to learn of these lifesaving missions, when viewed in the context of the grinding poverty which sometimes beset this tough, hardworking, seafaring community, through no fault of their own. From time to time appeals for donations appeared in the local press, hoping to be received sympathetically for 'so deserving a class of men.' A particularly poignant one appeared in September 1867: 'An appeal is made to the benevolent on behalf of the Widow and nine Children of Edward Williams, of Porthleven, who are left utterly destitute by his sudden death, through heart disease, in the *Agar Robartes* Lifeboat, while assisting in the launch of the *Daniel Draper* [Mullion's new lifeboat] Lifeboat, at Penzance, on the 10th instant. Donations on their behalf are earnestly solicited.' In 1886 and 1888, the fishermen of Porthleven were indebted to this lifeboat's successor, the *Charles Henry Wright*, for saving lives and livelihoods when the fleet was in jeopardy *en masse* by sudden, unexpected storms, which made the re-entry of the difficult harbour mouth particularly treacherous. Sea and storm were not the only hazards around these parts, apparently, for it went on record that a lady approaching her confinement was so frightened by the maroons firing for a night emergency, that she was taken ill and died, and that the Institution granted her husband £25 on account of the tragedy.

Launching Problems
There had long been problems launching from the boathouse above the harbour at Breageside, which required tight and tortuous manoeuvres of the lifeboat on her carriage according to variable water levels in the inner

harbour and the prevailing weather conditions so, in 1897, a new boathouse and slipway were constructed on the rocks at the northern side of the harbour entrance, opposite the pier, at a cost of £1,395. But their problems were not over, for this boathouse took a battering from angry seas, characteristic of this area, which meant that they were not always able to get the lifeboat launched. The *John Francis White*, which arrived in 1900 and took part, with the Cadgwith and Lizard lifeboats in the epic service of the *Suevic*, was credited with saving eighteen lives. On various occasions she averted disaster by towing, escorting, putting pilots aboard and standing by. All except one of those aboard the *S.S. Tripolitania*, another casualty of the Loe Bar in December 1912 were saved by the Porthleven inshore rescue apparatus. The crewmen who lost his life had taken a gamble in jumping overboard at a favourable moment, only to be overcome by the turbulent waves.

Porthleven's Last Lifeboat

The *Dash*, the last of Porthleven's lifeboats, rowed by ten oars with a crew of thirteen, had been around quite a lot before she arrived here in 1926. She had

The lifeboat Dash, *built by the Thames Iron Works in 1902, was stationed at Blyth and placed in the reserve fleet before being sent to Porthleven in 1926. She was sold out of service in July 1930 and underwent various conversions for use as a pleasure craft. Here she is seen in a Cornish boatyard awaiting restoration (Photograph by Sheila Bird)*

been constructed in 1902, at a cost of £822, and was initially stationed at Blyth for nineteen years, during which time she had fourteen launches and saved fifty-seven lives. After an overhaul in 1923, she served in a temporary capacity at Brighton for a year and was returned to the reserve fleet at Cowes before being sent to Porthleven, in what turned out to be her last permanent posting as a lifeboat. But she never made a launch from here, and as the motor lifeboats from neighbouring Penlee and the Lizard provided adequate coverage of the area, the station was closed in 1929, and the lifeboat again returned to Cowes. After being sold out of service for £40 in 1930, she underwent conversions at various times, with a cabin subsequently being added. As an exhibit of *The World's Boats,* attention was drawn to the strong diamond shaping of her hull, with the planks going diagonally in opposite directions internally and externally, and to the forward remaining self-righting compartment.

Although the station had closed in 1929, the story of lifesaving here was not yet over, for the Institution awarded a Bronze Medal to Mr. T.H. Matthews, the Harbour Pilot in 1943, who, at great risk to himself, went to the aid of an Army Officer, who was in distress after attempting to assist a Sergeant who had got into difficulties while bathing in the sea; the pattern of which had a slightly familiar ring about it.

LOOE LIFEBOAT STATION
(1866-1930)

Whitesand Bay [also known as Whitsand Bay], so called from the whiteness of the sand, abounds in beautiful and romantic scenery, but is justly dreaded by sailors as the scene of many a fatal disaster.

(*Murray's Hand-book,* 1865)

Early Prestige
Prestige arrived early in the Looe estuary, with its ancient twin boroughs of East and West Looe on each side of the river. Much of their wealth derived from fishing, particularly the export of pilchards to Catholic countries for consumption during Lent, supplemented by a useful bit of free trading. Although the halcyon days were over by the end of the seventeenth century, the quaysides remained active with coastal traders, shipbuilding and the fishing industry, and a century ago Looe's fishing fleet created a stunning spectacle as lamps were lighted in the town. The potential for tourism had been recognised here by the turn of the century.

To Guard and Guide in a Beautiful Setting

To the east of Looe, a semi-circular range of cliffs fringing Whitsand Bay turns sharply southwards to terminate in the famous headland of Rame, just this side of Plymouth Sound. The headland is crowned with a ruined chapel, which has served as a landmark for generations of seafarers, itself commanding majestic views of the south Cornish coast right down to the Lizard. Coastguard stations were set up here and on Looe Island, while offshore the romantic Eddystone lighthouse bears witness of Man's endeavours to prevent the loss of life from shipwreck. Many a desperate sailing ship trying to make for the protection of Plymouth Sound became embayed in this beautiful setting, having not been able to round Rame Head. Furthermore, this historic section of seaway is one of the busiest shipping highways in the world, becoming more so, and creating problems of stress for today's hi-tech mariners.

Knowledge of these waters did not preclude disasters, as demonstrated by various fishermen, including Benjamin Christopher of Looe Island, who was lost from his open boat in the course of taking lobsters to Plymouth in January 1816. The seemingly gentler Channel coast of Cornwall has experienced some horrifying storms, as in January 1817, when conditions 'scarcely equalled by that which carried away the Eddystone lighthouse many years ago,' caused flooding and destruction in the town, also tossing a sixty ton vessel onto the quay and sweeping it off again.

A Proud Tradition of Saving Life from the Sea

Wrecks were all too frequent here, but Looe men had established a proud tradition of saving life from the sea before the lifeboat station was set up. In 1824, Boatman John Miller received the Institution's Silver Medal, and three others gained cash awards for saving seven lives from a vessel named the *Harmonie,* wrecked in Whitsand Bay. Ten years later another Silver Medal went to a local pilot, with monetary rewards to others responsible for saving twelve men from the *Konigsberg.* Commissioned Boatswain William Jennings displayed great heroism in November 1838, by swimming through angry seas to get a line aboard the stricken brig *Belissima,* when all else had failed, thus saving thirteen men, and bringing another Silver Medal to Looe. Sadly, another brig in distress, the *Albion* of Exeter, brought tragedy to one of the coastguard rescuers, as well as to four of her crew in September 1839. However two were recovered on that occasion. Service to yet another brig in February 1851, the *Fletan* of France, brought forth a further Silver Medal.

Desirous of having a Lifeboat

In view of the regular catalogue of casualties in Whitsand Bay, it is a little surprising that a lifeboat station was not established here sooner than 1866. The *Life-Boat* reported in July 1867:

A life-boat station has been formed at Looe, on the coast of Cornwall. It had frequently happened that the boatmen at this port, being ever ready to go off in their open boats to save the lives of shipwrecked crews, had run great risk in so doing. Indeed, on one occasion, some of them were returning from saving a fishing craft, when their boat was upset in the breakers, and several lives were lost. The inhabitants were very desirous, therefore, to have a life-boat — there being a large number of vessels frequently entering and quitting the harbour. There were plenty of fishermen available to form the crew; and, as every kind of co-operation was offered, the Society readily decided to establish a life-boat at Looe. A boat-house has been erected, and being in a public position, it is somewhat ornamental in character, and has over it a reading and assembly room for the use of the pilots and fishermen of the town. A thirty two feet life-boat, pulling ten oars, with a transporting carriage and the usual equipment of stores, has been placed therein, the Great Western, Bristol and Exeter, South Devon and Cornwall Railway Companies kindly taking them free over their lines to Liskeard. The cost of the boat, &c., was benevolently contributed to the Society by the late Sir John Pollard Willoughby, Bart; and, in accordance with his request, the boat was named the *Oxfordshire*, after his native county. On the 28th December she was inaugurated in Looe with the usual ceremony. After being drawn through the principal streets, she was named by Mrs. Carew, the wife of W.H. Pole Carew, Esq., President of the Branch, and launched, giving much satisfaction to the crew.

LIFEBOAT LAUNCH, LOOE.

Launching the lifeboat at Looe (Sheila Bird Collection)

Some might say that she made her unofficial mark before the ceremony of inauguration, trying to get through the narrow streets and around tight corners. Her presence here gave many endangered fishing boats, schooners, luggers, ketches and other vessels the chance to sail another day, for hers was of the sure and steady style.

Delighting All Hearts

Readers of the Empire building, highly popular *Boys' Own Paper*, who thrived on rollicking, rousing tales of adventure and heroism, raised money for lifeboats, which were placed here and at Poole. Thus *Boys' Own No.1*, also built at Shadwell, arrived in 1882, and after an efficient and dependable service record, must have delighted all hearts, aligning dreams with reality by saving nineteen lives from the fully-rigged *Gipsy* of Nantes, wrecked off Downderry on her last service in December 1901. And in equally satisfying story book style, the French Government showed its appreciation by awarding Coxswain Edward Toms a Gold Medal, Second Class, with Silver Medals for his crew. There were diplomas for all.

The following year saw the arrival of Looe's last lifeboat, the *Ryder*, built by the Thames Ironworks at Blackwall, which achieved an admirable record of service under Coxswain Thomas Toms, brother of Edward Toms, who had held that position for sixteen years or so. Thomas Toms, who was proud to have served in lifeboats for fifty years, recalled when the station closed down in July 1930 that his first trip was on October 22nd, 1880, in the *Oxfordshire*; when they rescued two lives from the fishing boats *Ada* of Devonport, and the vessel itself.

He recalled every service with clarity and detail, including a fateful day, February 13th 1900. 'The Looe crabbing boats were out in the road, when the seas rose faster than the tide was flowing. I was on one of the crabbers, and the lifeboat came out to *me*, then!' When asked about his worst experience, he replied, 'When our *Anemone* was wrecked (in September 1903). I never remember it blowing harder, barring the two gales the winter before last. We saved the crews of the *William* and the *Anemone* that day. Our boat got ashore off the Longstones, a mile the other side of Downderry, and the *William* dropped her anchors off Plaiday. They held while the wind was blowing from the land, but when it changed, the *William* went ashore.' The lifeboat saved six lives that day, in a service demanding highly skilled seamanship. Another particularly outstanding service occurred on 3rd March 1922, when the lifeboat ventured through the hazardous, rocky waters of Talland Bay in strong winds and heavy seas to rescue the entire crew of twenty-one from the French trawler *Marguerite* which, perhaps, did not get the recognition it deserved. The Ryder's final call out on April 18th, 1929, proved to be something of an anti-climax, to the aid of the *S.S. Paris*, aground on the Eddystone Reef, on a windless day, with thick fog and smooth seas. After the long trek out to the reef, she arrived to find that the liner, with 1,500 passengers aboard, had managed to get away, and it had not been possible to get a message to the lifeboat.

A Sad Farewell

Local people tried desperately hard to retain their lifeboat at Looe, but the RNLI remained adamant in its resolve to withdraw it, on the grounds that the area could be adequately covered by the motor lifeboats of neighbouring Plymouth and Fowey. Thus the farewell launch was an emotional occasion, tinged with feelings of sadness and pride. *The Cornish Times* reported:

> The signal rocket was fired punctually to time at 5.30 p.m., and out of her home came in majestic pride our honoured friend, fit for another fifty years duty....The launch was then quickly and skilfully accomplished, indeed she took the water as if she was determined to show that age cannot wither her, nor custom stale her infinite sea worthiness. Thus our lifeboat has passed into the history of Looe, after so many years of excellent service.

The reporter then grew reflective:

> There is an undoubted blank in Looe with no lifeboat, and one cannot help feeling a certain sense of insecurity without it. Its absence must bring once again to the fore the necessity of a buoy on the Rannies: skilful as our fishermen are, knowing every rock, even the most adroit is liable to place his boat in peril during the thick fogs which suddenly spring up; there would be no Looe lifeboat to 'stand by them'. Because, happily, no lives have been lost during the reign of the *Ryder* but many saved — the services of its crew deserve our admiration, gratitude and thanks, for their readiness to answer to the call of duty whenever the signal summoned them. There was no 'Heave Ho'ing' on the part of the passengers in the *Ryder*, but there was a very suspicious 'resting on their oars,' just beyond low water mark outside the Banjo; is it possible there was 'cargo' aboard, and that though there were no 'dead men,' there was a 'Yo Ho, and a bottle of Rum!' Well, '*Vale Ryder,* morituri te salutamus.*

The *Ryder* Lives On ...

The station may have been closed for over sixty years, but the lifeboat *Ryder* was not destined for oblivion; she was sold out of service and converted for pleasure use, with a cabin added. In October 1987, a dilapidated craft, which had been bobbing up and down in the Fleet lagoon, landward of Chesil Beach in Dorset, was discovered on the beach in the course of litter clearance. She would have been burnt along with other debris, had it not been for the timely intervention of a lifeboat enthusiast, who notified the RNLI, who notified Lt. Commander Barney Morris, Honorary Secretary of the Weymouth Lifeboat, with the result that she was restored as part of an employment training scheme, and put on display in the Devenish Brewery's museum at Hope Square in Weymouth. By a strange coincidence, Lt. Col. Ron Overd, Commandant of the Royal Engineer Training Camp at Wyke Regis, who organised her removal from the beach as a recovery exercise for his men, unaware of the identity of the boat, was a descendant of the Toms family which served in her for so long. Not only that, but Peter Tamlin, the Weymouth Harbour Master, also concerned with the renovation project, was similarly a Looe lad.

HAYLE LIFEBOAT STATION
(1866-1920)

The sea at Hayle forms an estuary, flowing over an immense area, which is dry at low-water, and weak in places called quicks. There is a bar at the mouth, impassable in certain states of the tide, but its further accumulation is held in check. About 60 years ago, Phillack Creek was converted into a back-water, and this has effected such a considerable reduction in the sand, that vessels of 200 tons can now enter the harbour.
(*Murray's Hand-Book For Travellers In Devon & Cornwall,* 1865).

A Place of Great Industrial Importance
Hayle, deriving its name from the Cornish word for 'estuary', was one of the few anchorages along the inhospitable north coast, and a place of early importance. For Irish and Breton sailors ventured here in early times to collect tin, to create bronze for the fashioning of tools and weapons, and a succession of Celtic missionaries landed here. It evolved into a place of great industrial significance, with copper smelting and an iron foundry served by a busy harbour. This increased the volume of shipping in the area, which was reflected in the number of ships coming to grief, principally on the bar. Ironically, the industry which brought prosperity was partly responsible for its own decline, in that its waste materials aggravated the build up of sandbars, strangling the harbour and adding to the navigational hazards.

The Need for a Lifeboat

In June 1816, Manby's apparatus was sent to Hayle and St. Ives. Ten years later, there was a bizarre sequence of events whereby the French ship *Ocean*, which had put into St. Ives in distress and undergone very expensive repairs, while awaiting a fair wind to sail, parted her cables and drove on shore on Hayle Bar. While the pilots and seamen of St. Ives risked their lives in rescuing the crew, some of the nearby villagers flocked to the scene to plunder the ship, and got exceedingly drunk in the process. The local seafaring fraternity, particularly the pilots, organised some splendid rescues. But a spate of disasters, notably that of the French brig *Providence*, wrecked on Hayle Bar in 1865, when the St. Ives lifeboat overturned while going to her aid (*see* St. Ives), and of the *Bessie* of Hayle the following year, when lifeboats were brought out from St. Ives and Penzance (*see* Penlee), led to the establishment of a lifeboat station here in 1866. This ten-oared, self-righting lifeboat, built by Forrestt of Limehouse, funded by Oxford University and named the *Isis*, was transported free of charge by rail, and received in rousing processional and musical style at Hayle. She was launched from her boathouse down the carriage slipway into the harbour creek at Copperhouse, and recovered by capstan. To overcome restrictive local conditions, she was sometimes assisted through the harbour by steam tug.

The Hayle lifeboat on her carriage outside the boathouse, situated in a quarry (Acknowledgements RNLI)

A Certain Healthy Rivalry
The new lifeboat and her brave, determined crew soon proved themselves, battling through daunting seas to rescue the crew of eight from the brigantine *Nicholas Harvey* of Hayle, which had run onto the Bar after a collision in St. Ives Bay, then saving another eight lives from the brig *Lizzie* of Newport three years later, as the St. Ives lifeboat *Moses*, which had come partly overland, and raced to the scene, stood by. This area had previously been their preserve, and human nature being what it is, a certain healthy rivalry manifested itself from time to time. A degree of this had been apparent in the old days, when the pilots from St. Ives and Hayle had vied with each other to be first on the scene with incoming vessels to secure the contract, with Mr. Trevaskis, Coxswain of the Hayle lifeboat, much in evidence. He was admired for his daring exploits, alone in his sixteen-foot gig, whatever the weather, and took a fiendish delight in scoring over the St. Ives men. The story goes that on one occasion, when a cargo vessel was expected from Bristol, the St. Ives men checked that his boat was in harbour, before setting off to intercept the ship. It was, but Trevaskis, unusually, had accepted a lift up to Newquay and set off in another gig, to board the vessel off Fistral Bay. So when the St. Ives hopefuls came alongside, Trevaskis gave a nonchalant smirk and offered them a tow to St. Ives.

Daring Deeds and Recognition
A particularly fierce battle against the elements in November 1874, with a partial volunteer crew, eventually brought them in sight of the casualty, the lugger *Jeune Ceres*, and the St. Ives lifeboat speeding towards her with the wind and waves in her favour. This time their rivals beat them to it. However, the shipwrecked captain and crew refused to be taken off, and disaster almost overtook the lifeboatmen on their return trip. The drogue rope snapped and two crewmen were hurled into the water. One was promptly recovered, but the other was submerged twice before being hauled to safety. In a December gale of 1881, the *Isis* rescued a total of ten men from the battered three masted Welsh schooner *Constance*, which had made for Hayle and grounded on the Bar, having taken St. Ives pilots aboard. A year later the crew narrowly avoided becoming morbid statistics while attempting to assist the schooner *Susan Elizabeth* of Dartmouth, for the lifeboat capsized when alongside, throwing all of them out. Matthew Trevaskis, one of the Coxswain's two sons, swam ashore; Zacharias Chinn and John Warren were drawn ashore by rocket line, another swam ashore and nine were able to get back to the boat. And it turned out that the shipwreck victims had already been saved by the Rocket Apparatus. The following year the Committee of Management voted £30 to the widow of John Warren who it was claimed had died as the result of his injuries. In 1886 Coxswain Edwin Trevaskis received a Silver Medal for his long and gallant service, with a clasp being added when he retired three years later.

The Wrecking of the 'Squirrel'

The trusted and familiar lifeboat, *Isis*, which had been instrumental in the saving of fifty-one lives, was succeeded in 1887 by a larger lifeboat called the *New Oriental Bank*, subsequently renamed the *E.F. Harrison*. She was here when the well known wrecking of the *S.S. Escurial* occurred on Gull Rock, Portreath, during a north-westerly gale in January 1895. Distress flares were fired, and frightened sailors jumped overboard or sought refuge in the rigging. Lifeboats launched from Newquay and St. Ives did not reach the scene, while the Hayle lifeboat, after being laboriously transported eleven miles overland encountered difficulties in trying to launch at low tide in soft sand. The coastguards' attempts to get a line aboard in these terrible conditions were similarly abortive, and the survivors were those who took a chance in swimming through the raging waters, to be dragged from the surf by helpers on the shore. Others, who had bravely clung to the rigging for many hours, dropped one by one, as exhaustion overcame them, or were overwhelmed by the sea as the masts were carried away. The sombre wreck of the *Escurial*, known to one and all as the *Squirrel*, was poignantly revealed at low water, while her copper, brass and ironwork was salvaged by divers. This tragic episode attracted some criticism of the rescue services, most of it unjustified.

A Knock-on Sequence of Events

The situation of sailors refusing to leave endangered ships must have been particularly frustrating to lifeboatmen in the days prior to ship-to-shore communication, having already expended time and effort and often placed their own lives in jeopardy. This was the case in January 1899, when the *S.S. Olivia* of Portreath, which had signalled for assistance in entering Hayle harbour in stormy conditions, collided with the summoned pilot gig. Fortunately the pilots succeeded in getting aboard, but there was a knock-on sequence of events, for she stranded on a sandbank, summoned assistance, then wasted the lifeboatmen's time when her crew declined to be rescued. The delay resulted in the lifeboat being flung against her side, then tossed ashore, fortunately without serious injury to the men. The St. Ives lifeboat, which was then summoned, had another mishap, when crewmen were washed overboard, but safely recovered. Furthermore, the accurate aim of the inshore rescue team was treated with disdain. When the weather abated, the men came ashore themselves. However, the ship's owners, Messrs. Bain & Sons of Portreath had the decency to make monetary gifts to all concerned.

This lifeboat, with a record of thirty-four saved lives, was superseded by the *Admiral Rodd* in 1906, credited with saving another ten lives, all of them from the *S.S. Hayle* of Penzance, in March 1913. By now the port of Hayle was in decline, and the sailing vessels which the establishment of a lifeboat here was designed to help had disappeared from the scene. Launching from here had never been easy, and in the changing situation it was felt that emergencies could be handled by neighbouring St. Ives, so the station closed down in 1920.

MULLION LIFEBOAT STATION
(1867-1908)

Some of the principal landowners have also been generous supporters of the Institution. Amongst the foremost of them is Mr. Agar Robartes, M.P. From a letter received from him a few weeks since, it is quite clear that no benevolent work in Cornwall had given him greater satisfaction than the help he had so bountifully extended to the lifeboat cause. He was its friend from the beginning, and he has continued ever since to be its most liberal supporter. The lifeboat that is about to be stationed at Mullion, in memory of the late Rev. Daniel Draper, who unhappily perished from the ship *London*, has been principally contributed by the Wesleyan Methodists of Cornwall. Thus the Cornish people in this as in every other good cause, have nobly done their part.

(Richard Lewis, RNLI Secretary, on the occasion of the inauguration of the Falmouth Lifeboat, as reported in the Falmouth Packet: August 1867).

Tragic Romanticism

The eastern shores of Mount's Bay have collected a catalogue of shipwrecks down the centuries, as sombrely testified in local churchyards. Indeed, legend has it that the lonely, atmospheric, salt-sprayed, sand-enveloped church of Gunwalloe was built in thanksgiving by a survivor of shipwreck, who vowed it should be sited where sounds of praise and prayer should mingle with the rhythm of the ocean.

Mention has already been made of the incredible number of vessels lost on Loe Bar, and countless sailing ships, many of them foreign, met their doom between Gunwalloe and Lizard Point. With the passage of time, these gruesome happenings are viewed with fatal fascination and mellowed into local folklore. Examples include the Dutch barque with a cargo of tea, which struck the Vradden in thick fog in July 1815, and became known as the 'tea wreck'; her coffee carrying counterpart in 1832, which came on shore between Kynance Cove and the Rill, and the slender and graceful Neapolitan barque, wrecked at Polurrian in June 1838, with the loss of all hands, thereby qualifying for the sad title of the 'dead wreck'. But it was not only strangers who succumbed to the perils of alien shores, for local pilchard seiners were sometimes caught out by sudden changes in weather conditions. Although Mullion Roads could afford shelter in some situations, it was also a maritime trap by which small sailing vessels driven before the wind, could become embayed.

An Ill-Wind

The possibility of placing a lifeboat at Mullion, offering coverage of the Lizard, had been under consideration following a recommendation of the Northumberland Report of 1851. But indecision and dissension caused delays, and the casualties continued. It was an ill wind that kept a number of vessels lying at anchor in Mullion Roads in September 1858. When it changed direction, most succeeded in weathering the Lizard headland; the brig *Glencoe* of Whitby did not. After dragging her anchors and being driven on shore at Polurrian, the crew took to the rigging, and lines thrown to them by coastguards fell short. Despite this and similar happenings, it was not until the wreck of the Austrian barque *Padre* in 1862 that a coastguard casualty report drew the *Board of Trade's* attention to the need for a rocket-fired apparatus here. According to a contemporary account by the Rev. E.G. Harvey, 'Lord, then Mr. Robartes on hearing the report, sent his steward to make enquiries whether a lifeboat would not prove equally beneficial; but the reply returned from the parish then was that, a lifeboat would be useless, unless the rocks at the entrance of the Cove were cleared out.' A Manby Rocket Apparatus, with its carriage arrived later that year, and was soon to demonstrate its worth. As to the establishment of lifeboat coverage, the site at Polpeor was thought to have better launching prospects, with the advantage of easier operation each side of the Lizard peninsula. So a lifeboat was emplaced there in 1859. But ships continued to be wrecked and lives lost in the vicinity.

There was an eerie incident just before Christmas 1862, when the deserted schooner *Arwenack* of Truro reached these shores, having had her sails blown away in a storm. It transpired that her entire crew, who had taken to the ship's boat had been drowned when the boat capsized. The men of the *S.S. John McIntyre* of London were more fortunate after their ship sustained damage off the Lizard in fog in April 1865, and came ashore at Gew-graze. But it took a triple tragedy in January 1867 to bring things to a head, and to acknowledge that a lifeboat was necessary to cope with the situation at that time, in a knock-on sequence of events which went from bad to worse, after a number of vessels had sought shelter in Mullion Roads during a strong easterly gale. When the storm veered to the south west and intensified, they were all placed in jeopardy. Some were able to effect an escape; others became victims of the frantic manoeuvres of other shipping. In terrifying conditions, the schooner *Cherub* of Swansea struck another schooner, the *Ebbw Vale* of Liverpool, then the schooner *Margaret* of Teignmouth. The crew of the *Ebbw Vale* abandoned ship and were taken to Plymouth by the smack *Hearty* of Jersey, and one sailor from the *Margaret* got aboard the *Cherub*. Those aboard the *Cherub* abandoned their ship, which had become a mass of debris strewn around the coast by the following morning, and got safely ashore. But the remaining four aboard the *Margaret* were in a perilous situation. Attempts were made to reach them with a rocket line fired from the shore, and lifeboats laboriously transported overland arrived too late, for all had gone down with their ship. In the aftermath of the tragedy emotions ran high, and a positive decision was made to have a lifeboat emplaced here, with the Wesleyan Methodists leading the way with their memorial fund to the Rev. Daniel J. Draper, a recent victim of shipwreck in the Bay of Biscay.

Improving on Nature
The Institution was instrumental in carrying out engineering works, blasting rocks away to widen the entrance to the cove, and using this material to replenish the beach and divert the course of the stream to prevent it causing further beach erosion. These improvements also benefitted the fishermen and made the harbour safer for everyone. Nevertheless, history was to demonstrate that the lifeboat's potential was hampered by the exposed nature of this beach.

The Arrival of the Daniel J. Draper
The inaugural ceremony for Mullion's new lifeboat, fittingly named the *Daniel J.Draper*, was in the context of a regatta at Penzance, alongside established local lifeboats as part of the festivities surrounding the opening of the public buildings on 10th September 1867. Three days later she was brought to Mullion and put through exercises under the command of Captain J.R. Ward, the Institution's Inspector. Her boathouse was a few yards up the road and, after launching, she was hauled up by capstan, and turned at right angles to be re-housed. Her first service occurred a month later, when she saved three men from the barque *Achilles* of Glasgow, after she had stranded at Polurrian Cove. The remainder were recovered by the inshore rescue team. One of the saddest occurrences was the wreck of the iron barque *Boyne* of Scarborough, on her way to Falmouth for orders, when she struck the rocks on the eastern fringe of Mount's Bay as the result of a navigational error, for her plight went unnoticed until a clifftop farmer heard cries of distress many hours later and alerted the lifeboat crew. A coastguard was on the scene attempting to get a line aboard when they arrived, but the ship had split into two sections by this time. Most of the shipwrecked seemed mesmerised with fear, and unable to co-operate when a line was successfully thrown aboard. Despite the lifeboatmen's efforts, all were drowned, apart from four who had escaped in their ship's boat on the orders of the captain at the onset of the emergency.

The lifeboat Daniel J. Draper, *her crew and local folk in relaxed pose outside the boathouse at Mullion (Sheila Bird Collection)*

Neither the *Edith,* which came on station in 1887, nor the *Nancy Newbon* which followed her in 1894 performed any services, and the station was closed in 1908.

FALMOUTH LIFEBOAT STATION

(Established 1867)

Falmouth Harbour has been celebrated from a remote period for its extent and commodiousness. Its entrance, about 1 m. wide, is defended by the castles of Pendennis and Mawes. In the middle of the passage lies the *Black Rock*, an obstruction of little import, as, though covered by the tide, its situation is marked by a beacon, and there is on either side of it a broad and deep channel. The sea, having entered through this opening, immediately expands into a basin, so capacious, that, during the French war, buoys were laid down in it for 16 sail of the line, and in 1815 a fleet of 300 vessels, including several of large size, took shelter within it, and rode out a gale without a casualty.

(Murray's Hand-Book of Devon & Cornwall: 1865)

The Multi-Functional Port of Falmouth

Falmouth, one of the finest and safest natural harbours in the world, has played a proud role in our maritime history. Besides being a famous port of refuge, this deep water haven in its advantageous *first in, last out* situation enjoyed the prestige that went with being chosen as a Post Office Packet port in 1688, while 'Falmouth for Orders' became famous the world over. This success gave rise to ship building, ship repair and other maritime industries. The *Coasting Pylot* of 1693 stated:

If any Ships have occasion to haul ashore to wash, tallow, stop Leaks, or load or unload Goods, Sir *Peter Killigrew* hath been at very great Charges in building a very good, convenient and safe Mole or Pier, where are Keys with Cranes and good Store-houses, or Ware-houses, to load or unload Goods, the Ships lying by the Key-side close by the Store- house. Many *Virginia* Ships have here unloaded their Tobacco, and is very convenient for that Purpose. The Tides rise and fall here at a Spring-tide 18 and 20 Foot, and 12 and 14 at a Neap-tide. It floweth here at Full and Change five Hours and a quarter.

161

Sailing in and out of The Haven

On the face of it, this gentler southern Cornish coast, with its beautiful, wide river estuaries, hospitable looking bays and protective headlands, might be more benign to the mariner than some of the awesome, dramatic sections of the north coast, where the hazards are quite obvious. But this impression is deceptive for, in conditions of fog or storm, sailing ships sometimes ran headlong into disaster on the shores of blind headed bays, thinking they were making for a safe haven, having confused the headland of St. Anthony, the Dodman and the Gribbin. However, the situation improved after the erection of a lighthouse on St. Anthony at the eastern approach to Falmouth harbour and a striped red and white beacon on the Gribbin, which also served as a leading mark to the port of Fowey. The Dodman, to the east of Falmouth, and the configuration of partly concealed rocks known as the Manacles to the south, have been responsible for countless shipwrecks.

The beacon of St. Anthony, mounted on tall scaffolding, stands sentinel at the mouth of the Fal estuary (Sheila Bird Collection)

Not everyone would agree with Murray, in the opening quotation, about Black Rock in the harbour entrance being 'of little import', particularly those who have been its victims. The seventeenth century *Coasting Pylot* makes mention of it as the mariner is guided into this safe haven:

There is a Rock which lieth in the Harbour's Mouth, and lieth nearer the West-Shore than the East-Shore; this Rock is called *Falmouth Rock*, and sheweth itself above Water at Half-tide; there is a Pole placed on it, to shew where it lieth when it is under Water. You may sail in and out of either side of this Rock; the East-side is the best. Being past the Rock, and you would anchor in *Carreck Road*, which is the place where great Ships ride, you may sail up in the Fair-way, keeping your Lead; for there is a narrow deep Channel which hath eighteen Fathom Water all the way up to *Carreck Road...*

But having got thus far, the seafarers' problems were not necessarily over.

Disasters inside The Haven

Such is the nature of ships and the sea, that despite every precaution, the sea will always have its way, and shipwrecks will continue. Even the seemingly safe waters inside Falmouth Haven can become treacherous at certain times, particularly when winds funnel up from the south through the harbour entrance. The worst disaster occurred in very severe weather conditions in January 1814, when the transport *Queen*, returning from Spain with invalided soldiers, French prisoners, women and children, was driven from her anchors onto rocks at Trefusis Point, becoming a complete wreck in twenty minutes. Most of the 330 or so swept overboard or crushed by masts, planking and flying debris were buried at Mylor Churchtown, Budock and St. Gluvias. The inhabitants of Flushing were very distressed by the mangled bodies and wreckage washed up on their shores. Fourteen years later, when the brig *Sarah* was in peril on nearby rocks, they burnt furze and tar barrels on the hill to illuminate the scene as masts were cut away and shipwreck victims hauled ashore in an empty cask. This earned Lloyd's agent William Broad the Institution's Gold Medal for his endurance and initiative in saving eleven people by means of an open boat, and was an example of the many brave rescues carried out by coastguards, pilots, fishermen, boatmen and others of the seafaring community around Falmouth and St. Mawes.

Moved by Compassion

In the days of sail, violent gales from the Atlantic caused many vessels to make for the shelter of Falmouth Haven, when the coasts of Cornwall were left littered with shipwrecks, and the local press proudly commented on Falmouth's effectiveness as a port of refuge. The vessels in the harbour survived the hurricanes of December 1830, when the open seaboard was strewn with casualties, including the recently built brig *Bacchus* of Gloucester, which became a victim of the Gull Rock off Nare Head. The brig *Bon Père*, which had found herself in difficulties in trying to make for Falmouth was more fortunate, for her plight had been noticed by the coastguards, who summoned assistance before she was driven on shore at Towan Beach to the north of Killigerran Head. As darkness fell, and the anguished sailors cried for help, Lieutenant William James, R.N., of St. Mawes, moved by compassion, heroically plunged into the billowing surf and got a line aboard, thus saving ten lives. He was awarded the Gold Medal of the RNLI.

Recognition for the Heroic Rescue of Shipwrecked Cannibals
A Gold Medal and three Silver Medals awarded by the Institution in 1836 similarly recall heroism in classical style, after a bizarre sequence of events. The story surrounding Case No. 525 is best told by quoting the records of the time:

> Messrs. Robinson, Brooking, and Garland, 36, Old Broad Street, transmitted a memorial, signed by several Magistrates of the county of Devon, and other persons, stating, 'That on the 17th December last, the brig *'Angerona,'* John Jellard, master, left St. John's, Newfoundland, for Teignmouth. On the 22nd December, in lat. 47 N. Long. 37 WW. a sail was discovered in distress. The *'Angerona'* immediately stood towards her, and found her to be the *'Francis Sparght'*, J. Gorman, master, from St. John's, New Brunswick, to Limerick, dismasted and waterlogged. At this time it blew a strong gale, with a tremendous sea running, which frequently broke over the vessel, and rendering it extremely dangerous to board her; but seeing a number of persons on the poop, the captain of the *'Angerona'* resolved on making an attempt to rescue them; the boat, the only one on board, was lowered, when Capt. Jellard, William Hill, mate, John Fowell and Samuel Hicks, seamen, entered the same; they made for the wreck, which, after much exertion and difficulty, they gained, and from it they took six human beings, in a state of suffering too horrible for description, and wholly incapable of exertion: with these they returned to the *'Angerona'*, and having placed them on board, nothing undaunted (although the small boat had shipped much water) these brave men, cheered on by their shipmates, again pulled for the wreck, and ultimately saved the remaining five of the eleven miserable and helpless creatures, of a crew of, originally eighteen. They had been on the wreck nineteen days, without provisions or water. Three had been washed overboard, when the vessel first became a wreck; on the 15th day, lots were drawn for a victim, and ultimately in four cases, human blood had been shed for the sustenance of the survivors. Owing, however, to the kindness and attention paid to these unhappy sufferers, by all on board the *'Angerona'*, they soon recovered, and were put on shore at Falmouth, on the 7th January, 1836.

Although this case does not come within the Rules of the Institution, which is limited to cases of Shipwreck that occur on the 'Coasts of the United Kingdom', yet in consideration of the very meritorious conduct and exertions of Capt. Jellard, and the three other persons who assisted him, as before mentioned, which are highly appreciated by the Committee, they have voted the 'Gold Medallion' of the Institution to be presented to Capt. Jellard, and the 'Silver Medal' to Mr. William Hill, to John Fowell, and to Samuel Hicks, to be sent to Messrs., Robinson, Brooking, and Garland.

Facilities for Ships and the Shipwrecked

In 1838 the Institution voted a Silver Medal to Lt. W.G. Fields, R.N., for the rescue, by means of a boat, of two crewmen from a coal barge wrecked at Falmouth. Many of the ocean-going vessels which had taken a battering in the storm of February 1840 came to Falmouth for repairs, thus reinforcing the tradition of ship repair, which led to the development of the docks. The terrific gale of 1859, said to have been the worst since 1823, again caused havoc to shipping, while Falmouth proved its worth. Falmouth, with its Missions to Seamen, Seamen's Bethel and wide ranging facilities was well equipped to deal with the aftermath of shipwreck.

The Arrival of Falmouth's First Lifeboat

In view of all this, it is rather surprising to find that when the people of Gloucester had wanted to bestow a lifeboat on Falmouth (possibly recalling the sad fate of the *Bacchus*), the mayor of the time, Mr. Webber, declined on the grounds that Falmouth harbour was so land-locked that it did not require a lifeboat, and suggested that one might be more effectively positioned on the coast to the south or east. But Captain Ward, Inspector of Lifeboats, who knew the coast well, insisted that Falmouth was indeed the best place for a lifeboat station, particularly in regard to the treacherous Manacles. A special meeting was convened to persuade the mayor to accept the lifeboat, which carried the responsibility of keeping her well housed and properly maintained. Subscriptions poured in for the building of a boathouse on a site in the area of the docks, while the railway companies concerned demonstrated their goodwill by conveying the lifeboat free of charge.

The leading gentlemen of the town formed themselves into a committee and, determined that the opening of the lifeboat station would be an occasion to be remembered linked it to the presentation of the Albert Medal to Theophilus Jones, on behalf of Queen Victoria, in recognition of his courage in rescuing disabled seamen from the *Marmion*, wrecked on 17th March, 1867. As the *Falmouth Packet* reported:

Shortly before twelve o'clock, the lifeboat, mounted on a carriage drawn by twelve fine horses, kindly lent for the occasion by Mr. Wills of Constantine, left the Docks, where it had recently been stationed, and where the Life-Boat House had been erected, and, preceded by a band, took its way through the principal streets of the town en route for Penryn, followed by a large concourse of people. In the boat were seated the whole of the crew, attired in their life belts, and above their heads was suspended an attractive banner, on which was inscribed in prominent letters, 'Success to the Gloucester Life boat.'

The citizens of Gloucester donated money for a lifeboat to be based on the coast of Cornwall, and a Cornish committee member contacted the influential Mr. Charles Fox and then the Mayor, with a view to it being emplaced at Falmouth. The photograph shows the newly constructed lifeboat taking the name of The Gloucester, *in 1867 (Acknowledgements RNLI)*

Having perambulated around the main streets of Penryn, the lifeboat returned to the Greenbank, where spectators jostled with each other and took up vantage points at every window, balcony and porch to witness the splendid procession of maritime, military and civic dignitaries in full and colourful regalia, wending their way through the crowded streets to the docks, accompanied by the stylish brass bands. Here Mr. Jones received his award, to the rousing strains of 'See the Conquering Hero Comes', lengthy speeches were made and the lifeboat was launched. In the afternoon she was to demonstrate her self-righting qualities, and in the evening a prestigious dinner was held at the Falmouth Hotel. In reply to the Mayoral speech, Mr.

Richard Lewis, Secretary of the Institution made his point when he said, 'Let no one say after the shipping disasters of last winter in this neighbourhood, that a lifeboat is not wanted at Falmouth.' And he added, 'I believe she will never lack willing hands to go afloat in her in the stormiest weather. Indeed, Cornish sailors and fishermen have stood forth conspicuously in manning these lifeboats.'

At that time it required around £600 to establish a lifeboat station, and Richard Lewis impressed on the people of Falmouth that lifeboats, not properly maintained, tended to become death boats, and that about £50 a year would be needed for her upkeep. He suggested that the citizens of Gloucester might like to maintain their interest in the boat they had so nobly financed. On his return the following summer, he watched the *City of Gloucester*, along with other Cornish lifeboats demonstrating their skills in racing each other, with Looe emerging victorious on this occasion.

A framed, enamel plaque inside the boathouse, refurbished by ex-Coxswain Vivian Pentecost and crewmember Trevor Wilsham commemorates the arrival of that first lifeboat, which was launched on ten occasions during her time on station, but did not save any lives. During this period there was an award winning service carried out by Mr. N.G. Hatch, Mate of the *Berkshire* of London, the Harbour Master and others in their respective boats who assisted in saving life from the brig *Marys* of Whitby, which became a casualty of Black Rock on 22nd October 1880, during a heavy east-north-

The crew of the Jane Whittingham *(1887-1894) then based within the Docks, prepare for a practice launch (Acknowledgements Maurice Osborne, Sheila Bird Collection)*

-easterly gale. The Mate received a Silver Medal of the Institution. Falmouth's second lifeboat, the *Jane Whittingham*, launched twice, with no record of having saved life. However, Falmouth fulfilled its valuable role as a port of refuge during the severe storm and blizzard of March 1891, and the port's tugs kept busy rounding up casualties in conditions so severe that giant icicles hung suspended from the rigging of stricken ships, and chronometres went awry.

'Have a Care of the Manacle Rocks'

Danger lurked on the approach to this safe haven, and the *Coasting Pylot* cautions: 'In sailing in and out of this Place, and when you come from the Westward or are bound to the Westward, you must have a Care of the *Manacle Rocks* which lie South by West from the Mouth of *Falmouth* Harbour 2 Leagues, some of them lie above Water and some under Water, and lie about three Miles East away from the Land into the Sea.' Modern technology has vastly reduced the number of casualties of the Manacles, but countless sailing ships and quite a number of steamships came to grief here, usually after rounding the Lizard and making for the port of Falmouth.

Fine and Fulfilling Services

The arrival of the *Bob Newbon* in 1894 heralded the beginning of Falmouth lifeboat's fine and fulfilling record of service, which has received official recognition at various times. This lifeboat assisted some of the most memorable casualties of this coast, and found herself in a hazardous situation after going to the aid of the *S.S. Renwick* of Newcastle, which had gone ashore on rocks near Gyllyngvase Beach in a south-westerly gale in February 1903. The excited spectators cheered as the crew of the stricken ship was rescued by coastguards with their inshore rocket apparatus, but the lifeboat, which was in danger of being driven ashore, let down her anchor, hoping it would withstand these ferocious conditions, and rode out the storm, while would-be rescuers kept cold and uncomfortable vigil on the beach, with lifelines in readiness.

An event which finds an illustration on the pages of many a maritime book, with funnels protruding through the waves in a horrifying, riveting manner, took place in October 1898, when the New York bound passenger cargo ship *S.S. Mohegan*, on a wrong course, was in collision with the *Manacles*, sinking within forty-five minutes, with great loss of life. The Porthoustock lifeboat played a memorable role, rescuing forty-four of the one hundred and fifty or so aboard, with Falmouth, Cadgwith and the Lizard lifeboats converging on the scene in an unsuccessful search for survivors (*see* Porthoustock). A year later the American passenger liner *S.S. Paris* of New York, (formerly named the *City of Paris*), went aground at nearby Lowland Point in thick weather with calm seas. Once again Falmouth lifeboat, having been towed out by tug, worked in conjunction with the Porthoustock lifeboat, but with a happier outcome. The passengers and crew, who were taken off by lifeboat, transferred to the tug *Triton* and landed at Falmouth, realised how fortunate they had been in their near-miss at the Manacles; when the fog cleared, they gained a salutary sighting of those funnels and masts jutting above the surface of the water. The liner was refloated.

The disaster of the four-masted barque *Hera* of Hamburg on 1st February 1914, gave rise to one of the most dramatic rescues ever carried out by a Cornish lifeboat. After ninety-one days at sea the magnificent, fully-laden German barque, which was making for Falmouth for orders, misjudged St. Anthony Light, carried on past the harbour mouth and met her doom on the Whelps, a submerged reef surrounding Gull Rock in Gerrans Bay. The crew set off distress signals, as the ship rapidly foundered, and took to their boats. However, the more heavily loaded one capsized with nine of the twenty-four crewmen battling their way through the icy, swirling waters and clambering onto the sloping jigger mast. Coastguards and others gathering on the clifftop witnessed a scene of rising pathos by the light of car headlights and hurricane lamps, as exhausted men lost their grip and vanished beneath the cruel waves. The lifeboat *Bob Newbon*, under Coxswain S. Hingston was on her way, being towed through the heavy seas by the Falmouth tug *Perran*, accompanied by fellow tugs *Victor* and *Triton*.

The *Falmouth Packet* reported: 'In 25 minutes of the first firing of the signal, the Falmouth lifeboat *Bob Newbon* was on her errand of mercy. Nineteen souls had perished before the appeal for help reached port. *Bob Newbon* saved five. 'Sadly, three sailors, who had clung to the rigging so bravely slipped into the water a few minutes before the lifeboat arrived. Some of the victims were buried in the churchyard at Veryan, while the wreck, which constituted a hazard to navigation had to be blown up. A lifebuoy from the *Hera* was put on display at the Falmouth Seamen's Bethel, where it remained as silent witness to seafarers' vulnerability. After prayers during the ceremony of inauguration, the Reverend Strong, a former sailor himself, commented that despite the bashfulness and retiring disposition of sailors, they were very appreciative of all that was done on their behalf. Furthermore, Mrs. Fox of the notable Quaker family, pointed out that this institution offered a protection to those, 'who, when leaving the dangers of the deep, came to the dangers of the land,' and warned of moral temptations.

Secured to the Masts and the Stanchions

The Seamen's Bethel found itself looking after some colourful characters of the sea shortly afterwards, when the Chilean transport *Malpo* reached Falmouth in a disabled state, after taking a battering in the Bay of Biscay. The Second Officer of the *Northam*, a Welshman named Evans, got a line aboard the stricken ship by heroically jumping overboard in a lifebelt and getting onto the ship, to enable a tow to be undertaken. However, the hawser broke when they were under tow, and they were met by the tugs *Victor, Triton* and *Dragon* as they limped towards port. Water had penetrated her cabins and crew's quarters, and she had developed a heavy list to port. Devoid of anchors and cables, she was made fast to the *Northam.* The *Falmouth Packet* reported: 'Those who went aboard next morning found men on deck, with hands behind their backs and tied to the masts and stanchions. Rumours of a mutiny were dispelled when it was discovered that they were Chileans, being given a lift home, who had been caught looting the stores and cargo, while the officers and crew were busy looking after the ship.'

Feathers in Nautical Caps

Wartime conditions left the rescue services depleted, so it was particularly creditable that when the call to rescue life from shipwreck came in February 1915, the undermanned Falmouth and Mevagissey lifeboats and the Portscatho Rocket Brigade set out in daunting circumstances to assist the four-masted barque *Andromeda* of London, which had struck Killygerrans Head, and had heavy seas breaking across her. It proved to be a great feather in the nautical cap of the inshore rescue team, who succeeded in getting the twenty-seven survivors ashore in three quarters of an hour, in gale force, south-westerly winds, in darkness, when it had been impossible for a lifeboat to get in close enough. The following year, the *Bob Newbon* saved nineteen from the Auxiliary tanker *Ponus*, which had gone ashore and later caught fire on Gyllyngvase Beach. It was a strange service, involving three 'call outs', with the crew refusing to abandon ship at first, taking off nineteen men, then being summoned again after fire had broken out, endangering the life of the Second Mate, who had been ordered to remain aboard by his captain, while others had been allowed ashore in the ship's boats. He escaped death by fire in jumping overboard, and was lucky to escape death by drowning by being snatched up by two officers who had heroically launched a small boat into terrifying conditions. It was impossible to get him into the dinghy, so they tied him to the stern and pulled for the shore with all their strength. Lt. E. Badger R.E. and Lt. S.C. Stephens, R.N.R. received Silver Medals for their courageous conduct. It was during the *Bob Newbon* era, in 1918, that the Council terminated the Institution's tenancy of the lifeboat house, which had to be removed, and the lifeboat placed afloat.

Leading up to the Era of the Crawford and Constance Conybeare

The *Bob Newbon* was followed by four second-hand lifeboats, the *Jane Anne,* formerly stationed at Irvine, and the seasoned *Herbert Sturmy,* which had seen service at Swanage, and was later transferred to Cadgwith. Each was to launch on one occasion, without performing a service. *The Brothers,* which followed, was a forty-five foot Watson motor lifeboat, previously used at Penlee; then followed the *B.A.S.P.*, of the same class and size, also built at Cowes, which had served at Yarmouth, Isle of Wight. But it was the arrival of a new Watson for Falmouth in 1940, the *Crawford & Constance Conybeare*, that marked the arrival of another particularly fine period of service for the Falmouth station, coping with a variety of wartime casualties when Falmouth was a reserve naval port. The new lifeboat, which cost £9,000, and which had two forty horse-power diesel engines and was capable of a speed of eight and a half knots, was a gift of Mrs. Constance Conybeare, whose husband, Rear Admiral Crawford Conybeare had taken part in the Discovery & Alerte Arctic expedition in 1874. She was named and dedicated in a ceremony held on Custom House Quay by Bishop J. Holden, on January 13th.

Her initiation was to be swift, for on the morning of January 19th, Coxswain 'Janner' Snell and his crew were summoned to the aid of the *S.S. Kirkpool* of West Hartlepool, which was dragging her anchors off Castle Beach and in danger of being driven on shore in south-easterly gale force winds and heavy seas. Two tugs which were standing by in the heaving waters had been unable to get a line aboard but, in these terrible conditions, Coxswain Snell manoeuvred skilfully alongside, first to port and then to starboard to engage a line; this accomplished, the line was transferred to a tug, which started to haul without gaining purchase. But this attempt had to be aborted when the casualty grounded, settled broadside on to the breakers, and let out a horrible hiss was her boilers lifted and her engine room filled with steam. The Falmouth crew was now confronted with an even greater challenge, being requested to remove a stretcher case and some firemen from the casualty. In a bold feat of seamanship in the grand tradition, the lifeboat synchronized the dramatic rise and fall of the waves to dart between ship and shore, and hold alongside, to enable the injured man and fireman to be taken aboard. The lifeboat landed them, then returned to pull off a second coup, thereby rescuing a total of thirty-five lives. This service brought a Silver Medal to Coxswain 'Janner' Snell, a Bronze Medal to Motor Mechanic C.H. Williams and Thanks on Vellum to the crew.

John Snell and the *Jean Charcot*

'Janner' Snell's son John, who joined the Institution in 1939 as an engineer, became a reserve travelling mechanic. His happiest and most memorable times were during the war, when he served around the western coast of Britain with the French lifeboat *Jean Charcot* in which refugees had escaped from Ile Molene, Finistere, in June 1940, with her Coxswain and Mechanic aboard. She made landfall on St. Mary's, Isles of Scilly, and was handed over to the Institution by the Ministry of Shipping for the duration of the war. John Snell overhauled her engines at the Little Falmouth Boatyard, but Tommy Pratt, a travelling electrician who had been working on her, was killed when a German bomb struck the Wayside Cafe in Falmouth. John spent five years with the *Jean Charcot* and formed a very close relationship with her. 'She was a lovely boat; she was a part of me. Nearly broke my heart when I had to give her over,' he recalled poignantly in 1990. 'She was painted the Institution's colours, which were red, white and blue, then I took her on reserve duty all around the coast. The crew would always find accommodation wherever I went, and I had to be somewhere where they could call me within a few minutes in case of the lifeboat being wanted, because no maroons or radios could be used during the war. The Secretary of every station would have the calls from the coastguards; he would inform the Coxswain who would organise tellers to go around and call the crew out. We were all trained in gunnery and supplied with rifles, just in case you picked up a German airman who was himself armed and who might take charge of the boat. They said if I didn't take this gunnery course, they would send soldiers to go out with me.' So, to preclude such a possibility, he learnt to handle a machine gun. When the *Jean Charcot* was handed back to the French on May 10th 1945, they acknowledged her to be in very good condition.

The Wartime Situation

The port of Falmouth came under the jurisdiction of the Admiralty at the beginning of the Second World War, commandeering various adjacent and seafront hotels, with the Membly Hall their Chief Naval Base. They also requisitioned the services and boat of highly experienced Boatman Leonard Morrison, who was also Second Coxswain, having joined the lifeboat service around 1930. Much secret work took place at night, and Leonard Morrison was ordered to carry out a variety of services, including the towing of landing craft and the delicate business of mines being laid in Falmouth harbour and the Helford river. There were many restrictions, and ships were ordered into the port and searched. All vessels, including lifeboats, had to report their movements and seek Admiralty clearance.

Falmouth Bay saw many wartime casualties, mostly blown up by mines or sunk while being towed into the port, but occasionally they fell victim to German aircraft, which also attacked the harbour and points around the Fal and Helford rivers. One air raid on the docks on July 10th 1940 set three ships on fire. One of these, the *Marie Chandros,* which had a highly inflammable cargo of raw cotton, was towed still blazing to be sunk off St. Anthony. An obliging service was carried out by the *Crawford and Constance Conybeare* on November 10th the following year, when she responded to the call to take salvage men off that wreck, who were unable to get away in their own boat in a southerly gale with rough seas. They were thanked and rewarded by the Salvage Company. March 31st, 1941 was also a memorable day for the lifeboat crew when, in conjunction with the tugs *Goliath* and *Northgate Scott,* they gave assistance to the Dutch steamers *Vliestroom, Kalso* and *Karanan,* which were victims of air attacks and stormy seas. In 1944 this lifeboat and a reserve lifeboat were successful in saving lives and landing craft.

Romantic, Rollicking Real Life Drama
Falmouth's catalogue of wartime services, often carried out in conjunction with the port's tugs, was followed by an increasing peacetime pattern of mishaps with the 'Birminghan Navy' in all its guises. However, if the call out in August 1949 to the schooner *Hispaniola*, which had been used in the filming of Treasure Island and other projects, added a touch of romantic, nautical fantasy, this was nothing compared with the rollicking, real life drama of the *S.S. Flying Enterprise* in January 1952, which had the *Crawford & Constance Conybeare* waiting in the wings, and captured the imagination of the world. Many vessels in the Channel found themselves in trouble during the week of storms around Christmas 1951, when very high winds gusted up to ninety miles per hour, and the ocean-going tug *Turmoil*, under the command of Captain Dan Parker, arrived in Falmouth Bay with the *Mactra* under tow and had to make a swift turnaround, to go to the aid of the American freighter *Flying Enterprise*, lying with a heavy list 350 miles off Land's End, and took nearly two days to get there. During this time, it was reported that the list had worsened and that the thirty-seven-year-old Dutch Captain Kurt Carlsen, a fine seaman who had gone to sea as a ship's cook at the age of thirteen and worked his way up, had ordered his crew to abandon ship, but insisted on remaining aboard himself. Why, everyone wondered, did the Captain stead-fastly refuse to leave his doomed ship? And what was the significance of her cargo?

Having battled her way to the scene of the casualty, where other ships were standing by, the raging seas thwarted repeated attempts to get a line aboard. Then, after a near collision, Ken Dancy, the fair and youthful mate of the *Turmoil*, daringly leapt aboard the stricken ship with a tow rope, thus allowing a tow to get underway as weather conditions worsened. It was a difficult operation, requiring all the tug skipper's skill and resourcefulness. But the tug with the casualty in tow, and an escorting destroyer close by, were forced to heave -to as conditions deteriorated still further, about sixty miles from Falmouth. The following day, as the storm raged on, the tow line broke and the vessels drifted apart. In the teeth of a force eight gale, it was decided that they would try and hook her anchor. She was lying flat on her port side with her bow lifting from the water and her smoke stack almost awash. Just as she was about to make her final plunge, Ken Dancy leapt from the top of the stack, and started swimming towards the tug, and Captain Carlsen, taking a final glance at his sinking ship, jumped for his life. The skipper brought the *Turmoil* in as close as he dared, swung her stern into the swell and lowered the Jacob's ladder, which the men reached after about nine minutes in the water.

The tug returned to Falmouth on the evening of January 10th, after ploughing her way through the continuing storm. Crowds braved the rain to see her arrival, hoping to catch a glimpse of the already legendary heroes. However, they stayed on board that night, bracing themselves to step ashore and face a heroes' welcome amidst a blaze of publicity the following day. This colourful sequence of events, still remembered with relish by many, was commemorated in Holland by the building of a lifeboat in 1975, aptly named the *Curt Carlsen*. And what was the nature of the cargo which compelled the Captain to remain with his ship until the last possible moment? Components for a nuclear submarine.

Falmouth's Coxswains and Outstanding Services

Bertram West, who joined the Falmouth crew in 1948 and took command in 1961, was coxswain when the lifeboat performed a difficult service on December 13th of that year, saving the crew of fourteen from the steam tanker *Allegrity*, in distress off Greeb Point. He was also involved in a particularly harrowing service following the *Darlwyne* disaster of 1966, when thirty-one people lost their lives off the Dodman while out on a pleasure trip. The next year brought him, Assistant Mechanic R.F. Twydale and Shore Signalman C.J. Barnicoat framed letters of thanks, for rendering assistance to the French trawler *Martine Jean Paul*, aground on Trefusis Point in a westerly gale with short, choppy seas. During this year evaluation trials were carried out at Falmouth with the fast rescue/boarding boat 18-01, of the Hatch type. So 1967, which also saw their Centenary award, was quite an auspicious year for Falmouth.

Wally Brown had taken over as coxswain in August 1972, when the lifeboat *The Princess Royal* (Civil Service No.7) went to the aid of the Swedish schooner *Mina* which, with damaged rudder and anchor cable parted, was drifting onto a lee shore under Dodman Point in gale force winds and rough seas. The crew of ten was saved, while skipper Per Engwall has subsequently made a point of entertaining his rescuers aboard his vessel whenever he passes this way. The Institution voted a Bronze Medal to Coxswain Brown in recognition of his courage, determination and seamanship.

Arthur 'Toby' West, who became Coxswain in 1975, was awarded the Bronze Medal for gallantry, skill and determination displayed when the jack-up barge *Mer D'Iroise* in tow of a tug was in distress off the Lizard on 28th November 1977. Although the deck of the huge barge was under water and moving violently in the north-easterly gale and heavy seas, Coxswain West successfully held the lifeboat alongside while the six stranded men were taken off. Two years later came recognition for the Falmouth crew's part in the Fastnet Race services, when numerous yachts got into difficulties. 1980 created a precedent here in that the McLachlan lifeboat A508, which had been used as a boarding boat, was redesignated as a lifeboat for service during the

The Crawford and Constance Conybeare *with her flag at half-mast, having picked up some bodies after the Darlwyne disaster off the Dodman in August 1966 (Acknowledgements RNLI)*

summer and winter. This led to the distinctive situation of Falmouth being the only place in Cornwall to have an Arun Class lifeboat and an Atlantic 21 on station.

Vivian Pentecost was coxswain in 1985, when the lifeboat *Elizabeth Ann* went to the aid of the French trawler *St. Simeon* which was sinking thirteen miles south of the Lizard, during a violent storm with very rough seas and snow and rain squalls on February 15th. The Institution awarded him their Thanks on Vellum for his skill and leadership. Two years later a Chairman's letter of appreciation went to Mr. John Pentecost for his assistance to the Falmouth McLachlan lifeboat, after he had rescued four people from the sea in his working boat after their dinghy had capsized, and transferred them to the lifeboat to be taken ashore to waiting ambulances.

Falmouth Coxswains have been paid prestigious compliments from time to time, including private visits by royalty. And no doubt it will be a very long time before Dr. Robert Runcie, former Archbishop of Canterbury and Vice President of the RNLI forgets his uplifting experience between the Falmouth lifeboat and a Wessex helicopter from RNAS Culdrose, from which he emerged safely to declare it 'a wonderful experience.'

John Barton was appointed coxswain in September 1989, when Vivian Pentecost retired.

Wessex Mk. 5 of 771 S.A.R. Squadron lowers the Archbishop of Canterbury on to the Falmouth lifeboat. All of 771 Squadron's Wessex 5 helicopters have been replaced with Sea King War Mk. 5's (© Crown copyright 1991/MOD reproduced with the permission of the Controller of HMSO)

CADGWITH LIFEBOAT STATION
(1868-1963)

Cadgwith is a tiny fishing village some distance from the Lizard. There is a bench against the white walls of the cottages right in the centre of the village , from which the whole of the bay can be seen, and from which the boat is watched that is perpetually on the look our for signs of pilchards. On this bench the fishermen sit in patience and wait for the harvest, they scarcely turn their eyes from the sea.

(The West Briton: 1885)

A Tradition of Fearless First Class Seamanship

The sturdy, seafaring community at Cadgwith, whimsically described as 'a romantic fishing village' in a guidebook of 1865, has long enjoyed a well earned reputation for fearless, first class seamanship, with a strong tradition of sons following fathers, not only into fishing, but every branch of maritime service. Mellowed fishermen and ex-lifeboatmen still occupy the famous bench today — capable of accommodating about twenty, and known to one and all as 'the stick'.

This seaboard has always been notorious shipwreck territory, and back in 1859, following the tragedy of the *Czar*, Polpeor Cove had been chosen as the place to site a lifeboat for the Lizard (*see* The Lizard). The Institution awarded a Silver Medal to Mr. John Ridge for his part in the rescue by shore boats in saving eighteen of the thirty-one men. However, experience was to demonstrate that it was not viable to transport this lifeboat overland, hampered as they were in this remote area, with narrow lanes, farm gates, hedges and other impediments.Clearly, back-up was required on each side of the Lizard peninsula, and if anyone had any doubts, these would have been dispelled by the triple tragedy off Mullion in January 1867, when the lifeboat arrived too late (*see* Mullion). So stations at Mullion and Cadgwith, which had a wealth of potential lifeboat talent, and which was already supplying crewmen for the Lizard lifeboat, were established in September of that year. A boathouse was constructed, and the ten oared *Western Commercial Traveller*, built by Woolfe of Shadwell arrived, having derived her name from those who financed her. But she was to have her name changed to *Joseph Armstrong* in 1878. A mercury barometer , made by Messrs. Negretti & Zambra, which was also sent here at that time, is now on display inside, along with other lifeboat memorabilia. For in the days before national weather forecasting, each station was responsible for ascertaining the likely pattern of the weather; decisions which could have far reaching implications for any seafaring community. As an aid to this, it has been Institution policy since 1861 to provide barometers and manuals for each station, and to appoint someone to record daily readings and keep charts up to date, for the payment of a penny a day. It cost the Institution £6 to equip each station with a high quality barometer, which represented a considerable outlay at that time.

The *Western Commercial Traveller* soon proved her worth, and local fishermen had reason to be thankful for her protectiveness, which on two occasions meant obligingly securing their seine nets, and thus their livelihoods. Captains of brigs, barques and steamships were similarly indebted to her for assistance and standby services, sometimes carried out in conjunction with the Lizard lifeboat and tugs, and saving ships as well as those who sailed in them. This being the case, it seems a particularly cruel quirk of fate that Cadgwith's dedicated first coxswain, Edwin Rutter, who had preserved so many lives from shipwreck, was claimed by the sea when his fishing boat capsized in 1891.

In February 1869, the experience of the cable-laying ship *Calcutta* of London had been an epic one before the lifeboat came on the scene. During a nocturnal gale 150 miles south-west of the Lizard, the *Calcutta* had discerned a dim light ahead, and had slackened her speed to pass to the stern of the vessel. But, in stormy conditions, she misjudged her progress and sliced the brig *Emma* of Memel amidships. Four crewmen were hastily hauled aboard, but others were lost as their ship went down. Unfortunately, distress signals displayed by the disfigured survivor of the encounter drew no response from passing shipping. Some of the ship's boats were successfully launched, but the captain and several others were killed as one was being lowered, which left just eight exhausted men aboard when the Cadgwith lifeboat approached, and faced the daunting task of coming in close to the casualty which was oozing cable and hazardous debris in heaving seas. And, having accomplished this clever feat of seamanship, she and the Lizard lifeboat, which had been standing by, had to make for Falmouth, as weather conditions made it impossible for them to return to their own stations. Of those who had taken to the boats, some were safely picked up by a Greek brig and a French schooner, and landed at Falmouth; some made landfall at Eastern Green, Penzance, but others lost their lives in a capsize off Mullion. There was keen competition for the prize ship *Calcutta*, which was towed to Plymouth by HMS *Terrible*. Small monetary awards were made to both lifeboat crews and to the RNLI.

Important Services on a Busy Shipping Route
In view of its situation on the principal shipping highway up and down the English Channel, it is hardly surprising that services involved prestigious shipping, including early steamships and liners. All sections of the local seafaring community turned out to assist in September 1879, when the *S.S. Brest* of Glasgow fell victim to fog, with the Cadgwith lifeboat being acknowledged as saving forty lives in two trips. Four years later accomplished lifeboatmen played a significant part in saving the Glasgow steamer *City of Venice;* a service recalled inside the boathouse today, including a photograph of binoculars awarded to Coxswain Edwin Rutter. September of that year saw this fine old lifeboat performing her last service, and saving twenty-one lives from the *S.S. Suffolk* of London (*see* The Lizard).

Cadgwith's second lifeboat, rowed by twelve oars, and requiring an extended boathouse, arrived in 1887, and took over the name of *Joseph Armstrong.* Her first service, in March 1893, was in conjunction with the Lizard lifeboat, which had been alerted to the plight of the *S.S. Gustav Bitter* of Newcastle, which had struck the Callidges Rocks in thick fog, by the lighthouse keepers. Three of four men found clinging to the rigging, fit enough to get aboard by line, were taken ashore, and the Lizard lifeboat returned to the scene. The *Joseph Armstrong* picked up those who had taken to the ship's boat, which was experiencing difficulties in the Race, off the Lizard. These included Captain David Ball, who had inadvertently left his ship by being washed overboard, then been recovered by the ship's boat. He was concerned about the fourth man, incapacitated by arthritis, still lashed to the rigging, and insisted on getting aboard the stricken ship with lines to secure his release. This fine feat of heroism, involving him swimming back to the lifeboat through treacherous waters without any safety equipment, earned him a Silver Medal of the RNLI.

The *Joseph Armstrong* was replaced by a yet bigger lifeboat in May, 1898. constructed by the Thames Iron Works at Blackwall, taking the engaging name of the *Minnie Moon* from the donor's wife. She was to reinforce the fine traditions of seamanship and dedicated service established at Cadgwith, saving a total of 282 lives. Twenty five of these occurred in August 1906, in three trips out to the fully-rigged *Socoa* of Bayonne, which had struck the Craggan Rock in poor visibility, after a navigational miscalculation. Although considered a write-off, she was towed to Falmouth a few weeks later, after her weighty cargo of cement had been jettisoned, to undergo repairs. The lifeboat's next service was to stand by the *S.S. Highland Fling* of London, which had struck rocks in thick fog shortly after calling at Falmouth for repairs. As her bow section was stranded and her aft section was watertight and floating several days later, the salvage company decided to remove this latter section and tow it to Falmouth. So *Minnie Moon* was employed to escort half a ship back to the place she had so recently left in a wholesome state.

An Epic, Record-Breaking Service

This salvage experience was to come in useful two months later, when the homeward bound White Star liner *Suevic* of Liverpool struck the Clidges Rock off the Lizard in dense fog, giving rise to an epic, record breaking service, also involving lifeboats from the Lizard, Coverack, Porthleven and Falmouth tugs (*see* the Lizard). Cadgwith is credited as having recovered the largest number of people – two hundred and twenty-seven in successive trips. Silver Medals acknowledged key roles played in this rescue, and a notice inside the boathouse tells us: 'this R.N.L.I .Silver Medal was awarded to the Coxswain Edward Rutter for the part he played when the Cadgwith lifeboat rescued 227 survivors from the wreck of the *Suevic* in 1907. Edward Rutter was the son of Edwin Rutter, the first Cadgwith Coxswain.' This was the last voyage of Captain Thomas Jones, after thirty-nine years at sea; seventeen of them in command of a ship. The Court of Inquiry concluded that: 'The vessel was not navigated with proper seamanlike care after 10 p.m. on March 17 last.' As for the vessel, her bows were removed, and the stern section was towed off to Southampton, where she was renovated, and the pride of the White Star Line's Australian fleet remained afloat for many more years. After serving as a troopship in the First World War, she was bought by a Norwegian and converted into a whaling factory ship. Then in 1942, when it was feared she might fall into enemy hands, she met with the arguably more honourable fate of being scuttled by her crew.

After the wrecking of the White Star Suevic *on the Maenheere Reef on 17th March 1907, from which a record-breaking 456 lives were saved by four Cornish lifeboats, local people were paid salvage money to retrieve wool and leather from the water (Sheila Bird Collection)*

A Time of Contrasts

There was thick fog and a calm sea when the splendid, fully rigged barque the *Cromdale* of Aberdeen was wrecked at Beast Point in May 1913, and the surprised crew hastily took to their boats, fearing that she might capsize. On this occasion the Cadgwith lifeboat rescued twenty people, while those who had gone aboard in an attempt to salvage some possessions, were thankful that the Lizard lifeboat was standing by when water covered the decks, and they had been obliged to make for the rigging. During the First World War, the *Minnie Moon,* and later motor fishing boats under the RNLI War Emergency Rescue Scheme of 1918, saved lives and assisted casualties of war. After the war there was a lengthy lull, and on her last service in March 1932, the veteran lifeboat saved six trawlermen from the wrecked *Omer Denise* of Ostend, who were in peril after taking to the ship's boat.

The Dunkirk Connection

In 1932 the *Minnie Moon* was replaced by the *Herbert Sturmy,* a pulling and sailing type, previously on station at Swanage and Falmouth. Cadgwith had been in line for a new motor lifeboat, but the loss of the St. Ives boat in 1939 and the outbreak of war, when boatbuilders were obliged to turn their attentions to the War Effort resulted in the proposed Cadgwith boat being sent to St. Ives. Their boat, now scheduled to come here was requisitioned for

The Guide of Dunkirk *served at Cadgwith from May 1941 until the station closed in May 1963. This lifeboat, built in 1940 and originally destined for St. Ives, was requisitioned for the evacuation of Dunkirk. She was financed by the Girl Guides Association and named during a ceremony in 1947 (Sheila Bird Collection)*

the evacuation of Dunkirk, and arrived here in May 1941. As she was financed by a gift of £5,000 by the Girl Guides of the Empire, it was agreed that she would be appropriately known as the *Guide of Dunkirk*. Fifty years later her war service was recalled when she sailed across the Channel as one of the Little Ships of Dunkirk. During her wartime period here, she was called out on three occasions, to search for missing R.A.F. aircraft and an unknown vessel in distress. In January 1952, she and the Lizard lifeboat launched when the *S.S. Flying Enterprise* of New York was in difficulties, but neither was required to perform a service in the subsequently headline hitting sequence of events (see Falmouth). She assisted holidaymakers in trouble and saved seventeen from the *M.V. City of Ghent*, of Dublin, before being sold out of service to John Moore of Mevagissey, whose family had crewed the Cadgwith lifeboats.

Amalgamation with the Lizard Station

It was a tremendous blow to this proud seafaring community, which had always provided crewmen for the Lizard station, when their own station was closed down in 1963, and amalgamated with that at Kilcobben, which had opened two years previously (*see* The Lizard). But there was some consolation in having an Inshore Rescue Boat inside their boathouse for a while, and in having Cadgwith's name incorporated in that of the new station for a while longer. Today the noble history of Cadgwith's lifeboat is recalled inside the boathouse, with an interesting display and reminders of those who served in them.

PORTHOUSTOCK
LIFEBOAT STATION
(1869 —1945)

The winter gales shriek over Black Head, and the vivid fury around the Manacles is as the face of death.

(A.G. Folliott Stokes: *The Cornish Coast & Moors*)

The Dreaded Manacles
Many a hardy mariner has looked into that face of death, for of all the navigational hazards to be encountered around the coast of Cornwall, these sinister rocks must have claimed the biggest toll of shipping, ironically so close to the welcoming portals of a safe haven (*see* Falmouth). In the days of sail, vessels leaving Falmouth with easterly winds and ebb tides were particularly vulnerable, but proposals in 1825 to construct a lighthouse on the Manacles, and renewed from time to time, fell on stony ground. However, the erection of St. Anthony lighthouse did improve the situation, and a bigger buoy was emplaced on the eastern side of the Manacles.

At Peace in Fiddler's Green (the Sailors' Heaven)
At any season of the year, strong winds whistle and howl around the handsome church of St. Keverne, whose steeple tower has been a navigational aid to mariners for centuries, and whose brooding, atmospheric churchyard in this poignant maritime setting provided a last resting place for scores of shipwrecked victims. Among them were those aboard the transport *Dispatch*, which struck Lowland Point with the loss of 120 lives on January 22nd 1809, and the brig of war *Primrose*, which became a casualty of the Manacles the same night, with the loss of 125 lives.

Locally Organised Rescues
Local fishermen, coastguards and others went to the aid of distressed ships in their own boats, often risking their own lives in trying to save others. In 1828 Porthoustock men saved the five crewmen from the schooner *Auspicious*, wrecked on the Manacles, and nine years later four lives were saved from the schooner *St. Ives* by the smack *Mary Ann* and local boatmen. On the

occasion of another major disaster, on May 3rd 1855, when the emigrant ship *John* struck the Manacles and drifted towards Lowland Point, the future lifeboat coxswain James Hill was among the fishermen who put to sea to help save ninety-one of the 286 on board. (There is a memorial to him inside St. Keverne church.) At the Inquest he stated:

I went out to Porthoustock half dressed and got two boats out; finding we could not clear the point we returned. Three of us went out again and met the other boat returning, and we were told it was impossible to reach the wreck. About an hour later we launched the boats again and succeeded in getting to the ship. We picked up one man from a boat, and a woman and nine men from a raft, and landed them at Tom's Cove, where they were helped up the cliffs by neighbours. We made three other trips to the *John*, and saved fifty lives. Our crew were myself, my son James, William Matthews, Thomas Pearce, Henry Tripconey and James Conner.

Coastguard Thomas Clear of Coverack reported:

We arrived at Porthoustock about 12.30 a.m., and joined the fishermen there. We launched three boats, but the boat I was in was overmanned, and the sea so rough we were obliged to put back. We tried again with fewer men with no better result. An hour later with Coastguards......a fisherman of Porthoustock and myself, we made three trips to the wreck and saved thirty-five lives.

The Situation of the Boathouse

In view of the recurring tragedies, it is surprising that a lifeboat station was not established in this little fishing cove, adjacent to the Manacles, until 1869, when the disaster of *H.M.S. Despite* again focussed attention on the local dangers. When the boathouse was constructed at the head of the creek, the sea was not too distant, and launching over the beach was relatively easy. But waste material from the adjacent quarries, which washed back into the cove, caused the floor of the inlet to build up and increased the distance to the now sharply shelving water's edge and imperilled launching, particularly when the wind was in the east. This situation also had an adverse effect on the fishing industry and hastened its decline as an anchorage.

Porthoustock's First Lifeboat

The Station's first lifeboat, the *Mary Ann Story*, thirty-three feet long and rowed by ten oars, arrived that September and was put stylishly through her paces after having been displayed through the streets of Helston with her crew decked out in their lifeboat gear. Her first service was in January 1872, when she saved five lives from the barque *Cabinet* of Newcastle, and the following year she escorted the Danish brig *Alexander* away from the danger of the Manacles, thereby preventing loss of life and shipwreck, demonstrating the practical advantages of a lifeboat station in close juxtaposition to the navigational hazard. An intimate knowledge of home waters and expert seamanship also paid off, in saving twenty-three lives from the *Ceres* of Greenock and five from the schooner *Georgiana* of Liverpool in 1877 and 1881. Her last service was in April 1884, when she helped the shipwrecked crewmen of the *S.S. Lady Dalhousie* of Greenock to help themselves in salvaging possessions and stores before their vessel slid beneath the waves, after an encounter with the reef. She was replaced in 1886 by the larger lifeboat *Charlotte,* constructed by Forrestt of Limehouse.

Porthoustock's second lifeboat, the Charlotte, *which was on station 1886-1900 (Acknowledgements Frank Curnow; Sheila Bird Collection)*

The Great Blizzard of March 1891
James Henry Treloar Cliff, who succeeded James Hill as coxswain in 1907, after serving as second coxswain for thirteen years, was an expert swimmer and instrumental in saving many lives. As the Great Blizzard of March 1891 was just beginning to make itself known, James Cliff noticed a distressed small smack, which turned out to be the *Dove,* making a run for the beach at Porthoustock, and ran to assist. Then, backed up by helpers on the shore, he coiled a rope around his waist and waded through the boiling surf to rescue

two men and a boy, who were then looked after at his and a neighbouring cottage.

The inhabitants of nearby Rosenithon alerted the lifeboat crew to two vessels anchored to the north of the cove, which turned out to be the ketch *Edwin* and the dandy (sloop with a special rig) *Aquilla* of Guernsey, but it was unable to launch in such tremendous seas. Coverack rocket brigade was summoned, and James Cliff again roped himself up and was lowered down the cliff abreast of the vessels. But they were forced to witness the sad spectacle of the two little ships and their doomed crews being battered and claimed by the cruel seas. Things went from bad to worse as the blizzard raged on, with the disastrous wreck of the four-masted fully-rigged *Bay of Panama* on Nare Head, to the north of Porthallow. Once again, James Cliff, accompanied by two others, headed off over the cliffs with ropes and grapnels to see what they could do, and the rocket apparatus was summoned from Coverack. From the adjacent clifftop they saw the once grand, now pitiful ship in disarray, with angry waves washing over her, and they clambered down the cliff to join the Porthallow men who were trying to get a line aboard to the few remaining survivors. For many had either been carried away with the after mast or frozen to death in the rigging, as had been the fate of the Captain and his wife. Those who had survived thus far had been off duty, below deck, and were hauled ashore by the line fired by rocket apparatus and subsequently taken to Falmouth. Communications had gone awry in these outlandish conditions, and a well known tale of heroism tells of the butcher's boy who fought his epic way through the snow to Falmouth in order to alert the authorities to the disaster. Being a lifeboatman was never easy; questions were asked as to why no lifeboat was launched on these occasions, and the crew's stated ignorance of an emergency and their reservations about launching gave rise to the possibility of emplacing a smaller lifeboat here, requiring fewer men to crew her. But in the event, the *Charlotte* went away and returned with two drop keels.

The Mohegan Disaster

Seven were saved from the ship's boat of the brig *Dryad* of Whitehaven, and twenty-eight from the *Andola* of Liverpool, and there were standby services with a barque and a steamship before the major disaster of the *S.S. Mohegan* of Hull occurred in October 1898. This modern and luxurious ship, which was felt to be unlucky from the start, was described by one of her captains as 'a whore by name and a whore by nature' (in a conversation with Hartley Peters of Helford Passage). Constructed for the Wilson, Furness, Leyland Line by Earle's Shipping Company of Hull as the *Cleopatra*, she was sold to the Atlantic Transport Company of London before launching, and her first trip across the Atlantic was beset with problems. Overhauled and renamed the *Mohegan*, she left Tilbury for her second crossing on October 13th 1898

Few lifeboats sold out of service have been put to such practical and picturesque use as the one sent to Porthoustock on reserve. For this lifeboat, upturned, became a dwelling on the foreshore, in use for many years (Acknowledgements Frank Curnow; Sheila Bird Collection)

under the command of Captain Griffiths, with fifty-three passengers, ninety-seven crew, seven cattlemen and a general cargo. On their way down the Channel elegantly attired passengers were settling down to dinner or preparing for sophisticated shipboard socialising as their vessel inexplicably set on the wrong course struck the outer Manacles. Incongruously, and in quick succession, the metal plates of the engine room lifted, water rushed in, the lights went out and the ship went down, to the accompaniment of the anguished screams of humanity.

James Hill, the coxswain of the lifeboat, who had noticed the lights of a large vessel on a danger course close to the shore, summoned his crew, and the lifeboat was underway in less than half an hour, in moderate conditions. Not surprisingly, there was no response to their white light, and the casualty was difficult to locate at first. Assistant Coxswain James Cliff, who had been up at St. Keverne, was told of the disaster and requested to take out a back up crew in the old lifeboat. But as this was battered and ill-equipped, he opted for the best boat on the beach, and with a volunteer crew of four, headed in the direction from which the cries of distress had been heard.

Coxswain Hill and his men aboard the *Charlotte* came across an upturned boat, with two men hanging on to her. Then they heard cries coming from underneath, and after righting the boat with much difficulty, they found two women and a child. More cries alerted them to a battered ship's boat with twenty-four people, and almost filled with water. The lifeboat took the survivors ashore where they were looked after by local cottagers. The second coxswain's boat had located the wreck on the Maen Varses rocks, and James Cliff had signalled reassurance to the survivors by setting fire to his necktie and shouting that they were returning for reinforcements as their boat was undermanned. Fortunately their return to shore coincided with that of the lifeboat, which meant that James Cliff could transfer to the *Charlotte* and direct her to the wreck. As he recalled later: 'When we arrived back at the wreck they saw us, as we again burned a light and they all shouted. But it was a very difficult matter approaching her as on her starboard side were the Maen Varses rocks and a heavy sea breaking over them, and on the other side, when we tried to get near, the boats's derricks were sticking out of the water, also the awning poles. We were a long time manoeuvring to drop the anchor in the right position.'

Quartermaster John W.H. Juddery, one of the heroes of the rescue, who had assisted the passengers before the ship sank, eventually joined others in the mizzen rigging, and when the lifeboat arrived, he swam out to establish a line by which they were saved. Forty-four people survived this horrendous shipwreck, while one hundred and six, including the captain and most of his officers were lost. Contemporary newspapers chronicled a most harrowing sequence of events, leading up to a mass burial in St. Keverne's churchyard. Farmer James Pengilly, local agent of the Shipwrecked Mariners' Society, was instrumental in organising relief work for the survivors, and in recognition of this, the Society presented him with an inscribed aneroid barometer. The RNLI awarded Silver Medals to Coxswain James Hill and Quartermaster John Juddery for his gallant conduct. The bereaved King family of Cincinnati donated an inscribed memorial bell, which was incorporated in the peal of eight, inaugurated by Sir William Treloar, Lord Mayor of London, and cousin of Coxswain James Henry Treloar Cliff on 9th May, 1907. A memorial window was emplaced in the church and a granite cross inscribed *Mohegan* positioned near the north door.

Another Steamship with a distinctive Personality
In May the following year, the American liner *S.S. Paris*, bound from Cherbourg for New York carrying a general cargo, a crew of 370 and 386 passengers ran aground at Lowland Point, close to the site of the *Mohegan* disaster. Fortunately the sea was calm and, after a slight delay in locating her in thick fog, the lifeboat went alongside, allowing Second Coxswain James Cliff to climb aboard and advise on the situation. A tug was requested. The passengers, who were taken off by Porthoustock lifeboat transferred to the

tug *Triton* and looked after in Falmouth, realised what a lucky escape they had had, when the dispersing fog revealed that sobering wreck; her funnels and masts protruding above the surface of the water. At that time the *Paris* enjoyed the dubious distinction of being the largest ship to have stranded on our coasts. This ran true to form, for she had a flair for individuality. The *Paris*, which had begun life as the *City of Paris*, emerged from this predicament with the aid of fleet of tugs, and was towed to Falmouth for temporary repairs. After extensive renovations in Belfast, she was renamed the *Philadelphia*. In 1917 she became the United States armed transport *Harrisburgh*. After being sold to the New York Naples Steamship Company in 1925, she served briefly as an emigrant ship before being scrapped.

After the S.S. Paris of New York ran aground at Lowland Point, on 2nd. May, 1899, in thick weather, the Coverack rocket team got a line aboard and the Porthoustock and Falmouth lifeboats transferred the passengers to the tug Triton, *which took them to Falmouth. The liner was eventually refloated (Sheila Bird Collection)*

Coxswains and the Changing Scene

The lifeboat *Charlotte*, which had also experienced a colourful life, was replaced in 1900 by the *James Stevens No. 17*, but the heyday of the station had passed. John George had been the initial Coxswain in 1869, and James Hill took over nine years later, at the age of thirty-four. He, a tough lifeboatman of the old school retained the position of Coxswain until he reached seventy, which meant that James Henry Treloar Cliff, who had served as Second Coxswain for so long, was Coxswain for only three years. William Henry Tripp took his place in 1908, and was superseded by George Martin Tripconey in 1922, and Joseph William Tripconey in 1935. But by this time the decline of sail, the increase of steamships and the improving technology were playing their part in reducing the toll of the Manacles. The *James Stevens* performed standby duties in 1919, and saved the *S.S. Dolphin* of Manchester and eight lives, placing a crewman aboard and escorting her to safety. Later that year the twenty-year-old lifeboat *Queen Victoria*, constructed by Roberts of Mevagissey, arrived here, having formerly been based at Bembridge. Another secondhand lifeboat, the *Kate Walker*, which had served at Lytham, replaced her nine years later. A lifeboat constructed for Porthoustock in the yard of Groves & Gutteridge was destroyed in an air raid during the Second World War. However, times were changing, and the increased difficulty in getting the lifeboat across the greater distance to the water's edge, the shortage of men to crew her and the decreasing demand for her services, which could be covered by Falmouth's Watson Class motor lifeboat led to a temporary closure in 1942, and a permanent shut down in 1945.

PORT ISAAC LIFEBOAT STATION
(1869-1933: ILB Station 1967-)

The harbour is a comparatively busy one, but it requires a good deal more courage to be a fisherman on this harsh coast than it does at Polperro or Mousehole. Apart from Port Isaac there are few ports of refuge in a storm. The streets are so narrow that the natives have the greatest difficulty in hoisting their life-boat through them.

(S.P.B. Mais: *The Cornish Riviera*, 1929)

A Formidable Section of Coast
The fishermen of Polperro and Mousehole might take issue with this landsman's comparative assumption, but there is no denying the problems caused by the narrow streets. Indeed, it is difficult to believe that the lifeboat was manoeuvred between the overhanging houses without getting wedged; but battle scars on masonry along the way told a story of tight fits and determined squeezes, and came to be regarded as a source of historic pride.

Until the lifeboat station was established, the exceptionally tough breed of seafarer along this formidable section of coast was traditionally on the alert

353 A Tight Fit with the Lifeboat at Port Isaac

Negotiating the steep, narrow streets of Port Isaac with the heavy lifeboat was tantamount to achieving the near-impossible, but there were always plenty of willing hands (Sheila Bird Collection)

for emergency at sea, which occurred all too frequently. Rather unusual victims of shipwreck in May 1845 were young James Rounseval, newly rich from an inheritance, and his three friends who took a boat out to indulge in shooting seabirds, and got very drunk when they called in at Port Isaac. In merry mood for their homeward trip, they ignored local advice to take on a bag of sand as ballast, and demonstrated their bravado by taking on more beer instead. When the predictable happened, and their small boat capsized, Port Isaac men were ready in their gigs. Two of the revellers were saved, but the transient young heir, dragged down with pockets full of lead weight, and one of his friends were drowned. During the Great Gale of October 1859, 'almost unprecedented in its severity,' which created havoc with shipping all around the Cornish coast, Charles Mitchell, a local fisherman was awarded the Institution's Silver Medal for courageously putting off three times in fishing boats to rescue the crew of four from the sloop *Busy* of Newquay.

The First Lifeboat Joyfully Received
The Life-Boat reported in January 1870:

> Port Isaac, Cornwall. The third life-boat placed by the Institution within a few weeks on the coast of Cornwall has been forwarded to Port Isaac, the people in that locality having asked to be provided with a life- boat, which, it was thought, would probably be useful there, especially to the crews of fishing boats, which sometimes had to run for the port at great risk. There were also sufficient boatmen to act as the crew of the boat, and a Local Committee of resident gentlemen was readily formed to look after the station. The site for the boat-house was presented by Lord Robartes, who has ever been ready to help forward the life-boat cause in Cornwall. The boat sent was a thirty-two feet ten-oared one, with seven and a half feet beam and is provided with a transporting carriage.

There was great excitement when this lifeboat, the *Richard & Sarah* arrived, having been sent by rail to Bodmin Road Station (now Bodmin Parkway), and drawn the rest of the way by teams of eight horses, with an overnight stay in Wadebridge. A mile or so outside the little town at Trewetha, they were greeted by the RNLI Inspector Captain Ward, coastguards, local organisations and local dignitaries, backed up by military music and crowds in festive spirit, to set up the triumphal entry into Port Isaac. Then, as *The West Briton* reported,

> From Trewetha to Port Isaac the boat was preceded by the coast-guard of the district in full costume; the crew of the lifeboat in their 'canonicals'; the chairman of the Sunday school and the teachers; the Band of

Hope adherents, confident and cheerful; the members of the Foresters' Society, armed *cap-a-pie*, all walking two and two; and the Pengelly band, of course, giving time and impetus to the onward march. Some little difficulty was found in passing one corner of Port Isaac street, but the difficulty overcome, the boat was soon on the beach ready to be launched.

The crowds were thrilled to watch the new lifeboat and crew, made up of local boatmen from this isolated, tight knit little community, demonstrate their prowess, including the self-righting characteristic.

Lifeboats and Fishing of Premier Importance

The original boathouse in the main street was not ideally situated, and getting the lifeboat launched was a cumbersome business. Mounted on her carriage, she was guided and restrained by a team of helpers, who gritted their teeth and hoped that she would not run away with herself as she bumped her way down the steep slope to the harbour. Because things were so tight, anyone wishing to extend their house could only do so above lifeboat level, a situation giving rise to some novel innovations which now add extra character to the streets. In Port Isaac lifeboats and fishing were paramount, to the extent that a public health recommendation of 1894 that each house should provide its own closet or that public conveniences should be erected was resisted on the grounds that they were very strong and healthy, and that

Fishing and the lifeboat were of paramount importance in Port Isaac, and getting the lifeboat launched was a complex team accomplishment (Acknowledgements RNLI)

193

the proposed site interfered with their 'fish washing stream' and the launching of the lifeboat. In 1927, a new boathouse was established at the harbour slipway.

A Highly Creditable Record of Service

The first service of the Port Isaac lifeboat brought a Silver Second Service clasp to Charles Mitchell, for his gallantry in assisting with the rocket apparatus to save five from the brig *Stephano Grosso* of Genoa in October 1870. Ten years later this lifeboat capsized whilst on exercise, fortunately without loss of life. But the *Richard & Sarah*, sometimes taken on her carriage over steep terrain, achieved a highly creditable record of service with fishing boats, the barque *Ada Melmore* of Maryport, the schooner *British Queen* of Wexford and the *S.S. Indus* of Dundee, thereby saving fifty-seven lives. She was replaced by another lifeboat taking the name *Richard & Sarah* in 1887. She also rendered services to fishing vessels, a schooner, a barque and a steamship, and saved twenty-eight lives. Port Isaac's third lifeboat, which was the secondhand *Charles Witton*, became the third *Richard & Sarah* when she arrived here in 1905. She was replaced by another secondhand lifeboat, the *Ernest Dresden* in 1927, which remained here until the station closed in 1933. The station had been honoured by another Silver Medal back in 1895, when the Institution recognised the good service rendered by James Haynes over many years.

The Changing Situation and the Establishment of an Inshore Lifeboat Station (I.L.B.)

The station was obliged to close down towards the end of the First World War as a temporary measure, when so many of its able bodied men had been called up, and there were problems caused by the silting of the harbour. However, the changing social pattern brought increasing numbers of holidaymakers to the area, who found themselves in trouble along the shoreline and, on July 10th 1967, Port Isaac was established as an Inshore Lifeboat Station, with an Inshore Rescue Boat donated by Cullumpton (Devon) Rotary Club. Ten years later she was replaced by another, courtesy of the Cornwall & Isles of Scilly Round Tables.

In 1975 the station was awarded a Certificate of Merit by the R.S.P.C.A., for the assistance rendered by the inshore lifeboat after thirty bullocks plunged over a cliff at Port Quin. Two years later Thanks on Vellum were accorded to Helmsman Clive F. Martin in recognition of his skill and determination in taking the inshore lifeboat among submerged rocks through heavily breaking surf to rescue a badly injured man after a cliff fall at Jackets Point. Vellum service certificates were presented to the rest of the crew. In 1978 Thanks on Vellum went to Helmsman Mark J. Provis and crewman Edward J. Fletcher in recognition of their skill and determination when rescuing a boy trapped on a narrow ledge near the base of the cliffs at Bossiney. Edward Fletcher made a leap for the rock when the inshore lifeboat was close to the cliff, but lost his grip and fell backwards into the sea. The next wave lifted him ten feet to a ledge just below the boy and flung the inshore lifeboat against the rocks. Life is never dull around this station, and in 1991 lifeboatman Andy Walton stepped ashore after picking up a windsurfer in trouble, to crowds on the beach toasting his hundredth rescue in the inshore boat.

MEVAGISSEY LIFEBOAT STATION
(1869-1930)

Every road in Mevagissey leads to the sea, the harbour, and the town, where the life of the sea, the tang of the ocean, fish, and subdued romance and subtle strength awes and captivates one's soul. The picturesque is fully attained when the fishing fleet, at anchor, coming in or going out, sails spread, dot the beautiful double harbour in a riot of colour and shadow, and all their various appeal.

(The Cornish Guide: c. 1930)

Vulnerable to the Easterlies
Falmouth and Fowey were long established harbours of refuge on Cornwall's south coast, but the section between them presented hazards, particularly when the wind was in the east, and vessels were driven on shore before the storm. The Dodman collected casualties in all weathers, and the Gwineas or Gwinges Rock off Gorran Haven presented another hazard. The *Coasting Pylot* of 1693 refers to these as the Deadman and the Windhead Rock, which 'lieth three Miles from the Deadman, and a Mile from the nearest shore,' adding that 'small vessels that are well acquainted sail within this rock.' A bell buoy was emplaced here. Other aids to navigation include a beacon tower on Gribbin Head, harbour lights and a lighthouse on the Eddystone Rocks off Rame Head, whose flashing light across the waters still provides a reassuring sight in these parts.

'Fishy Gissey' — A Place of Some Importance
The volume of shipping was quite considerable in the last century, with vessels regularly plying up and down the English Channel, the local fishing fleets and the increasing number of ships carrying china clay in and out of the

ports of St. Austell Bay. In former times Mevagissey was a busy fishing port of some importance, with a brisk export trade. Pilots and preventive men were based here. As an aid to safety, the Board of Trade had supplied the port with a barometer in 1859. The local seafaring community made outstanding efforts to save the crew and cargo of the Russian brig *St. Nicholas* wrecked at Port Holland in December 1830, and it is particularly heartening to learn that 'two poor fishermen of Mevagissey' received fifty ducats each, together with others rewarded and thanked by the Emperor.

Stricken by Pestilence
Pestilence was another hazard at sea, which could be encountered by those going to the aid of shipping in distress, and Mevagissey was almost wiped out in the late 1840s, when cholera swept over Europe from Russia. This may or may not be associated with the stormy night of January 1846, when the brave pilots of Mevagissey boarded the schooner *Mary Pope* of Waterford, which was in a distressed state, displaying the yellow flag, her crew stricken with sickness and exhaustion. They were taken into Mevagissey where repairs were carried out on their battered vessel.

More Early Rescues
Pilots, coastguards and others rushed to the assistance of the French schooner *Rochellaise*, which was driven on shore to the west of the harbour in a south-easterly gale in June 1857. After abortive attempts to refloat her, the crew was taken off, but the captain refused to leave his ship until the situation was really crucial. With much difficulty, he was brought ashore by line and hauled up the cliff. The Institution recognised this brave service by awarding Silver Medals to Henry Pomeroy, Chief Boatman of the Coastguard, and pilots William Cloke and Joseph Lee. The RNLI also awarded a Silver Medal to Richard Johns, mate of the *Mystery*, in 1873, creating a total of four Silver Medals for the station.

Protection between Fowey and Falmouth
Lifeboat stations had been established at Polkerris, on the eastern side of St. Austell Bay in 1859 and at Falmouth in 1867. Having emplaced lifeboat stations at key points around the Cornish coast, the RNLI's attentions were drawn to places where casualties were occurring beyond the reasonable range of sailing and rowing lifeboats, which took some time to reach the scene, and offered no weather protection or facilities for lengthy services. So this was an obvious gap to be plugged. The *Life-Boat* of January 1870 reported:

> Mevagissey, Cornwall. This place has been chosen as one of the stations of the Institution, the local residents being of the opinion that

it was highly desirable to have a life boat establishment there, and giving their hearty co-operation in its formation. The boat sent is a sister one to that at Porthoustock, a transporting carriage and boathouse being also provided as usual. The boat is the gift of Sir Robert N.C. Hamilton, Bart., K.C.B., and his friends and others in South Warwickshire, and at the desire of the donors it has been named the *South Warwickshire*. The demonstration on the occasion of the launch was of a most pleasing character. It took place at Mevagissey on the 2nd October. The Honourable Mrs. Tremaine performed with much *éclat* the ceremony of naming the boat. In addition to the usual prayer given by the vicar of the parish, the Rev. H.A. Baumgartner, a harmonium has been brought to the beach, and an appropriate 'Hymn for those at Sea' was sung by the children of the national school. The Institution was again indebted to the kindness of the Directors of the Bristol and Exeter and South Devon Railway Companies for the free conveyance of this lifeboat from Bristol to the nearest railway point to its station.'

Lifeboat Initially Based at Port Mellon

Mevagissey's first lifeboat station was actually based at Port Mellon Cove, just to the south, where Roberts the shipbuilders were then based. They carried out some lifeboat construction in the 1890s, and occasionally visited the station to carry out repairs. The boathouse was built by W. Body at a cost of £141, on ground leased free of charge from the Earl of Mount Edgcumbe. *Murray's Thorough Guide* of 1895 mentions this lifeboat station and the large coastguard station above Gorran Haven. There was also a coastguard station on the Dodman and the Greeb and above Mevagissey, from which six of its most able men were drafted into the Royal Navy to serve in the Baltic Fleet in 1854.

On her first service launch, to the aid of the French brigantine *Girondin* in December 1869, the lifeboat was thrown back on the shore immediately, and was then relaunched with the utmost difficulty and rowed out into the teeth of a terrible gale. The lifeboatmen discovered six sailors desperately clinging to the rigging of their wrecked ship, and carried out a painstaking and dangerous operation, recovering the victims one by one as the lifeboat was flung about in the surf, disconcertingly close to the casualty. The *South Warwickshire* was beached at Par, her crew numbed and exhausted, and recovered the following day. It was said that the fishermen of Mevagissey took greater risks when manning the lifeboat than they would ever have dared to do in their daily lives on the sea.

Getting the Message

Communications were improving here, for as a place of some consequence, Mevagissey Post Office was included in the telegraph system in March 1871.

Mevagissey's first lifeboat, the South Warwickshire, *pictured at Port Mellon, to the south of Mevagissey, where the boathouse was then situated (Acknowledgements RNLI)*

After trials by local coastguards, the RNLI forwarded a cannon to the lifeboat station in March 1873, to alert the crew to night time emergencies at sea. The station was situated at Port Mellon, whereas most of the crew lived the other side of Polkirt Hill, at Mevagissey. Ten years later, the *South Warwickshire* answered a telegraphed request from Charlestown to go to the aid of the lugger *Bacchus* of Nantes, which had taken a battering in a violent gale while waiting for conditions to moderate before entering dock to load up with china clay. This was another example of a captain declining to leave his ship, thereby placing lifeboatmen's lives in jeopardy and, on this occasion, the Polkerris lifeboat had already been out to offer assistance. He and two crewmen were taken off by the Mevagissey lifeboat, which, unable to return to the home station on such a dark, foul, night, was lucky in making a blind, safe landing on the Porthpean shore with her cold, tired and hungry crew. Those who put their lives on the line for the sake of their fellow men usually bring out the best in others, but on this occasion the lifeboatmen, who needed assistance in getting their boat hauled up the beach met with unco-operative local people, including one who first wanted them to name their price and a coastguard reluctant to leave his nice warm bed on their behalf. So horses were summoned from St. Austell, and the rescued and rescuers went to Charlestown, where they enjoyed a warm and kindly reception.

Lifeboat Based in Mevagissey Harbour

A larger lifeboat, the *John Arthur*, built by Hansen of Cowes, which came on station in 1888, was kept afloat in Mevagissey harbour. She performed one service saving two lives from the sloop *Jessie* of Truro and escorting the vessel to the safety of the harbour. The arrival of the steam tug *Petrel* in 1895 made for greater efficiency in the fishing industry, in that she could tow the mackerel boats to and from the fishing grounds. Work started on the new boathouse and slipway in the outer harbour in 1896, and Mevagissey's third lifeboat, built by Rutherford of Birkenhead arrived the following year, taking the name *James Chisholm*. She was to be Mevagissey's last lifeboat, none of which was constructed here.

Most of the Mevagissey families had relatives aboard the lifeboat, which at one time had two Coxswains, a Bowman and enough men to muster three crews, and everyone turned out to watch their lifeboat zipping down the slipway. Recovery was by handwinch, operated by ten men. They were paid five shillings (25 pence) to take part in the regular practice launches, which to them was a considerable sum to swell the fluctuating family coffers.

During the period (1888-1896) that the lifeboat was kept afloat, a certain amount of damage had been sustained by wind and weather, but these troubles were not over when the boathouse was built in the supposedly sheltered outer harbour, for it was subject to batterings by storm, as in 1917 when the main doors were smashed by exceptionally heavy seas. The motor fishing boat *Margaret* operated here under the RNLI Emergency Scheme in the latter part of the First World War. The career of the *James Chisholm* mostly involved fishing vessels, but during this time she saved twenty-two lives in difficult circumstances from a small boat of the *S.S. Eastfield* of London, which had been torpedoed, with the U boat in question remaining uncomfortably close by. Another notable war service was carried out by the *Margaret*, when twenty-one lives were saved from the torpedoed *S.S. Butetown* of London.

After Fowey was provided with a motor lifeboat, able to cover a much wider range, the adjoining stations of Mevagissey and Looe were seen as being surplus to requirements, and so they were both closed in 1930.

PORTLOE LIFEBOAT STATION

(1870-1887)

Portloe is a little fishing village at the mouth of two narrow converging combes, and is well known for its lobsters. The cove is rock girt, and the Coastguard station, as at Gorran Haven, is about the only tidily kept domain.

(Thorough Guide: South Devon & South Cornwall, 1895)

Great Tradition of Maritime Service

In the days of sail, the sea regularly cast up wrecks upon the shores of Veryan Bay, with vessels driven helplessly before an easterly wind, or casualties which failed to round the Dodman. In addition to this, many fell victim to a hazard pinpointed in the seventeenth century *Coasting Pylot*: 'Between the Deadman and Falmouth, lieth a Rock above Water, called the Gull Rock.' As if to repay this toll of the sea, but more probably on account of grinding poverty, there was a strong tradition of local lads joining the Navy, and thus spending their days in foreign waters. Or perhaps they were emulating Peter Carder of Veryan, who was a crewmember aboard the *Elizabeth*, the last of Drake's fleet to accompany the *Golden Hind* when she rounded Cape Horn. This was a real life adventure in swashbuckling style, for the ship was wrecked on the mainland of South America, and the crew attacked by savages. Having managed to evade the cooking pot, this son of Veryan gave himself up to the Portuguese, sailed on slave ships, and eventually escaped and returned to Britain, where he was substantially rewarded by the Queen.

The seafaring theme is recalled by the attractive Homeyard almshouses, built for the widows of sailors by Mrs. Letitia Kemp Homeyard, a relative of Canon Kemp, in the style of Veryan's famous round houses in 1956. The church of St. Symphorian supports the missions to Seamen. Inside the church is a model of the *Olivebank*, presented in 1936 by the Rev. E.C. Alston, in memory of the men who lost their lives around these coasts. This ship, perhaps the most famous of the Bank Line, ended her days under the Finnish flag during the Second World War. Veryan's tranquil and beautiful church-yard is the last resting place for many seafarers over the centuries.

200

Life-Saving Endeavours

Back in December 1830, when a hurricane littered the Cornish coast with battered shipping, the French schooner *La Mayenne*, the Danish galliot *Catherine Margaretta* and the Russian brig *St. Nicholas* each carrying valuable cargo, were wrecked at the head of Veryan Bay, where no lifesaving facilities existed. With great heroism and initiative, five young fishermen boarded a boat which had washed towards the shore and saved seventeen men from the Russian and French vessels. The crew of the Danish vessel also managed to get ashore, and the three ships broke up in a remarkably short time. Those who flocked to the scene the following day, intent on gaining the spoils of shipwreck, may have ignored the entreaties of magistrates and other officials, but they took the hint after the revenue cutter *Adder* let fly with warning shots above their heads.

Ill-Positioned for a Lifeboat Station?

In 1870, when the legacy of Jacob Gorfenkle allowed for a lifeboat commemorating his name to be emplaced on the Cornish coast, Portloe was chosen as the new site, much to the dismay of the seafaring folk of Portscatho, who considered Portloe to be ill-positioned for a lifeboat station. Hindsight shows they may have been right, for there were on-going problems in positioning a boathouse and launching in this tight situation, and in the event the station was closed in 1887 without a single service launch being performed. However, it did not follow that the closure of the station indicated a cessation of disasters, for casualties between St. Anthony and the Dodman included the *Carl Hirchenburg* and *Dundella* (1891), *H.M.S. Thrasher* and *H.M.S. Lynx* (1897), *Lady Wolseley* (1906), *Agnes* (1911), *Gustav* (1912), *Hera* , (1914) *Andromeda* (1915), *Burnside* and *U 113* (1920) and *Sambra* in 1926. But when motor lifeboats arrived at Falmouth and Fowey, the area between the stations could be adequately covered.

ST. AGNES, ISLES OF SCILLY LIFEBOAT STATION

(1890-1920)

I have known Scilly Pilots put to sea when, to a landsman, it seemed sheer madness. Nothing was to be seen but a mass of broken water, nothing to be heard save the screaming of the gulls and the boom of the surf breaking on the deadly ledges. Yet, slipping their buoy behind the shelter of some friendly reef, these brave men would go forth apparently into the very jaws of death, to assist some helpless ship in distress and guide her into a haven of safety.'

(Scilly and the Scillonians: J.G. Uren, 1907)

Well-Positioned for the Western Rocks

In 1890 a lifeboat station was established at St. Agnes, better positioned than St. Mary's to deal with the horrifying casualties of the Western Rocks, which occupy an area of about ten square miles, and was generally regarded as the most dangerous in the British Isles. This had been the scene of colossal shipwreck, particularly before the St. Agnes light was emplaced in 1680, which the *Coasting Pylot* had referred to, and which William Borlase had described, in 1756, as 'the greatest ornament on this Island'. Experience demonstrated a need for warning lights on the western extremity of these rocks and Bishop Rock, adjoined by other dangerous rocks and reefs was chosen as the site for a new lighthouse. But this protector of shipping, erected on one of the most difficult sites in the world, was to measure itself against the full force of the Atlantic storm. The first tower, of 1847, was of open construction to minimise wind and wave resistance, was destroyed before completion. The replacement tower of 1858 was subsequently strengthened and re-structured. Warning lights were emplaced on Round Island, to the north of Tresco in 1887, and Peninnis Head in its southerly situation on St. Mary's in 1911.

An Inspector from the Institution had visited St. Agnes shortly after the *Schiller* disaster in 1875, with a view to establishing a lifeboat station here, but local men had given him to understand that they preferred to use their gigs for rescue work. However, when the Inspector returned in April 1889 they were keen to have a lifeboat. So a boathouse and slipway were constructed at Priglis Bay, on a site provided by Mr. Dorrien Smith. The new ten-oared, self-righting lifeboat was christened the *James & Caroline* by Mrs. Dorrien Smith at the inaugural ceremony in August 1890, and Mr. Abram Hicks became the first coxswain. William G. Mortimer took over from him in 1901, and Osbert B. Hicks, St. Agnes' last coxswain replaced him in 1912.

Launching and recovering the lifeboat on St. Agnes, Isles of Scilly, always presented great difficulties (Acknowledgements RNLI)

A Most Distinguished Record of Service (*see also* St. Mary's)
The St. Agnes lifeboat performed a most distinguished record of service, often working with St. Mary's lifeboat and local craft, and going to the aid of smacks, schooners, luggers, barques and steamships in daunting circumstances. The Institution awarded its Silver Medal to Frederick C. Hicks in recognition of gallantry and seamanship displayed during the service to schooner *Thomas W. Lawson* on December 13th, 1907. The United States Government gave him a Gold Watch and awarded Gold Medals to the whole crew of the gig *Slipper* (*see* St. Mary's).

The original lifeboat had been replaced by the *Charles Deere James* in 1904, which was replaced by a Watson Class lifeboat taking the same name in 1909. The second *Charles Deere James* performed particularly fine services to the *Ardencraig*, saving fifteen lives, the *Thornliebank*, saving a ship's boat and twenty-five lives, and to the *S.S. Gothland* of Antwerp, when seventy-one people were rescued. This lifeboat also distinguished herself in the First World War, but the most memorable service followed an incident which achieved world-wide notoriety at the time; namely the torpedoing of seven neutral steamers, six Dutch and one Norwegian by a German submarine shortly after they had left Falmouth in company. The St. Agnes lifeboat, which arrived on the scene after being alerted by the keepers of the Bishop Rock Lighthouse, saved forty-seven lives and three ships' boats. Each crew-member was presented with a Medal by the League of Neutral Countries (Haarlam), which also made awards to other seamen taking part in the search.

Launching from St. Agnes had never been easy, despite the erection of a second boathouse and long slipway in 1902, and many subsequent alterations and repairs. This factor, the increasing difficulty in finding enough eligible crewmen among this small population, and the arrival of St. Mary's first motor lifeboat *Elsie* with its increased capabilities, led to the closure of the station at St. Agnes, which had saved 206 lives during thirty-four service launches in the short period of thirty years.

COVERACK LIFEBOAT STATION
(1901-1980)

Chynhalls Point is locally known as the Meres Point, because, years ago, a French ship and all of her crew, together with the Captain's wife and four children , were all lost without trace.
Coverack's old time fishermen reckon that when a gale is blowing and the moon is full, they have heard the French mother crying for her children.

(Austyn Pengilly: November 1982, aged 88)

Of Sea and Storm and Shipwreck
To the early tourist, Coverack was a remote and popular village noted for its bass, pollack and magnificent rocky scenery, 'An added fascination is the fact that you have the dreaded, though to the outward eye quite inoffensively mild, rocks of the Manacles practically at your door,' states a G.W.R. guide-book of 1929, demonstrating a failure to relate to a coastal environment in real terms; a situation all too familiar to today's lifeboatmen. The patronising text continues: 'And the natives will show you places on the cliffs where you may

sit and see the hulks of old wrecks fathoms deep under the crystal clear water.'

Countless tales of the sea and storm and shipwreck must have been recounted around these cottage firesides of a winter's evening, to become absorbed into the folklore of the Lizard. For Coverack is in shipwreck territory, with Black Head, Chynhalls Point, Lowland Point and the Manacles on its maritime doorstep. As January came round each year, thoughts must have returned to that fateful January in 1809, when the transport *Dispatch* drove ashore at Lowland Point and rapidly broke up in heavy seas. As local folk rushed around to organise a rescue, news came that another vessel, which turned out to be the transport *Primrose*, had been wrecked on the northern side of the Manacles. Despite the endeavours of local fishermen, which met with some success, around 200 people lost their lives. The emigrant barque *John* of Plymouth became another victim of the Manacles in 1855, ending up broadside on to the rocks at Lowland Point. When the weather moderated slightly, the Porthoustock lifeboat and the Coverack coastguard's longboat were able to reach her and rescue seventy people. But 193 were lost. The Coverack coastguards demonstrated their vigilance in October 1898, when they observed the *S.S. Mohegan* set on a disaster course for the Manacles, and fired a warning rocket. Although they fancied she altered course slightly, her fate was sealed. She struck and rapidly began to sink. The stranding of the *S.S. Paris*, albeit without tragic loss of life, occurred just a year later (*see* Porthoustock). This wreck is recalled in the naming of a local hotel.

To Cope with Casualties on the Grand Scale

Lifeboat stations had been established at Cadgwith and Porthoustock, but at that time, with increasingly large passenger steamers plying these waters, the navigational hazards seemed to be collecting casualties on the grand scale, somewhat out of proportion to the little sailing and rowing lifeboats. So back-up was needed. Consideration had previously been given to Coverack as the place to establish a lifeboat for the Manacles, but Porthoustock had been chosen instead. Now it was Coverack's turn to have a lifeboat station, with launching down a very long iron slipway off the rocks at Dolor Point, constructed at a total cost of £1,800. The 35 ft. *Constance Melanie*, rowed by ten oars, arrived in February 1901.

The new lifeboat's first service occurred a year later, when she and the Porthoustock lifeboat launched in response to the sound of distress rockets, to discover the former tea clipper *Glenbervie*, now with a cargo of spirits, stranded near Lowland Point. The Coverack lifeboat, the first on the scene, could not get in close, but succeeded in hauling the sixteen crewmen aboard through the sea by means of a rope. Some of the vessel's cargo was removed before she disintegrated a few days later.

In March 1907, the *Constance Melanie* played her part in the epic service of the *S.S. Suevic* of Liverpool, saving forty-four lives (*see* Cadgwith and The Lizard). Further prestige came with the service to the German barque *Pindos*, best told in the words of Austyn Pengilly, who was there at the time.

About 10.00 p.m., on Saturday 12th February 1912, we heard rockets signalling the launching of the Coverack lifeboat, *Constance Melanie*, of a ship in distress from our farm overlooking Coverack Bay. My father and I made haste across the cliff footpath, and we saw a four masted ship on the Meres Point, with a tug to the east of her that had tried to hold her against the gale force south-easterly wind. We found out that Mr. Billy May, the Lloyd's agent had gone with helpers, carrying a large acetylene powerful searchlight. This was a great help in the pitch darkness. The lifeboat crew got all of the wrecked men twenty-eight souls, to harbour safely at about 4.30 a.m. All of the lifeboat crew praised the usefulness of the light.

Meanwhile, Mrs. May had collected dry clothes and other things from the generous folk of Coverack, who always kept a store for such occasions. Mr. Eli Cultance, landlord of the Paris Hotel in Coverack, was also one of the lifeboat's crew, which was a rowing boat then. The twenty-eight Germans got off their wet clothes in the hotel's lounge, played the piano and sang German songs of praise for the good people of Coverack. Later on, my father, who was the Shipwrecked Mariners' representative, hired horse-drawn buses, and sent the German crew to the Sailors' Home in Falmouth, amid cheers from the large crowd of Coverack folk assembled there.

The *Pindos*, which had just left Falmouth, was being towed by the German tug *Ancona* when the emergency occurred, in a rising gale. And when the lifeboat arrived on the scene, two German sailors heroically leapt into the heaving waters to establish a lifeline. After four men were taken off, conditions were so bad that operations had to be suspended until daylight. It was placed on record that the provision of a powerful light, illuminating the scene, encouraged and reassured the victims and their would-be rescuers in this disconcerting situation. Having bided their time wisely, the remaining crewmen were saved. This fine service was acknowledged by the presentation of the RNLI's Silver Medal to Coxswain John Corin, who also received an inscribed gold watch from the Kaiser. The German Government sent a monetary award of £22. 10s. to the crew.

The Advantages of Falmouth's Close Proximity
This lifeboat's subsequent services reflected the increasing trend from sail to steam in its casualty list, and many potential headline-hitting situations were

Above: Coverack's first lifeboat, the Constanta Melanie, *was on station from 1901-1934 (Sheila Bird Collection)*

Below: The Coverack lifeboat performed an outstanding service in rescuing the crew of twenty-eight from the 4-masted German barque Pindos, *after she had gone ashore at Meres Point, near Coverack, in February 1912 (Sheila Bird Collection)*

207

averted by the lifeboat being there, offering advice, standing by, escorting and working in conjunction with other lifeboats and Falmouth tugs. Many a battered ship in this area was to experience the advantage of Falmouth's proximity as a harbour of refuge, offering facilities for ship repair. This included the collision casualties *S.S. Berville* and *S.S. Ugo Bassi* in September 1923 and the *S.S. Mansepool* and the *S.S. Horne* in October 1928; also strandings within a few minutes of each other in March 1932, with the *S.S. Ocklinge* at Lowland Point and the Belgian steam trawler *Omer Denise* at Perprean Cove, to the south of Coverack. The *Constance Melanie* launched on these occasions, and a repeat service to the *S.S. Ocklinge* turned out to be her last. Her sister ship, the *S.S. Lyminge* had been wrecked on Gurnard's Head in September 1931.

The Arrival of a Motor Lifeboat

The *Constance Melanie* was replaced in 1934 by the 35 ft.. Liverpool type motor lifeboat *The Three Sisters*, constructed at Cowes, and named in commemoration of sisters from the cultured, literary Couch family. The naming and dedication ceremony was quite a prestigious affair, with Sir Arthur Quiller Couch, the Bishop of Truro and the lifeboats of Falmouth and the Lizard in attendance. This lifeboat was geared to the type of emergencies which had been occurring in this area, particularly those involving steamships. The arrival of this lifeboat heralded a new era, with ongoing services to victims of leisure and pleasurecraft, many of whom had taken to the water with little or no knowledge of seamanship or local conditions. This was punctuated by wartime services, mostly in search of torpedo casualties or missing aircraft. A comparatively modern tavern yarn concerns the occasion in March 1941, that two German aeroplanes bombed the *S.S. Cieszyn* of Gdynia off Dolor Point, then machine-gunned the men as they took to the boats and their ship went down. The lifeboat succeeded in saving twenty-seven lives. Lifeboats were obliged to operate in darkness during those wartime years, and the light on the Manacles buoy, which had obviously been used as a 'fix' by enemy aircraft was also extinguished.

Spanish Recognition

There had been a lull in steamship casualties off Lowland Point, until just after the end of the war, in February 1946, when the *M. V. Fauvette* of London, with a cargo of empty shell cases, ran aground. The lifeboat stood by, but the crew of nineteen managed to get ashore as the tide receded and the vessel was towed clear by tugs. The lifeboat's next service proved to be a particularly notable one in November 1951, when the *S.S. Mina Cantiquin*, homeward bound for Spain with a cargo of pitch, struck rocks near Black Head in a south-westerly gale with lashing rain. Having sustained damage to her forward section, her crew fired distress signals as she was swept towards

The Coverack lifeboat launches into calm waters down the long slipway (Sheila Bird Collection)

Chynhalls Point. The lifeboat, which promptly launched, found waves breaking over the stricken ship, but succeeded in the difficult manoeuvre of getting close inshore and allowing the seventeen crewmen to jump as they made a run on the leeward side of the ship, which was bows-on to the shore. This was accomplished in the nick of time, for the casualty was drifting across Coverack Bay and, despite the lifeboatmen's attempts to get a man aboard or take the little steamer in tow, the inevitable happened, with Pedro, the ship's mascot, becoming a canine victim of shipwreck. Conditions were such that the lifeboat, unable to return to Coverack, made for Falmouth, where she was to remain for two days before it was prudent to return. The Spanish Lifeboat Society awarded Coxswain Rowe its Silver prize medal, with diplomas for him and his crew.

A Station Held in High Esteem

A ceremony of inauguration in September 1954, marked the arrival of Coverack's third lifeboat, the *William Taylor of Oldham*, which was constructed by William Osborne of Littlehampton. She was the first of her type, a 42 ft. Watson, and the first lifeboat to have commercial engines installed. The allocation of this splendid lifeboat, which had undergone rigorous testing around our coasts, was an indication of the high regard in which the Coverack station was held. Adaptions had to be made to the boathouse and slipway to accommodate her. A particularly memorable occasion on which she and her crew demonstrated their worth was in January 1956, when the stone-carrying, London-bound *M.V. Citrine* of Glasgow radioed that she was in difficulties three miles east of the Lizard in a strong north-westerly gale, with her hatches stove in. The Coverack and Lizard lifeboats promptly launched, and stood by, as requested by the Captain, who was attempting to beach the vessel. Things seemed to be going well until she struck the bottom and began to founder. Then the ship's lifeboat capsized as she was being launched, and several crewmen were flung into the water. The Coverack lifeboat rescued four of them, and the Lizard lifeboat picked up the other three. However, three frightened men remained aboard the sinking vessel, which was listing heavily towards them. Quick thinking Acting Coxswain Reginald Carey turned this situation to an advantage, by 'doing a Blogg.' In this extremely daring manoeuvre, the lifeboat went full speed ahead across the casualty's port quarter, then abruptly full speed astern, allowing the marooned men to grab the outer lifelines, and be hauled aboard. This brought the Coxswain a Bronze Medal of the RNLI, and the Maud Smith Award for the bravest life saving act of the year.

Sad Finales

The service of July 30th 1963 was a particularly poignant one, for it involved Coxswain William Archibald Rowe, who had helped to save so many lives, and his fishing boat *Bessy III*, which had struck a rock to the east of Coverack as he returned from piloting a stone-carrying vessel. He was able to swim to Lowland Point, and was given first aid by one of the lifeboat crew, and taken to hospital by helicopter, where he died. He had been an officer of the boat for thirty-two years, and Coxswain for nearly twenty-five.

The lifeboat was withdrawn in 1972, and a sixteen-foot inshore lifeboat was sent to the station. But in 1980 the station was closed down, as Falmouth, with its fast Arun and inshore lifeboat could now provide cover for the area.

ST. AGNES LIFEBOAT STATION

(1968 -)

St. Agnes is situated on the north coast, surrounded by several rich tin mines. It cannot be considered as a port, for, though a quay has been more than once erected for the accommodation of vessels, the violence of the sea has always soon demolished it; and the harbour is choked up with sand.

(Observations On the Western Coast of England: W.G. Maton, 1794-6)

Dangerous Waters

The grand and rugged coastline here seeks to defy the impetuosity of the Atlantic waves, but there can be few parts of Cornwall where the sea's destructive influence has been more graphically illustrated. Traditionally, the people of St. Agnes had depended more on the mineral wealth of their hinterland for their livelihood than fishing and the sea, and the harbours they sought to create were primarily concerned with the importation of coal for the mines and the export of tin. Nowadays this awesome area of shipwreck has become the haunt of holidaymakers, who take liberties in this coastal environment at their peril.

In 1967 a decision was made to establish a lifeboat station here, which materialised in 1968, with the cost of the ILB defrayed by the B.B.C. Blue Peter Appeal, and the lifeboat taking the name Blue Peter IV. She operated seasonally and was equipped with a V.H.F. radio telephone set.

On July 17th 1977 the lifeboat was skilfully manoeuvred through a very narrow, rocky channel in heavy surf to rescue an injured surf lifesaver in an award winning service, which brought a Silver Medal for gallantry to Helmsman Peter David Bliss and Thanks on Vellum to crewmembers Barry Garland and Roger Radcliffe. The crew also received the Ralph Glister award for the bravest inshore lifeboat rescue of 1977. In 1983 Helmsman Peter David Bliss was awarded a Certificate of Commendation from the Royal Humane Society for assisting in the rescue and resuscitation of a swimmer after he had waded out through the surf to help two lifeguards bring the swimmer ashore.

MARAZION
(1990 -   )

'Lifeboat weather', is no longer confined to gales and storms, and the lifeboatmen's service is in great demand even through the best of summer weather.

(The RNLI)

Back-up, Inshore Coverage of Mount's Bay
In April 1990 a temporary lifeboat station opened on St. Michael's Mount because of the increasing number of windsurfers and leisurecraft getting into difficulties during the summer season. The sixteen foot D Class inflatable, operating as an extension to the Penlee station included husbands and wives among its fourteen crewmembers, who mostly lived on the Mount, reported to be the first female and married crewmembers of a lifeboat in the West Country. After a successful trial summer season, in which they responded to sixteen calls, the station was set to become permanent, as a satellite to Penlee, with the appointment of an Honorary Secretary and a Deputy Launching Authority.

Opposite: The Oakley makes a splash! The James and Catherine Macfarlane, *constructed in Lymington in 1967, was initially allocated to the Padstow Station, served at The Lizard (Kilcobben) Station From July 1984-September 1987, and is now on display at the Land's End complex (Photograph T.P. Roskrow; Acknowledgements RNLI)*

THE LIFEBOAT

'Been out in the life-boat often?'
'Aye, aye, Sir, often enough.'
'When it's rougher than this?'
'Why, bless you, this ain't what we calls rough!
It's when there's a gale a-blowing,
And the white seas roll in and break
On the shore, with a roar like thunder,
And the tall cliffs seem to shake,
When the sea is a hell of waters,
And the bravest holds his breath,
As he hears the cry for the lifeboat
His summons may be to his death.
That's when we call it rough, Sir,
But if we can get her afloat
There's always enough brave fellows
Ready to man the boat.'

('Dagonet' The Life-Boat 1882)

A 771 Squadron Search and Rescue helicopter practises a tricky manoeuvre on Camel's Head (© Crown Copyright 1991/MOD reproduced with the permission of the Controller of HMSO)

RNAS CULDROSE TO THE RESCUE!

The deeds performed by SAR [Search and Rescue] flyers often demand quite extraordinary degrees of heroism and stamina. Like lifeboatmen, they are a special breed, driven by a flinty sense of duty, a readiness to serve others and a refreshing tendency to cut the cackle and get on with the job in hand.

(Drama In The Air, John Beattie)

West Cornwall has long played a vital role in national security and communication, and the 731 acre site at Culdrose, near Helston, acquired by the Admiralty in 1943 and commissioned as *H.M.S. Seahawk* in April 1947 has now become the largest helicopter base in Europe. It is the Navy's foremost training base for helicopter pilots, observers, aircrewmen and aircraft handlers as well as being the primary base for the Royal Navy's Anti-Submarine Sea King Squadrons. The functions of the Royal Naval Air Station at Culdrose have adapted to meet changing situations, and the Search and Rescue humanitarian operations involving the general public and sometimes animals in distress, evolved spontaneously to fulfil a need. For R.N.A.S. Culdrose, ideally positioned on the Lizard peninsula to deal with emergencies on land or sea, was increasingly called upon to render assistance, particularly to ships or sailors in distress in the South West Approaches and the English Channel, or to the escalating inshore incidents occurring in the 'Silly Season'. Between the early 1960s and the mid 1970s, rescues were carried out by Whirlwind and then Wessex helicopters but, as these were sometimes restricted by bad weather or short range capabilities, radar-fitted Sea King helicopters came to be used when they were available. These had a larger carrying capacity, a radius of action of 230 miles and the capability of operating at night in severe weather conditions.

These Naval helicopters, designed for other purposes, proved so versatile and effective in the Search and Rescue role, that it came to be felt that lives were needlessly being lost when helicopters were not available to respond to the call of civilians in distress. From 1975, after negotiation with the Department of Trade, R.N.A.S. Culdrose has provided continuous SAR cover as part of the U.K. S.A.R. organization. Today 771 Squadron, whose motto is 'Not for us alone', provides coverage for an area in excess of 200 nautical miles around the south-west peninsula, round the clock for 365 days a year, liaising closely with the Coastguard at Falmouth, the RNLI and the Rescue Coordination Centre at Plymouth. The Squadron is required to scramble within fifteen minutes by day and forty-five minutes by night, but in practice this is usually reduced to four minutes to take off by day and fifteen minutes by night, sometimes with a Naval doctor or medical assistant aboard. In such circumstances, the doctor can be winched down to the vessel to ascertain the medical situation, which might be to stretcher lift the case to be flown to Treliske Hospital in Truro, where there is a helicopter pad.

Some of the dramatic highlights include the incident of the *Ben Asdale*, on December 31st, 1978, in Force Ten blizzard conditions with nil visibility and technical troubles, when eight survivors were brought to Culdrose after achieving 'mission impossible', missions to the *Merc Enterprise* four years previously, the *M.V. Lovat* (*see* Penlee) in January 1975 and to the Greek vessel *Skopelos Sky* in 1979. This was the year when the disastrous Fastnet Race stretched the combined rescue services of the south-west to their limit, and brought recognition to lifeboat crews and further well deserved honours to Culdrose. This was their biggest Search and Rescue operation to date, with helicopters being airborne for 203 hours over three days, rescuing seventy-three people. March 1980 brought the fine mission of mercy to an injured crewman aboard the Liberian freighter *Penta* 165 miles south west of Penzance in sixty-five knot winds, and on the same day a Sea King launched on a similar mission to the Panamanian vessel *Grace V*. December 19th 1981 brought the heroic and harrowing service to the cargo vessel *Union Star* and the search in diabolical conditions for the ill-fated Penlee lifeboat crew, described by the courageous helicopter pilot Lt. Comndr. Russell Smith, USN, who was on attachment to the Royal Navy as being 'truly the bravest eight men I've ever seen who were also totally dedicated to upholding the highest standards of the RNLI.'

A classic rescue in March 1989 saw the combined rescue services in action after the wrecking of the Panamanian registered freighter *Secil Japan* (*see* St. Ives *and* Padstow) at the aptly named Hell's Mouth on the north coast, when Cornish lifeboats and two Sea King helicopters from Culdrose were joined by a third from RAF Brawdy. In stormy conditions and in pitch darkness, with waves breaking over the casualty and the three helicopters hovering perilously close to the cliffs, fifteen of the sixteen Korean crew were winched to safety (and then looked after at the 'Fishermen's Mission' in Newlyn). This courageous service was formally recognised by the presentation of the *Edward and Maisie Lewis* award by the *Shipwrecked Mariners' Society*. Lieutenant Darrell Nelson, who was on exchange from the US Coastguard, and who piloted 771's Sea Kings, was awarded the *Queen's Commendation for Valuable*

Services in the Air. Chief Aircrewman 'Smiler' Grinney, 771's most experienced diver was awarded the *Air Force Medal* for his part in the rescue as well as for his courage and professionalism in rescuing an injured Spanish seaman from a trawler in mountainous seas earlier that evening. In October of that year, one of the biggest rescues ever tasked to Naval Search and Rescue Air Squadrons brought George Medals to Petty Officer Crewmen Dave Wallace and Stephen 'Shiner' Wright for their part in the heroic rescue of forty people from the sinking Pakistani countainer ship *Murree*, in stormy conditions off Start Point (Devon). As the last survivor was being winched to the safety of a Sea King helicopter, the vessel began to slide beneath the waves, bows first, and the two rescuers leapt ninety feet into the raging seas and swam for their lives to avoid being sucked under by the casualty. A lifejacket given to the Squadron by the *Murree*'s First Officer bore the words he wrote upon it during the rescue: 'To the angels who come in the guise of men.' Laurels abound as these highly skilled courageous men coolly achieve the seemingly impossible, in a humanitarian service which makes increasing demands every year.

Note: There is an excellent section on Search and Rescue at Flambard's, Helston.

THE ROLE OF THE COASTGUARD

> When a wreck takes place on any part of the coast under the charge of
> the Coast Guard, every individual on the spot or within reasonable
> distance, is to use his utmost exertion to save the lives of the persons
> on board and also to take charge of the vessel and to protect such
> property as may be saved from embezzlement of any kind.
>
> *Coast Guard Instructions, 1829*

The Coastguard Service, initially set up to stamp out smuggling around our
shores has evolved to meet a variety of changing situations and continues to
do so today. Back in 1698, when smuggling activities were giving rise to
much lost Government revenue, armed Riding Officers were appointed to
patrol coastal and inland areas on horseback, as part of the Preventive
Service, working in conjunction with Customs and Excisemen and improvised patrols afloat. Despite strict laws and daunting punishments smuggling proliferated in the eighteenth and early nineteenth centuries, but after
the Napoleonic War the Government expanded its preventive measures to
include fast and efficient Revenue Cutters patrolling out at sea and Preventive Water Guards operating inshore, thus creating a formidable triple
catchment net to intercept the audacious 'free traders.' To maintain such an
ambitious scheme it was decided that the Preventive Water Guards should
come under the jurisdiction of the Treasury most of the Preventive cruisers
would become the responsibility of the Admiralty, while the Riding Officers,
who were to be disbanded in 1865, should be administered by the Board of
Customs.

The Preventive Water Guard, established in 1809 and regarded as the
forerunner of H.M. Coastguard, was well organised under Captain Han-
chett, RN, who selected the cream of the demobilised sailors to man the
service, and set high standards. Each station was supplied with a gig or rowing galley, and was manned by a Chief Officer, Chief Boatman and Boatmen,
trained in the use of firearms and subject to frequent inspections. Personnel
were required to make themselves familiar with the local terrain, to take part
in training sessions and combined exercises with the allied services, but not
to get too friendly with the community. Although their function was primar-

218

The nerve-centre of the Maritime Rescue Coordination Centre, Falmouth (Acknowledgements Falmouth School of Art and Design and MRCC, Falmouth)

ily to stifle smuggling, the situation of shipwreck inevitably presented itself on their patch from time to time and was part of their experience. Thus the saving of life from shipwreck became absorbed into their role. Each station was issued with Manby's Mortar Apparatus, which was capable of firing a lifeline to inshore casualties by rocket. Volunteer life-saving brigades also began to appear around these coasts.

After some years of triple administration with overlapping functions, a review published in 1821 led to certain sections of the Preventive Service being streamlined into the Preventive Water Guard, which was returned to the Board of Customs, albeit with the Admiralty retaining the right to appoint its officers. This new organisation, established on 15th January 1822, was to be known as the Coast Guard.

Coast Guard instructions of 1829 were concerned with discipline, good relations with kindred organisations and their responsibilities in regard to the prevention of smuggling and shipwreck, when the onus was on them to preserve life, take charge of the vessel and protect property. On land and at sea, the Coastguard's daily régime was harsh and the hours long. Basic training exercises included the strenuous musket and cutlass drill, and an armed nightly vigil was carried out in the open air. Coastguards, who tended to be moved on quite frequently, sometimes encountered hostility from local people who were inclined to view the bounty of the sea cast upon their shores from a rather different perspective. They lived afloat, in beached hulks or, if they were lucky, in specially constructed Coastguard cottages which had a look out in the Chief Officer's house and storage for arms and ammunition. Special success in thwarting smugglers was rewarded, while failure in any aspect of their duties brought punishment. Nevertheless, bribery was not unknown, nor the recording of fictional duties by certain Royal Naval personnel, who regarded a Coastguard posting as a soft option.

Throughout its varied history, the Coastguard has been many things to many people and in 1831 it was seen by the Admiralty as a convenient means of manning the fleet in time of war. Naval style uniforms were introduced, and as reservists the Coastguards were obliged to undergo naval training. All the able-bodied Coastguards in Cornwall were to be drafted into the Royal Navy when the Crimean War broke out in 1854, leaving their role of coastal watch unfulfilled. Replacements were urgently needed, and *The West Briton* of January 1854 reported:

> On Thursday Captain Sheringham, of the Royal Navy, assembled the fishermen and pilots on St. Mawes Quay, and addressed them on the advantages and necessity of their joining the new coast-guard force, lately proposed by government, to raise ten thousand men, to be drilled in gunnery duty for twenty-eight days in the year. He was accompanied by Mr. Barrett, R.N., the officer of the coast-guard at St. Mawes. He entreated them to consider the urgency which government would be placed under, of making extraordinary efforts to protect our shores during the impending contest. He made a forcible appeal to their loyalty and patriotism; pointing out the duties they owed to their native country, and to their homes and fire sides.

Two years later the Admiralty assumed complete control of the Coastguard, despite the protestations of the Board of Customs, which had the responsibility of protecting the Revenue.

This takeover by the Admiralty put the emphasis on seamanship and a well trained reserve, capable of tackling any emergency alongside the professionals in time of war. When it came to the test the Coastguards were able to demonstrate their worth, but tragically they were to be almost obliterated at the beginning of the First World War, when most of them were sent to sea in obsolete warships, ill-equipped to withstand the formidable German fleet and its U-boats. Furthermore, the removal of these highly trained Coastguards left our shores vulnerable, when it was essential for national security that a coastal watch be maintained to give warning of imminent invasion or detect the landing of spies or saboteurs. So the surviving Coastguards were restored to their duties. Their skills in signalling and communications proved invaluable for Intelligence, as well as their adaptability in coping with mine disposal and a host of other emergencies which came their way, working in conjunction with the police, military and rescue services, assisting vessels in distress, dealing with the aftermath of shipwreck and manning lifeboats. While under the command of the Admiralty they had collected an astonishing range of responsibilities towards various organisations, including the RNLI, Trinity House, the Fisheries, the Air Ministry, the Home Office, the Post Office, Lloyds and many others as well as weather forecasting; functions far removed from the original role of suppressing smuggling. Moreover, the Coastguard service may proudly lay claim to being at the forefront of conservation, in that it established an early responsibility towards the Society for the Protection of Wild Birds.

After the First World War, when events had demonstrated the need for Coastguards to remain at their posts in time of national crisis, it was not feasible for the Admiralty to maintain a service unable to fulfil a naval wartime role and a re-assessment in 1922 led to the Board of Trade assuming responsibility for the Coastguards on April 1st 1923, when, by Royal sanction, they retained the title His Majesty's Coastguard. Thus a hundred and one years on, the Coastguard became a professional life-saving force, keeping watch around our coasts and working in co-operation with the RNLI and other life-saving services. It was to be returned to the Admiralty for the duration of the Second World War, released to the Ministry of Transport and transferred back to the Board of Trade (now the Department of Trade) in October 1964. Since then there has been administrative stability, but a changing emphasis, requiring adaptability and a multiplicity of new maritime and shore skills.

Swift Emergencies at Sea call for Prompt Responses
The service developed as needs dictated and, as communications and technology improved the Coastguard assumed a co-ordinating role, backed up by its enthusiastic band of Auxiliaries, sometimes drawing on the expertise of the Royal Navy, Royal Air Force and other sections of H.M. services, and later filling any void by such measures as acquiring its own helicopters to be operated by private companies when services they had previously relied on were withdrawn. Today the key to saving life at sea depends on swift action, accuracy in locating the casualty, apt assessment of the situation and clear and efficient communication with the rescue resources, which include the Coastguard's own mobile rescue units, for the Coastguard still maintains a physical role at the sharp end of coastal rescue. But the emphasis is on communications and getting specialist help swiftly to the scene of the casualty which might be a small incident, or a major disaster involving

pollution. Traditionally the winter storms brought forth a crop of emergencies; today, with the escalation of tourism and pleasure boating, the 'Silly Season' is the busiest time for the combined rescue services.

In early times, when the only way ships in distress could communicate with the shore was by visual means, watch was kept from look-outs spaced along our coastline. But the development of radio (initially Morse Code signals transmitted by telegraph), telephone, voice radio and increasing use of VHF has led to vast changes in the Coastguard service, which has invested its resources in radio watch, rather than traditional, static visual watches, which have their limitations.

Throughout their history the Coastguards in Cornwall have played a proud part in preserving life from shipwreck, receiving much recognition from the RNLI and others, in the days when Coastguards were able to man lifeboats (as crewmembers, *not* coxswains), as well as for spontaneous rescues on their own initiative. This fine humanitarian tradition continues today, with the emphasis on the co-ordination of all maritime emergencies, meaning vessels or persons in need of assistance at sea and around the coastline within the United Kingdom Search and Rescue region.

In 1978 the Coastguard service was re-organised for operations to be centralised from Maritime Rescue Co-ordination Centres (M.R.C.C.s), such as that at Pendennis Point, Falmouth, opened by H.R.H. Prince Charles, the Honorary Commodore of H.M. Coastguard, on December 2nd 1981. This is the nerve centre for Maritime Search and Rescue for the coastal area from Dodman Point to the Isles of Scilly, and northwards to a point near Hartland, and extending half way across the Atlantic; an area of about six hundred thousand square miles. Brixham M.R.C.C. covers the area to the east of the Dodman. Vessels needing assistance, from the smallest pleasure craft to the largest liner equipped with V.H.F. radio, can summon the help of the Coastguard on V.H.F. Channel 16, the International calling and distress frequency. The Coastguard can also be contacted by telex, satellite or from the shore by the emergency telephone 999 system. Falmouth has the distinction of being the sole U.K. terminal for INMARSAT maritime satellite distress communications via the British Telecom Earth Receiving Station at Goonhilly on the Lizard Peninsula. Thus Cornwall, which has made such a significant contribution towards the development of maritime safety, is well poised to meet the demands of the future, with Falmouth M.R.C.C. at the forefront of the emerging Global Maritime Distress and Safety System.

This photograph, taken at R.N.A.S. Culdrose in June 1988, serves to illustrate the reliance on teamwork in today's Search and Rescue operations. For the rescue mission depends not only on the aircrew, who operate and fly the machine, coastguards, coxswains, policemen, firefighters and those in the medical services, but ancillary staff ranging from maintainers, who maintain aircraft, Operations Room staff and people engaged in essential back-up services behind the scenes such as chefs who provide food for the aircrew.

(© Crown copyright 1991/MOD reproduced with the permission of the Controller of HMSO)

BIBLIOGRAPHY

Beattie, John , *Drama In The Air*
Berry, Claude, *The Story of Padstow's Lifeboats 1827-1977*
Carter, Clive, *Cornish Shipwrecks; The North Coast* (1970)
Collins, Captain Greenvile, *Great Britain's Coasting Pylot* (1693)
Corin, John, *Sennen Cove and Its Lifeboat* (1985)
Corin, John, and Farr, Grahame, *R.N.L.I. Penlee*, (1981)
Corin, John, and Farr, Grahame, *Penlee Lifeboat*, (1983)
Esquiros, Alphonse, *Cornwall And Its Coasts*, (1865)
Folliott Stokes, A.G., *The Cornish Coast and Moors*
Folliott Stokes, A.G., *From Land's End To The Lizard*, (1909)
Harvey, E., G., *Mullyon, Its History, Scenery And Antiquities*, (1875)
Hillary, Sir William, Bart., *An Appeal to the British Nation on the Humanity and Policy of Forming A National Institution for the Preservation of Lives and Property from Shipwreck* (1823)
Howarth, Patrick, *The Lifeboat Story*, (1957)
Howarth, Patrick, *In Danger's Hour*
Jenkins, A.K. Hamilton, *Cornwall And Its People*, (1945)
Jenkins, Alf, *The Scillonian And His Boat*, (1982)
Kipling, Ray, *Rescue By Sail and Oar*
Lakeman, Mary, *Early Tide: A Mevagissey Childhood* (1978)
Langmaid, Capt. Kenneth, DSC, RN, *The Sea, Thine Enemy* (1966)
Larn, Richard, *Cornish Shipwrecks: The Isles of Scilly* (1971)
Larn, Richard, and Carter, Clive, *Cornish Shipwrecks: The South Coast* (1969)
Maddison, Arthur, *The West Country's Maritime Story* (1982)
Mais, S.P.B., *The Cornish Riviera* (1929)
Matthews, G. Forrester, *The Isles Of Scilly* (1960)
Mitchell, Percy, *A Boatbuilder's Story* (1968)
Morris, Jeff, *The Story Of The Isles Of Scilly Lifeboats* (1987)
Mumford, Clive, *Portrait Of The Isles of Scilly* (1967)
Noall, Cyril, *Cornish Lights And Shipwrecks* (1968)
Noall, Cyril, and Farr, Grahame, *Wreck and Rescue Round The Cornish Coast: Vols I,II and III* (1964, 1965 and 1965)
Pearce, Frank, *Mayday! Mayday! Mayday!* (1977)
Roddis, Roland, *Cornish Harbours* (1951)
Russell, W. Clark, *The British Seas* (1892)
Uren, J.G., *Scilly And The Scillonians* (1907)
Vince, Charles, *Storm On The Waters* (1946)
Walthew, Kenneth, *From Rock And Tempest* (1971)
Ward, C.S., and Baddeley, M.J.B., *Thorough Guide: South Devon and South Cornwall* (1895)

Warner, Oliver, *The Lifeboat Service* (1974)
Webb, William, *Coastguard! An Official History of H.M. Coastguard* (1976)

Life in Cornwall, Volumes I,II,III,& IV edited by R.H. Barton.
Early Tours In Devon and Cornwall edited by R. Pearse Chope (1918)
The Children's Encyclopedia edited by Arthur Mee
Murray's Hand-Book : Devon and Cornwall (1865)
International Code of Signals, (1969)
'Rescue 21': A Tribute To The 21st Anniversary Of The Solomon Browne And Associated Rescue Services (1981)
Kelly's Directories
Transactions Vol. 38: Apparatus For Saving Lives In Case of Shipwreck: Society For The Encouragement of the Arts
Old Cornwall, Vol. 6
Coastguard (The Magazine of Her Majesty's Coastguard)
Flash (The Trinity House Quarterly Journals)
Toilers Of The Deep (Royal National Mission To Deep Sea Fishermen)
Ships Monthly
The Lifeboat Journals
Archive records of the R.N.L.I.
Newsletters Of The R.N.L.I. Lifeboat Enthusiasts' Society
Grahame Farr archives
Western Morning News
The Cornish Times
Royal Cornwall Gazette
The Cornishman
The West Briton

I should like to thank the R.N.L.I., their officials in the south- west and the Coxswains, lifeboatmen and former lifeboatmen of Cornwall and the Isles of Scilly, who have co-operated closely with me and made the researching of this book such an enjoyable and fulfilling experience. Thanks also to the Société Nationale de Sauvetage en Mer, the Royal Naval Air Station, Culdrose, H.M. Coastguard Maritime Co-ordination Centre, Falmouth. William Osborne's Arun Shipyard, Littlehampton, Land's End Limited, Sennen, Flambard's Helston, and the staff of the Local Studies Library, Redruth and Falmouth Library; to Lt. Col. Ron Overd, Lt Cdr. Barney Morris, Austyn Pengilly, Frank Curnow, Catherine Bird and everyone who has assisted me. I am indebted to those who provided illustrations, particularly the R.N.L.I. in Poole and London, R.N.A.S. Culdrose, and to Brian Errington for his photographic work.

INDEX